Ontologies-Based Business Integration

Michael Rebstock · Janina Fengel · Heiko Paulheim

Ontologies-Based Business Integration

With Additional Contributions by
Christian Huemer, Klaus-Dieter Naujok,
Patrick Röder and Omid Tafreschi

 Springer

Prof. Dr. Michael Rebstock
Janina Fengel, MSc
Heiko Paulheim, BSc

Faculty of Economics
and Business Administration
Darmstadt University of Applied Sciences
Haardtring 100
64295 Darmstadt
Germany

rebstock@fbw.h-da.de
fengel@fbw.h-da.de
paulheim@fbw.h-da.de

SPONSORED BY THE

Federal Ministry
of Education
and Research

Funded by BMBF German Federal Ministry of Education and Research, No. 1716X04, Project ORBI (Ontologies-based Reconciliation for Business Integration)

ISBN 978-3-540-75229-5   e-ISBN 978-3-540-75230-1

DOI 10.1007/978-3-540-75230-1

Library of Congress Control Number: 2007943165

Production: LE-TeX Jelonek, Schmidt & Vöckler GbR, Leipzig
Cover design: WMX Design GmbH, Heidelberg

Printed on acid-free paper

9 8 7 6 5 4 3 2 1

springer.com

Preface

E-business integration is a vision we have developed over a long period of time. As we have worked in business practice for many years prior to and in parallel with our academic research, we have always thought of such integration not only as an intellectual challenge but also as a real business tool. Consequently, when we started our project on Ontologies-based Reconciliation for Business Integration (ORBI) in 2004, not only pure science but also business objectives were at the center of our research. We were very happy to be able to form a project consortium that consisted not only of renowned researchers but also of experienced business practitioners from a range of companies. Each played a specific role – as user, provider or co-developer of the application components that are based on the methods we have developed.

So may this book find its way not only to the desks of researchers and students, but also into the offices and minds of business practitioners worldwide who are dealing with the challenge of integrating their business processes, applications and information.

This book is, in the most general sense, about understanding each other – that is, what we do and think. Needless to say, within the project itself, and its environment, we had many opportunities to apply this underlying philosophy. In the end, the results prove it was worth the effort.

The book and the research it reports would not have been possible without the help and support of many people and organizations. We want to thank all of them for what they did for our work.

First, there are the present and past members of the ORBI project consortium. The academic partners include Gerhard Knorz from Darmstadt University of Applied Sciences, Martin Minderlein from Ansbach University of Applied Sciences, Michael Herfert and Ruben Wolf from Fraunhofer Institute for Secure Information Technology, Omid Tafreschi from Technische Universität Darmstadt, and Carlo Simon from University of Koblenz-Landau. The business partners include Boris Reuter from axentiv, Dietrich Jäger from i-market, Thomas Kummler und Mirko Doninger from Krombacher Brewery, Hubert Stockmeier from SupplyOn and Jan Matthes from EMB. Special thanks go to Klaus-Dieter Naujok and Christian Huemer from UN/CEFACT's and OASIS' joint former ebXML project as well as to Patrick Röder and Omid Tafreschi from Technische Universität Darmstadt, who agreed to contribute chapters to this book.

Our research was supported by many present and past student assistants and master's students. We want to thank all of them, especially Margrit Schaede who prepared the data for the system evaluation as well as Elzbieta Wieczorek and Martin Osuch who have helped to prepare the manuscript. Special thanks also to Martin Düpré for his technical support and to Melissa Nelson for proofreading.

We would like to thank the German Federal Ministry of Education and Research for the research grant that made this project possible. We are also grateful to the people both at AiF – especially Petra Mueser and Norbert Esser – and at Darmstadt University of Applied Sciences' Center for Research and Development – especially Ute Jochem – for their administrative support of the project.

We thank all the people at Springer who have helped to make this book possible. Special thanks to Ed Schuster from MIT for publishing the book in his Data-Driven Economy series.

Finally, a very big thank you to our families and partners who – especially in the last months – have endured seeing us even less than they normally do.

Darmstadt, November 2007

Michael Rebstock
Janina Fengel
Heiko Paulheim

Table of Contents

List of Additional Contributors

Klaus-Dieter Naujok
Former ebXML Chair
Illumonus, LLC
Founder and CEO
4410 Deermeadow Way
Antioch, CA 94531, USA
klaus@illumonus.com

Prof. Dr. Christian Huemer
Institute of Software Technology and Interactive Systems
Vienna University of Technology
Favoritenstrasse 9 – 11 / 188-3
A - 1040 Vienna
huemer@big.tuwien.ac.at

Patrick Röder
Omid Tafreschi
Technische Universität Darmstadt
Fachbereich 20 FG Sicherheit in der Informationstechnik
Hochschulstrasse 10
D - 64289 Darmstadt
roeder@sec.informatik.tu-darmstadt.de
tafreschi@sec.informatik.tu-darmstadt.de

1 Coping with Semantic Variety in E-Business

The globalization of everyday business and increasing international trade are leading to a growing need to improve national and international business collaborations and transactions. Emerging technologies for e-business transactions allow for new methods of process, data and application integration. Thus, business processes today commonly require electronic transactions between business partners. With the general objective of seamlessly coupling electronic information chains, process, data and application integration have become a major challenge in sustaining international trade and business development.

1.1 Semantic Variety and Ambiguity

Business partners almost always have different ways of systemizing the information needed to run a business, in terms of information syntax, structure and semantics. A growing number of these systemizations are based on industry, national or international standards. Currently, numerous e-business standards are already in use, and more are under development. Standards can be document standards, product taxonomies, business process blueprints and more, which differ in content, structure and methodology. In most business relationships, several of these standards are used at the same time, in parallel, within electronic collaborations and on electronic markets.

We term this ubiquitous, heavily parallel use of standards in electronic collaborations *semantic variety*, as it not only generates different syntactical requirements, but also, more importantly, creates the challenge of understanding the *meaning* of a business partner's messages. The consequences of semantic variety are mismatch and misunderstanding in electronic transactions, what we term *semantic ambiguity*. Too often, this results in the disruption of the electronic information chain and thus leads to negative cost, time and quality effects.

Semantic ambiguity in electronic transactions can occur on both the *schema level* and the *content level* of an electronic transaction. On the schema level, a data field "Terms of Delivery", for instance, can raise different expectations. Besides the question, in which format or syntax the field has to be encoded, it is substantial to know what information exactly should be transported in it. Is a statement wanted (only) about insurance and freight cost handling – or also about the mode of transport, about delivery time and schedules, about cold storage maybe? Then, on the content level, it has to be clear what entries are accepted for this field, and whether it is necessary to standardize this information, e.g., as foreseen by UN/EDIFACT (UNECE 2006). Using the standardized term "FOB Shanghai", for instance, would express that the seller cares for the delivery of the goods until they pass the ship's rail in the port of Shanghai. But can we be sure about the business partner's expectations without prior consultation?

We expect that semantic ambiguity will persist. At least three trends are driving the continuous development of new standards and thus hindering a convergence of standards towards a single one. These trends are new technologies, changing business processes and the globalized economy.

Although it might be expected that advances in technology and e-business application development result in a unification of standards, the opposite is the case. Before the advent of the commercial use of the Internet, at the beginning of the 1990s, it was expected by many that within a few years EDIFACT would be the general standard for electronic data interchange (EDI) communications. With the Internet, the Web and the Semantic Web, layers as well as scenarios of business communication multiplied, resulting in a need for new tools and standards. A large number of consortiums or companies have started projects in recent years in response to the challenge of process and information flow integration from different perspectives. UDDI (OASIS 2004), ebXML (ebXML 2007), Biztalk (Microsoft 2005), xCBL (xCBL 2006), BMEcat (eBSC 2005), eclass (eClass 2005), RosettaNet (RosettaNet 2007a), RDF Schema (W3C 2004d) and OWL (W3C 2004e) are some examples. All of these initiatives have contributed to standardization and created a whole new range of application and process possibilities. But this led to classical, EDIFACT-based EDI becoming less and less the standard scenario.

The development of new business process scenarios contributes to the growth of the visible number of standards. First, with the rising number of companies participating in interorganizational process chains, electronic markets and business transactions, an increasing number of once secluded inhouse standards now come into contact with other companies' information structures and content and have to be matched. Furthermore, changing process coordination needs stipulate new standards. Time-sensitive advanced-planning solutions for supply chain management (SCM) scenarios, for instance, call for a tight coupling of shop-floor automation systems with enterprise resource planning (ERP) applications. Web services further widen the options for these types of business communications and advanced process designs – but also necessitate additional, new standards. For some emerging business application areas, such as electronic negotiations, comprehensive standards are not even fully available.

Within the globalized economy, the business transactions of any company increasingly involve partners from other countries. In some of these countries, specific national or international standards are well established. This exposes companies to the necessity of dealing with the particular standards used by their business partners from abroad. Additionally, some large vendors still believe that establishing their own standards as an industry standard will grant them a competitive edge in the world market. This results in a number of want-to-be industry standards for emerging application areas. Even if many of those vanish over time, some winning standards last. Finally, the globalized economy drives the multiplication of standards at the national level. Evolving major players in the world economy – especially China – have discovered that setting a standard may be a powerful means of gaining economic standing and influence (Suttmeier et al. 2006).

1.2 Research Agenda

Thus the question of how to deal with different document standards, product taxonomies and other norms, all in use at the same time, reaches critical importance in today's world of open electronic communication, especially since these standards use different semantics.

Motivation

The exchange of and close adherence to field lists and formats does not guarantee that the – semantically – "right" fields with the "right" content are transmitted to a business partner. Technical standards or syntactic specifications obviously are not sufficient for semantic harmonization. Consequently and unsurprisingly, despite the hopes of IT managers worldwide, the "wonder-weapon" eXtensible Markup Language (XML) (Bray et al. 2006) did not solve the problem of sufficiently integrating process and information flows, even though it became a general syntactic standard.

How can businesses worldwide cope with the abundance of standards, and how can they achieve semantic interoperability under these circumstances? Past approaches have often been comprehensive. The development of and agreement on a universal standard is an often intended aim when dealing with semantic reference systems. Most of the consortiums and initiatives mentioned above subscribe to this aim. For exactly this reason, however, this aim proves impracticable. Other initiatives have tried to create a universal superstandard by merging existing standards into one. But because of the sheer number of existing and evolving standards and their dynamically changing nature, such comprehensive approaches have failed regularly.

Thus, with more and more e-business standards being used concurrently, complexity as well as time and cost requirements for building up electronic collaborations grow. Not only for small and medium-sized enterprises (SME) this fact can hinder the further and full development of electronic business integration, both conceptually and practically.

Approach

The challenge in electronic business transactions is to achieve *semantic interoperability*, i.e., to avoid mismatch and misunderstandings in integrated business processes, taking into account the parallel usage of standards. In this book, we identify *ontology management and engineering* techniques as an appropriate means for meeting these challenges. Information structures and standards for electronic business integration can be perceived as domain ontologies, as they contain domain knowledge in a structured form (Gómez-Pérez et al. 2004). Using ontologies and ontological engineering techniques, *semantic references* between information both on the structure and content level can be established.

The global Semantic Web initiative (Herman 2007) and networks such as OntoWeb (OntoWeb 2003) and its successor Knowledge Web (Knowledge Web 2005) have taken up the question of semantics and ontologies for information integration. The aim of these initiatives is the development of methods and procedures for managing semantic reference systems.

Often, document standards and object taxonomies are created for particular purposes or specific domains, for example the Dublin Core Metadata Element Set for cross-domain resource description (DCMI 2006), or biomedical (NLM 2006; OBO 2007), cultural heritage (Sinclair et al. 2006) and e-commerce focused ontologies. Conceptually, the significance of managing ontologies – meaning semantic reference systems for electronic business collaborations – has been discussed for a while (Gruber 1993a; Domingue 1998; Tennison and Shadbolt 1998). Still, methods and services for the practical use of ontology engineering techniques for e-business integration took much longer to be developed. Now, they have become highly necessary.

As it is very unlikely that companies around the world will simultaneously stop using different e-business standards, an approach that promises success should not try to create another "superstandard," but rather, to achieve semantic interoperability and thus business-to-business (B2B) integration through other means. In our view, this could be done by following an evolutionary, user-centered approach for building a knowledge base of semantic references. A successful approach to manage lasting semantic ambiguity in this sense will show three characteristics: it will be dynamic, evolutionary and based on open virtual communities:

- A dynamic method will accept the coexistence of a multitude of standards with references evolving dynamically and thus allow ongoing adaptation to changing standards.
- An evolutionary approach discards the idea of a complete initial reference base. In a world in which it is unclear where the next standard will originate from, this is a necessity. Moreover, if the complete initial building of a knowledge base is not required, ramp-up costs, and thus entry barriers, for companies wishing to participate in an electronic exchange are significantly lower, which is particularly important for SME.
- A community-based method relies on virtual social systems growing their knowledge base by means of collaborative user interaction and feedback (Almeida et al. 2007). As experiences with automated ontological engineering tools for semantically interlinking different ontologies show, domain expert knowledge is not only beneficial (van Harmelen 2006), but is needed for raising mapping quality to an acceptable level (Zhdanova et al. 2004). A collaborative social system supplies a platform for the necessary learning and quality improvement without raising costs to an unacceptable level.

1.3 Research Objectives

The general objective of the approach developed in our project (ORBI 2007) and presented in this book is to allow ontologies-based integration of e-business processes and information flows. In order to achieve this goal, not only conceptually but also in practice, the development of methods and modular application components for the referencing of e-business standards in electronic collaborations is required. We believe that these results will supply a yet missing but, in terms of application logic, very necessary next step on the way to integrated information and process chains.

In order to achieve the intended integration, several issues have to be considered. These include fundamental questions about the nature of business processes and business information flows on the one hand as well as thoroughly analyzed technical options for the necessary application integration on the other. Thus, our research objectives can be summed up as follows:

Establish Semantic Interoperability. In order to ensure a true common understanding about the contents of a communication between business partners, certainty regarding the semantics of the data transferred has to be established. Agreeing upon and deploying a syntax standard is not sufficient.

Enable Seamless Information Exchange. In business communications today it is still not unusual that some information is at times transmitted from one information system into another manually, i.e., by re-typing the data. Often, this is done intentionally in those situations where semantic ambiguity may arise, thus establishing a manual information quality control by a user. Methods for seamless information exchange should be able to refer to sufficient expert knowledge in order to render manual user interfaces unnecessary.

Integrate Business Processes. Many research projects addressing ontology engineering and management in the business area overlook the fact that information is never exchanged on a purpose-free basis, but rather, it always travels along with business processes – i.e., material, financial or coordination flows – and serves their specific objectives. The real purpose of ontological engineering methods in the business area is not information integration itself, but the integration of its underlying processes.

Allow Concurrent Usage of Multiple Standards. Based on their past experience, business practitioners, especially many IT managers, often assume that the ultimate information-exchange strategy is to get all business partners to communicate using the same standard. As argued above, this goal is even more unrealistic today than it was in the past. Modern methods for information integration must allow concurrent usage of more than one standard within electronic collaboration networks without additional implementation requirements.

Integrate Potentially Any E-Business Standard. Many initiatives restrict the range of standards they deal with for political, practical or technical reasons. For companies exposed to different national, industry or enterprise-specific standards – as is practically every business if all of its communications are addressed – this approach is clearly of low practical value. A universally usable methodology will avoid the predefinition of a range of manageable standards.

Supply a Reference Collection as Knowledge Base. Creating references between the elements of different standards means clarifying their semantics in a given context. Once created, this expert knowledge should be available to other users within the same or even other collaboration contexts. Methods for semantic referencing should preserve the knowledge created.

Allow Evolutionary Growth of the Knowledge Base. Establishing a complete reference collection as a knowledge base beforehand is very unlikely due to the number of standards, their evolution speed and the cost a complete analysis would create, if it were at all possible. Thus the knowledge base has to be flexible, in the sense that its evolutionary growth is not only possible but also a substantial building criterion. Clearly, an approach that does not start with a fully developed knowledge base shows weaknesses in the starting phase. Due to its initially small knowledge base, references supplied by the system might be erroneous and incomplete. But with the growth of the knowledge base, quality improvement occurs quickly – as many Web 2.0 projects demonstrate.

On a system-development level, the following supporting objectives can be added:

Supply Application Components for Semi-automated Referencing. User interaction is crucial for building a knowledge base that comprises domain expert knowledge. Still, manual user intervention should be as minimal as possible in order to achieve system acceptance. Thus the system should be able to perform standard operations in an automated mode.

Allow Integration into Arbitrary Applications. In order to allow access to the knowledge base from arbitrary process contexts, any process-supporting application should, ideally, be able to communicate with it. One possible way of achieving this goal could be to provide access to the knowledge base via a standardized interface, e.g., as a web service over the Internet.

Security and Privacy Issues. Adequate security engineering represents an important aspect of the conception and technical realization of semantic referencing, as data security, data consistency and confidentiality are of critical importance in the area of the e-business data interchange (Rebstock and Tafreschi 2002). This aspect includes access control issues as well as the trustworthiness of the information supplied by the knowledge base and the reliability of the underlying IT infrastructure.

1.4 Business Application Domains

In this book, not only do we discuss research results and develop novel methods and a methodological framework for ontologies-based business integration, but we also report on the development of application components based on web services that support the dynamic semi-automated referencing of information structures. The self-learning synchronization components introduced use methods of ontological engineering and artificial intelligence.

Thus, this book demonstrates what ontology management can do for e-business or, more precisely, for process, information and application integration under dynamic e-business conditions. Until now, ontology management and the Semantic Web have been intensively researched but rarely applied to business practice. In spite of the many research activities on semantics, not many projects address the question of how to deal with the parallel use of dynamically evolving semantic systems.

After the consolidation and more quiet growth of e-business activities in recent years, the advances of electronic business integration have entered a new stage and now proceed with changed speed. Application components and web services for ontologies-based business integration can foster this development by supporting a wide range of application domains including:

- Cross-company electronic collaborations
- International trade processes
- Enterprise-wide e-business integration
- Electronic marketplace transactions
- Electronic negotiation applications
- Enterprise application integration
- EDI integration

Following the design strategy developed above, such application components permit referencing standards without prior running of cost-intensive ramp-up projects or strenuous migration projects. Automated services can offer a substantial improvement and efficiency increase in building references between diverse ontologies since the complexity of their semantic structures can, to a large extent, be hidden from the user. As a result, the entry barrier for participating in electronic collaborations is lowered. SME in particular can thus intensify their activities in electronic collaborations and on electronic markets.

1.5 Book Structure

The remainder of this book is organized as follows: In Part I, we introduce the major concepts underlying e-business integration. Business processes, fields of application, and methods and standards for integration within different business and application domains are discussed. In addition, a case study sheds light on the process of creating and maintaining such standards, thus providing valuable insights as to how standards evolve.

Part II discusses knowledge management and semantic technologies, which are used throughout the remainder of the book to analyze and build the methodology and components for dynamic semantic synchronization. Ontologies, methods and tools for both ontology engineering and collective knowledge management are introduced, along with advanced methods and techniques for semantic synchronization. These include concepts from artificial intelligence as well as Web-2.0-like communities and context sensitivity.

In Part III, we develop the concepts and frameworks for e-business integration using semantic technologies. First, we show the functional requirements and application scenarios for the semantic integration of business processes and applications. Second, we show the importance of security management to these kinds of scenarios and develop an appropriate access control framework. As a case study of a practical application for dynamic semantic e-business integration, we describe the ORBI Ontology Mediator. In addition to its function and process design, application architecture and user interaction, we also discuss some key challenges in its application.

In conclusion, we discuss the future of business integration, including development trends and arising challenges.

Part I

E-Business Integration:
Processes, Applications, Standards

2 Integrating Processes, Applications and Information

By using electronic transactions to automate business processes, companies seek to optimize processes, accelerate the development of new products and services or access new markets or target groups. The facilitation of seamless electronic information processing is expected to add substantial economic value by generating cost-reduction potential and increasing the speed of process execution while at the same time enhancing the quality of processes, products and services. With seamless electronic communication inside an organization and across its boundaries, with partners, suppliers, and customers, business processes can be automated to an even greater extent, thus increasing their efficiency further.

2.1 The Business Case for E-Integration

Still, assessing the economic impact of information technology (IT) usage is not trivial. The reason for this is that IT generally does not add value directly. It is *business process performance*, defined by business strategies and enabled by IT, that creates economic value (Wigand et al. 1997, 159). Figure 2.1 shows these interrelations.

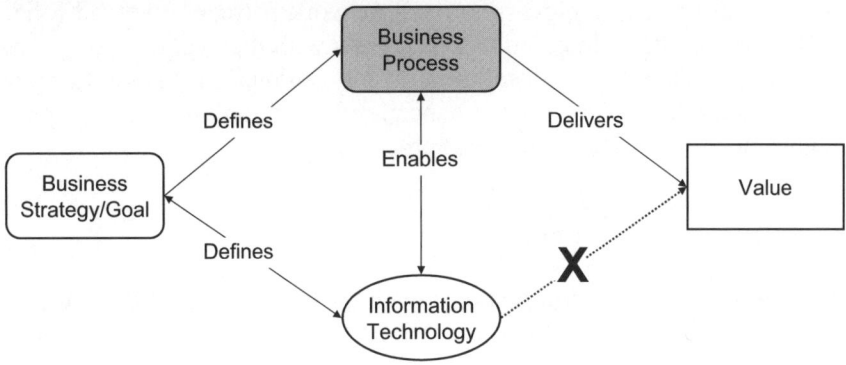

Fig. 2.1. IT and value added (adapted from Wigand et al. 1997, 159)

Thus, before discussing IT solutions, business processes have to be reviewed.

2.1.1 The Business Process Paradigm

The emergence of the business process view as a business paradigm has changed the perception and structure of companies and value chains. According to Hammer and Champy (1993, 35), a *business process* is "a collection of activities that takes one or more kinds of input and creates an output that is of value to the customer" A customer can be a market customer or an internal customer, for instance another department within the same company. A business process often crosses the boundaries of several organizational units or organizations. The objective of business process optimization is the creation of an optimal design for the process as a whole, not necessarily the optimization of every single task for itself. Task complexity may even rise in favor of more simple process structures (Hammer and Champy 1993).

The evolution of the business process view first moved from the optimization of single functional processes to the design of cross-functional processes, then, later, whole business domain processes and finally enterprise-wide processes. Major further steps included cross-enterprise approaches, especially SCM (e.g., Chopra and Meindl 2001) and electronic markets (e.g., Rebstock 2000; Bichler 2001; Ströbel 2003). With those approaches, business process analysis and design crossed enterprise boundaries. Major improvements in process lead time, quality and cost may be realized by implementing such processes (Hammer 2001).

A first step in integrating intercompany business processes can be for two companies to couple a single process bilaterally. The highest integration potential is realized by full supply chain network integration, i.e., by coupling all necessary processes of all network partners involved (Nieuwenhuis et al. 2007). Integration needs grow with the evolution stages between these two poles. With full process integration, information flows refer to a multitude of material, financial, and coordination (i.e., planning and business information reporting) processes.

2.1.2 Process Integration

For *routine processes*, information travels with the process flow upstream or downstream mostly along predefined routes. Information for those processes is stored in applications such as ERP, customer relationship management (CRM) or logistics execution systems (LES). Those applications are generally used by one or more processes. Process integration thus means information integration and, technically, application integration. The essential link between the tasks of a business process – company-wide or cross-enterprise – is information. Establishing non-disruptive information flows is thus the key challenge for successful business process engineering. Figure 2.2 shows a sample process chain with its respective applications and information flows.

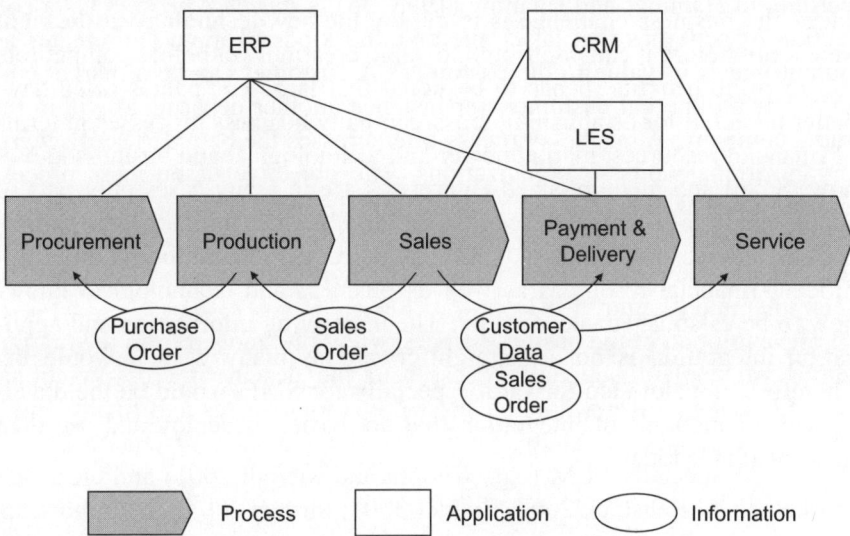

Fig. 2.2. Integration of processes, applications and information

For *ad-hoc processes*, in which structure and flow are not predefined, the applications used and information exchanged vary depending on the specific business case. Those kinds of processes form an even greater challenge for integration, as the methods and applications supporting these processes have to be much more flexible if they are to be interconnected in different business contexts. Most business process integration projects today still deal with routine processes, but there is a growing demand for the support of ad-hoc processes.

2.1.3 Business Processes and Information Technology

Information technology plays an important role within the business process paradigm. It is an *essential enabler* for organizational and management concepts (Hammer and Champy 1993). Without IT support, most process optimization concepts and projects would not be possible. In addition to being an enabler, IT also serves as an *accelerator* by allowing processes and information to travel more quickly through an organization than was previously possible. It is not surprising, then, that IT still is often referred to as a *key success factor* for business process optimization.

Because of this, IT is also a *challenge* for an organization. From a business perspective, every technological change or innovation poses the question of how it can contribute to further improving organizational performance. The business challenge is to deploy the new technology at the right time – not before it can contribute to value creation, yet before competitors can reap the benefits. It has to be noted that large companies often have better potential for establishing cross-company business processes in terms of financial resources, market power and technological and business know-how. Small and medium-sized enterprises are in many cases only part of supply chain or e-market networks if a large partner initiates their participation. The reason for this is that today's process integration requires significant financial resources as well as business and technological know-how to be established successfully. The underlying information and application integration is not as straightforward as many wish it would be. Therefore, a major step forward, especially for SME, would be the development of methods of integration that are easier to deploy and use than those available today.

2.2 Application Integration

Over the past 20 years, with the emergence of the Internet, application structures as well as the infrastructure for application integration have changed dramatically.

2.2.1 Networks for Application Integration

On a technical level, the exchange of information between applications is based on an electronic network infrastructure. Within companies, networks have been created and expanded over time. In the time of mainframes, data exchange was often triggered by departments processing mass data, such as production or accounting. With the dissemination of the personal computer (PC) throughout all company areas, computer nets for different purposes emerged and department nets were linked together, forming local area networks (LAN). With international expansion, company mergers or acquisitions, these nets were expanded to organization-wide nets – wide area networks (WAN) – that linked computers over a geographically scattered region. Before the ubiquitous availability of the Internet, proprietary data nets were set up to connect external business partners, usually by large international providers. Access to these nets was limited to subscribing companies. Hub services of value-added networks (VAN) were used for intercompany data exchange in electronic collaborations. With the growth of the Internet, VANs have lost their dominance in intercompany communication. Naturally, the use of the open Internet posed new challenges with regard to the protection of business data. When implementing integration solutions, the technical requirements for intracompany enterprise application integration (EAI) are very similar to those of intercompany scenarios, i.e., business-to-business (B2B) integration.

2.2.2 Business Applications

The use of the Internet has led to substantial business transformation and to the creation of what is now called "electronic business". Electronic business (*e-business*) denotes the support of communication and business processes through electronic communication services in potentially all functional business areas (Rebstock 2000). This involves data interchange in possibly all areas within an enterprise as well as across company boundaries. E-business encompasses electronic commerce (*e-commerce*), focusing on sales and distribution, as well as electronic procurement (*e-procurement*), focusing on sourcing. Furthermore, e-business also includes electronic communication services used in other enterprise departments such as human resources or finance and controlling.

Business application systems can be conceived of as tools for e-business activities. With respect to focus, we can distinguish roughly between *intraorganizational* and *interorganizational* business application systems. Intraorganizational applications include *lateral*, *operational* and *management applications*.

Lateral applications are used in potentially any workplace of the company for basic information processing and communication tasks, i.e., for word processing, calculation, presentation and personal electronic communication such as e-mail. Workflow management systems (WfMS) allow process flow automation, an even higher degree of integration than information flow integration.

Internal operational applications span a wide range of function-specific and industry-specific application components. Function-specific components support functions such as finance, accounting, human resources, sales or procurement. Industry-specific components support processes in specific industries, such as production planning and scheduling (PPS) applications, manufacturing execution systems (MES) or LES for discrete or process manufacturing, warehouse management (WM) for retail or wholesale companies or other specific solutions for the banking and insurance industry. Today, most of these application components are sold packaged as complete software solutions, especially as ERP systems, but also – often focused on only slightly different business aspects – as CRM or similar applications.

Management applications include planning, reporting and analysis tools such as data warehouses (DW) or business intelligence (BI) applications.

Interorganizational applications support intercompany information exchange. This information exchange takes place mainly through EDI, SCM and electronic market applications. Those are discussed in more detail below.

2.2.3 Intercompany Document Exchange – EDI

Electronic intercompany document exchange includes non-formatted personal communication such as e-mail – already mentioned above – as well as formatted data as part of business transactions. For formatted, or structured, business data, document exchange today normally is performed via EDI. Electronic data interchange denotes the automated exchange of structured e-business documents between applications (Rebstock 2000). The document types exchanged span a wide range of mostly operational business documents including procurement, sales, logistics and finance documents, e.g., requests, offers, orders, delivery notes, invoices, shipping documents or payment orders. As in traditional, non-electronic business relations, the document flows within market transactions follow comparatively stable patterns. EDI usually works asynchronously, as messages are sent to a partner to be processed according to their schedule, without direct real-time interaction of the application systems on both sides. Normally the data exchanged has to be converted to an in-house format after transmission to be usable in internal application systems.

Using EDI, an enterprise may communicate with many partners, such as suppliers, customers, banks, authorities or logistics partners. In doing so, the company may be part of a supply chain network with or without a dominating partner. According to Porter (1985), a company's process chain activities include primary and secondary, or support, activities. Both can operationally be supported using EDI, thus allowing the vision of an overall EDI-based process chain, as illustrated in Figure 2.3.

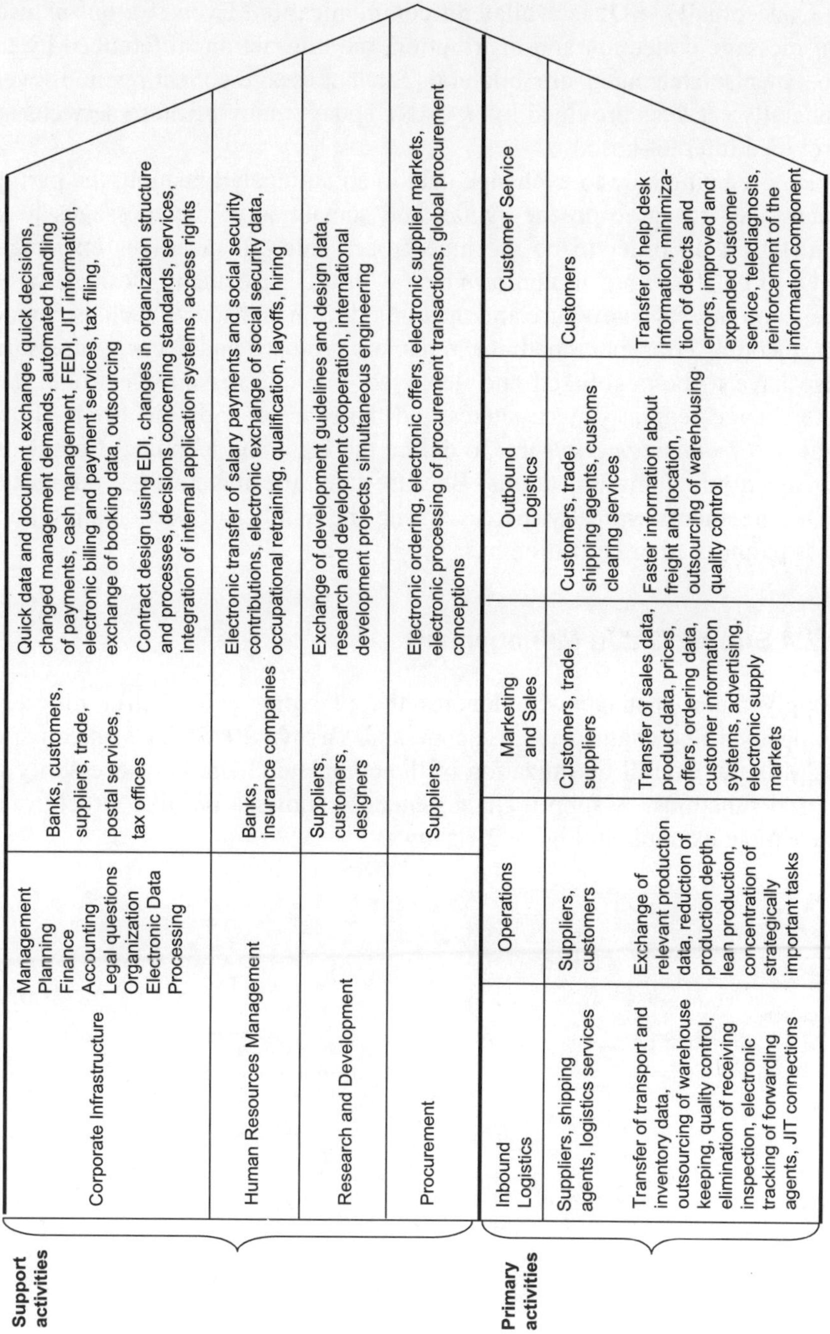

Fig. 2.3. Sample EDI-based value chain (based on Porter 1985, 37)

Conceptually, EDI is a bilateral communication. Even if a hub is used for message collection and distribution, the transactions referenced by the documents exchanged are bilateral. Such message-collecting hubs were generally services provided by a VAN. Today, many of these services are provided Internet-based.

Before being able to exchange data in an automated fashion, the participants need to agree on the syntax and semantics of the messages to be transferred. In order to be machine-processable, all messages exchanged need to be structured in conformance with this agreement. Besides agreements on message structure and meaning, technical aspects such as character encoding, transport medium, transport protocol and security measures also have to be negotiated and deployed. For this reason, electronic data interchange regularly necessitates and depends on (non-electronic) bilateral *EDI framework contracts* to define the legal and technical framework for electronic communications. Because they are bilateral, the number of EDI agreements typically increases with the number of participating business partners an organization has.

2.2.4 Supply Chain Management

Supply chain management denotes the planning and control of cross-company value chains (e.g., Lejeune and Yakova 2005). The objective of SCM is the overall optimization of the complete chain, not necessarily its partial functions. A supply chain generally shows a net-like structure, as the simple example in Figure 2.4 shows.

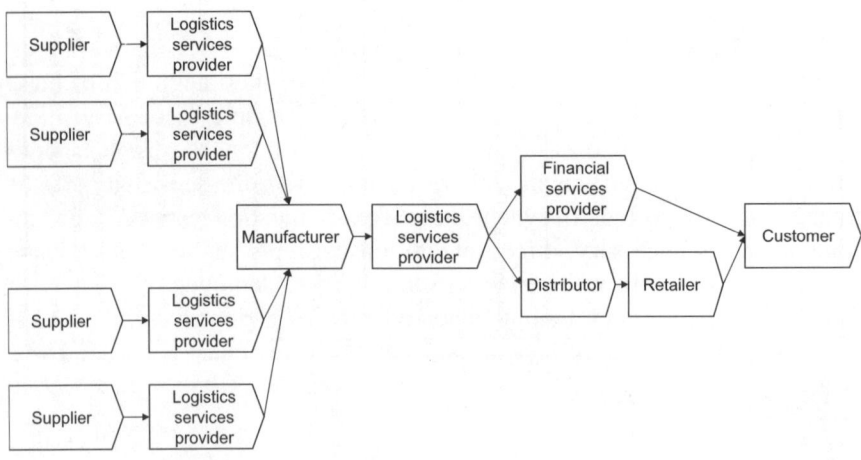

Fig. 2.4. Sample supply chain network

The general aims of supply chain optimization are quality improvements as well as time and cost reductions. The major focus of SCM is on the operations of the value chain. Potentially, SCM encompasses monitoring all value chain stages, from the procurement of raw materials, to semi-finished and finished products, to wholesale, retail and end customers. It includes logistics and other services involved. Thus, the process cycles of SCM encompass customer order, replenishment, manufacturing and procurement cycles with their respective planning and controlling activities. Figure 2.5 depicts those cycles for a sample chain.

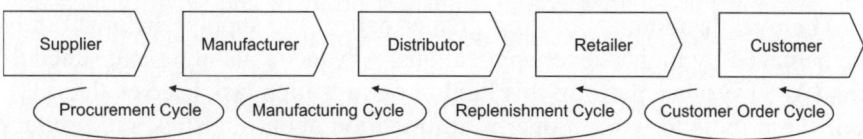

Fig. 2.5. SCM process cycles (based on Chopra and Meindl 2001)

To achieve SCM goals, complementary concepts like just-in-time (JIT) delivery (Vokurka and Lummus 2000) or vendor-managed inventory (VMI) (Simchi-Levi et al. 2004) are often implemented. Supply-chain management is primarily being realized as a closed system, where contractual agreements rule the handling of the supply chain. Such close cooperation needs to be based on clearly defined business processes and the exchange of well-defined, non-ambiguous messages and business documents (Quantz and Wichmann 2003b).

Supporting SCM by IT solutions is crucial, because only by applying interconnected, integrated information systems can its objectives be met. As SCM encompasses several companies, with their respective internal applications that manage parts of the chain's activities, the integration of these applications by means of information exchange becomes necessary. Electronic data interchange is an instrument used as long as asynchronous communication is sufficient with respect to the time-sensitivity of the transactions supported. If synchronous communication between applications becomes necessary, direct integration concepts such as EAI (Chang 2002) or synchronous web services (Sun 2002) are deployed.

A prerequisite – and a simultaneous challenge – of successful SCM is the quality of the data exchanged between the value chain partners. Three aspects have been identified as especially critical (Chopra and Meindl 2001, 337):

- *Accuracy* of information, as without exact information about the partners' plans and activities, the overall synchronization and optimization of the supply chain must fail.
- *Accessibility* of information, because if partners cannot access information necessary for their planning and operations, they cannot act as an optimized part of the chain.
- *Appropriateness* of information, since not sufficient information will hinder the value chain elements in the full coordination and optimization of their operations, whereas too much information will lead to additional coordination and clearing costs.

The overall optimization of a greater part of the supply chain can only be achieved by higher-level applications. Advanced planning and scheduling (APS) systems perform this kind of optimization task (Lee et al. 2002). For these tools to work properly, information about logistics and production planning has to be sent to the APS system from the internal applications of all partners involved and, after optimization computation, the results have to be sent back to the internal systems to update the planning data of these applications.

In EDI, communications are bilateral and have only one stage. In contrast, the information exchange challenge for SCM is to integrate several partners into the same information flow over more than one process step, as SCM higher-level coordination is multilateral and multi-staged. This requires higher integration capabilities of the companies and the applications involved.

2.2.5 Electronic Markets

An electronic market (*e-market*) is an application based on electronic communication services that supports the market coordination of economic activities (e.g., Schmid 1997; Rebstock 2000). On such markets, electronic transactions are performed by market partners. Thus, an e-market is an interorganizational application system. Such applications electronically support one up to all phases of a market transaction. In these virtual markets, business partners can perform either parts of or complete transactions electronically.

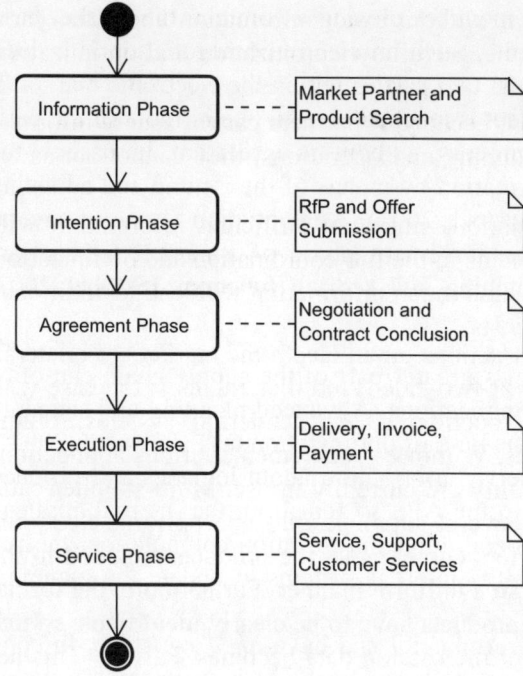

Fig. 2.6. Phases of an electronic market transaction

As illustrated in Figure 2.6, the model includes five phases (Rebstock 2000):

- Information phase, in which the relevant information concerning products, market partners, etc. is gathered.
- Intention phase, in which offers concerning supply and demand are submitted by the market partners.
- Agreement phase, in which the terms and conditions of the transaction are specified and a legally binding contract is closed between the partners involved.
- Execution phase, in which the market partners fulfill their duties according to the agreed-upon contract.
- Service phase, in which support, maintenance and other customer services are delivered.

Intercompany transactions are pursued in B2B marketplaces, where partners on both the supply and on the demand side are companies or organizations.

In order to reach an agreement for closing a contract, the market partners may negotiate its contents. Such an electronic negotiation is a decision-making process by at least two parties within the electronic market. It is performed until an agreement is reached or until one or more of the partners involved terminate the process, without an agreement. Its basis is the interactive exchange of information by means of the issuing and adjusting of offers back and forth (Rebstock 2001). A negotiation is one of several possible activities during the agreement phase of a market transaction. Other activities may be matching and scoring functions (Ströbel 2003; Bichler 2001).

Mostly, intercompany transactions on an electronic market are bilateral. They can also be (one-sided or two-sided) multilateral, as is the case with e-procurement applications, auctioning and tendering systems, online shops or electronic exchanges. Within e-procurement, various applications delivering different functionality are currently in use. Multi-supplier catalogs are bundling offers of several suppliers into one uniform electronic catalog. In order to make offers comparable, the products included in the catalog need to be described in a uniform manner. Furthermore, the format used has to be the same and products have to be clearly identifiable so that an automated consolidation of the catalog data becomes feasible. This necessitates semantically unambiguous product descriptions and the definition of message protocols for exchanging the respective data (Quantz and Wichmann 2003b).

During a specific market transaction, an information chain is formed between the market partners. If the flexibility of the applications used allows for it, such a network may be built dynamically and last only until the specific transaction is terminated. These networks have been referred to as *dynamic business webs* (Tapscott et al. 2000; Kalakota and Robinson 2000). Within such a business web, various applications may be linked together for exchanging information in an *ad hoc* manner. Figure 2.7 provides an example of a situation where three types of applications are participating in a web.

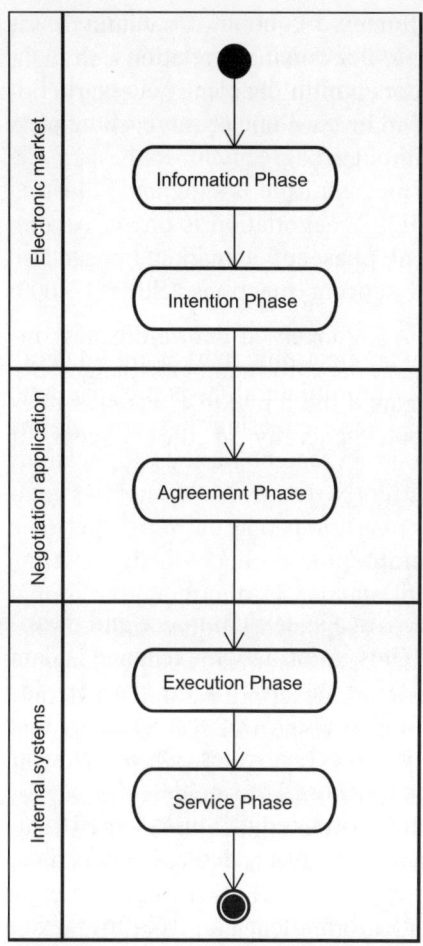

Fig. 2.7. Transaction phases and sample applications involved

The functionality supporting the information and intention phases is hosted by an e-market application. Components concerned with the execution and service phases are located within the respective internal enterprise systems, often ERP systems. The coordination process during the agreement phase is handled by an additional intermediate platform, a negotiation application. The example gives an impression of the wide range of other configuration scenarios possible.

In contrast to EDI or SCM consortiums, e-market networks are often more open and dynamic. Many e-market platforms permit the establishment of a new business relationship and the start of a transaction within this relationship from directly within the application. For EDI or SCM, the closure of additional, non-electronic framework contracts within a set group of partners still is the norm. In *ad-hoc* business relations, though, more dynamic types of application system coupling become necessary, because the partners might not have prior knowledge about each other's process and information integration requirements.

2.3 Information Integration

Having discussed the range of applications concerned with e-business integration, we will now take a closer look at the information exchanged between these applications. To fully understand the range of e-business integration options, we first need to look generally at the concept of information.

2.3.1 Information Concept and Typology

Information is purposeful data, i.e., data with a specific purpose and meaning for the recipient in a given context. Thus, information exchange is data exchange with a common understanding on the part of the partners involved regarding the meaning, purpose and context, i.e., *semantics*, of this data. Data is formed by signs following syntactical rules. On a technical level, electronically transmitted signs are composed of signals.

Digital data can be divided into character-oriented and bit-oriented data. Bit-oriented, or binary, data are either dynamic, like video and audio files, or static, like picture files. Character-oriented, or text, data can be formatted, like database files or XML files, or unformatted, like free-flow texts, letters or other text messages. An overview is shown in Figure 2.8.

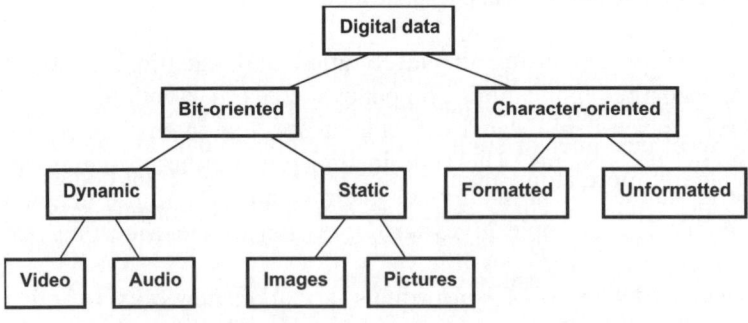

Fig. 2.8. Digital data typology

The main focus of business computing is and was mostly databases, i.e., formatted data. The transaction orientation of general business communication still calls for formatted data. Data for EDI, SCM data or data exchange on e-markets almost always is formatted. Information exchange between business partners thus almost always requires a joint understanding of the data exchange format applied. Internally, the transactional data exchanged is stored in database tables (more recently maybe also in XML files) within an application system. In recent years, with the rise of online catalogs or concepts like engineering data management (EDM), additional bit-oriented data in the form of product pictures, drawings or even videos are exchanged more regularly between business partners. The same holds true for electronic audio and video messages.

Depending on the type of usage of formatted data in an application system, we can distinguish short-term data on the one hand and longer-term data on the other. Short-term and longer-term refer to the period of time during which this information is typically valid and remains unchanged. Additionally, information can be distinguished according to whether it represents states or events, as illustrated in Figure 2.9.

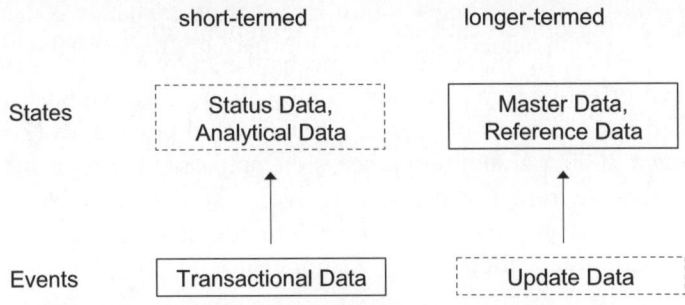

Fig. 2.9. Formatted data-usage types

Master data or reference data are longer-term data representing states; examples of master data are product data, including catalog or engineering data; employee, customer or supplier data. Reference data are quite similar, but generally more atomistic and often defined by external bodies. Examples for the latter are site codes, currency codes, payment-term codes and similar constructs. Update data, such as a price-update file for an electronic product catalog, is used to change master data.

Transactional data represent events in everyday business life. These are commercial events such as offers or orders; financial events such as invoices or other financial transactions; or logistical events such as dispatch advices, bills of loading, customs records and similar documents. Status data represent single short-term information states, such as an inventory status or an account status, whereas analytical data represent information about the actual state of an enterprise, or some of its objects, as a whole. Today this latter data is often also referred to as business intelligence data.

E-business integration today still focuses on transactional data and, to some extent – e.g., for catalog data – on master data. Information-intensive industries like banking or the airline business created some of the first globally interconnected information exchange applications in the 1970s, and were followed closely by the automotive, and later by the retail industry. Core transactional data like bookings, orders and invoices were the first documents to be regularly exchanged in an electronic way. Today, application domains span the whole range of industries, adding to the need for industry-specific information objects and structures. For manufacturing, retail, finance, logistics, tourism or healthcare, a wide range of standardized message types and data structures have been developed.

2.3.2 Integration Levels

In order to analyze the objects and modes of communication processes, semiotics can be applied. In linguistics this means the study of the formation, structure and effect of signs and sign combinations, i.e., symbols. It can be subdivided into the areas of syntax, semantics and pragmatics (Zemanek 1966; Sowa 2000). A semiotic process encompasses the transmission of a coded message from a sender to a receiver, who may then decode and understand the message. According to the semiotic model, three hierarchical levels of communication can be distinguished in this process as depicted in Figure 2.10.

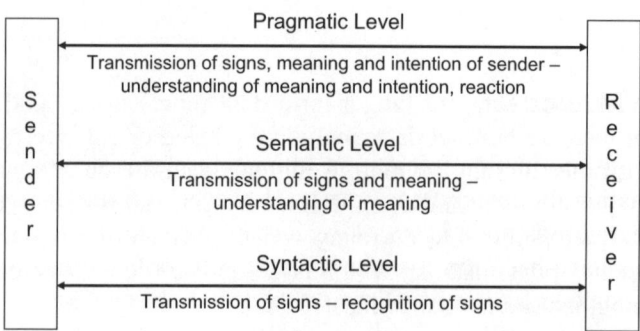

Fig. 2.10. Semiotic levels of information transmission (Wigand et al. 1997, 60)

At the syntactic level, signs are analyzed. Their combination is de-scribed by formal rules, the syntax. Syntax regulates the use of a language and the construction of sentences as word orders. Following these rules for sentence structuring, encoded signs are grouped into words and bigger functional units such as phrases and partial and full sentences, and their dependencies are formulated. On this level, heterogeneous sets of signs and data formats can lead to incompatible transmissions.

At the semantic level of an information transfer, the relation of signs to the designated meaning is set. Users assign meaning to signs and sign groups because they function as references to objects, events or conditions. Thus, a group of signs turns into a message and conveys signification of signs. Semantics is concerned with the meaning and intent of language and linguistic signs. When sender and receiver assign an identical meaning to transmitted signs, those can turn into a message and a semantic agreement exists. Heterogeneous meanings attributed to data transmitted, for instance because of differing data definitions, identification numbers or codes, lead to incompatibilities (Wigand et al. 1997).

At the pragmatic level, the intention and effect of messages is consid-ered. The message is supposed to trigger reactions from the recipient, turn-ing it into an action request, thus communicating intentions. The meaning of the signs transmitted, in combination with the consequence of actions invoked, turns message data into information, since there was a specific cause for sending it. This information is purpose-oriented knowledge and stimulates action. Thus, differing action and reaction patterns can also lead to incompatibilities in electronic transactions (Wigand et al. 1997).

To achieve full process integration, all of these levels need to be ad-dressed by a communication protocol. Still, most e-business transmissions today do not achieve this. Electronic data interchange, for instance, still the by far most popular e-business communication means, deals only with the syntactic level.

2.3.3 Integration Methods

Computer-supporting information integration ultimately means deploying methods for automating the integration process. However, the automation of information integration is not a new task by any means. Electronic data interchange projects have been run for many years. Still, conventional in-tegration projects – such as EDI or SCM projects – deal with static integra-tion problems: routine processes as well as application and information structures that remain more or less unchanged. These kinds of typical EDI scenarios still account for the vast majority of all information transfers in the B2B area worldwide. On some e-markets, also some processes with a less static process structure can be supported. But for the large rest of more dynamic integration situations, manual transfers – i.e., retyping the data – still remain necessary. Figure 2.11 depicts today's situation concerning the use of information integration methods.

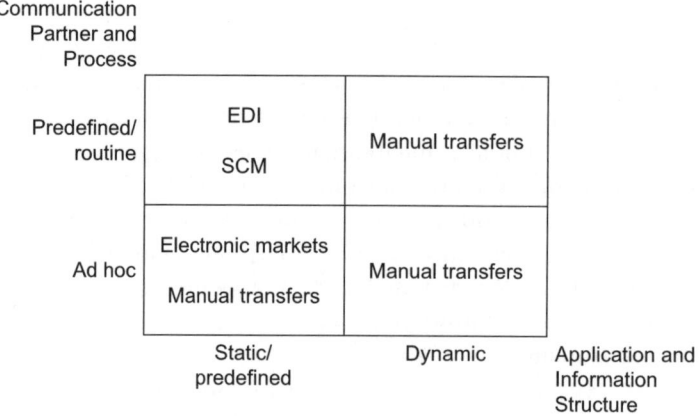

Fig. 2.11. Information integration methods today

If application or information structures change during or after deployment of a classical EDI solution, the project work must be partly redone and methods – normally static translation tables – must be reconfigured manually. In such cases, the semantics of the communication does not have to be revealed to the application systems involved as those systems do not have to interpret the information transmitted. Human actors perform this task while reconfiguring translation tables on the syntactic level. Even on e-markets that allow for a dynamic participation of market partners, those partners normally have to adhere to a prespecified set of messages in order to be able to participate in electronic collaborations.

Document standards today define messages mostly at the syntactic level. With the advent of the *Semantic Web* initiative, the work on semantic standards was launched. It can be expected that only semantic standards will help to build semantic synchronization services that will remedy today's limited information integration methods. Only with semantic standards the semantic synchronization task, which is performed implicitly today when syntactic reference tables are adjusted manually, can be made explicit and, thus, machine-processable.

3 E-Business Standards

The integration of interorganizational information flows is a key challenge for electronic business process coupling. For this integration task, standards play a major role. Without standards, and with the large number of business partners communicating electronically, integration tasks would be very complex, as exchange processes, content and formats would have to be negotiated for each bilateral communication relation. Agreed-upon information structures and transaction formats, and predefined document content, contribute to easing integration tasks.

As seen above, information integration needs to be achieved at different levels. In order for the partners to have the same understanding about transactions performed, the information exchanged needs to be unambiguous, i.e., carry the same meaning for both sender and receiver. Interoperability thus means not only merging data, but also clarifying and reconciling its meaning. Standards can supply this common ground.

In this chapter, we take a closer look at the e-business standards that are in use today and those emerging for tomorrow's use. We first provide an overview and develop a standard typology referring to the integration level concept introduced in the previous chapter. We then work along the typology, analyzing standards and standardization concepts associated with the respective levels. Finally, we discuss the standards situation today and draw conclusions for e-business integration.

3.1 Definition

A standard, very generally, is a rule that governs a specific situation. More specifically, the International Organization for Standardization (ISO) defines a standard as "a document, established by consensus and approved by a recognized body, that provides, for common and repeated use, rules, guidelines or characteristics for activities or their results, aimed at the achievement of the optimum degree of order in a given context" (ISO 2004). Since it is very precise, this definition may be too narrow for e-business practice, since not all standards used in e-business have been approved by a recognized body, if this means an official national or international organization. In e-business practice, we have to distinguish between official, or *de jure*, standards, in use on a legal basis, and a large number of *de facto* standards that are effectively in use without having been issued by a legal authority – such as standards developed by expert panels, industry consortiums or even individual companies. Thus, what we here term *e-business standards* includes official rules as well as non-official specifications or guidelines developed by companies, users, vendors or consortiums. Any agreed-upon information structure or transaction format, predefined document content, whether in-house, industry-specific, national or international, may be regarded as a standard.

In e-business, standards are intended for formatting data such as the descriptions of documents, transactions, processes, services, objects or conditions. Standards can offer both reference frameworks for information, transactions and processes on the structure level of an electronic communication – for instance by defining the structure of an electronic purchase order – as well as a common terminology and identifiers on the content level of such an exchange – for instance by defining unambiguous values for product groups, payment terms or terms of delivery.

3.2 An E-Business Standards Typology

Several approaches and models concerning the exchange and standardization of business data have been developed, each with its own focus. We will analyze relevant aspects before developing our own model.

3.2.1 Formatting Technical and Business Information

Establishing an electronic communication channel is, first of all, a technical task that is independent of the information content exchanged. The technical goal is to achieve correct and complete transmission of data from one application system to another. Technical standards facilitate message transport on this level. Data transported in a message can be differentiated into system information, required for the technical transmission procedure itself, and the business-related information, or *payload*, that is the actual transaction content to be exchanged between the business partners.

3.2.2 Levels of E-Business Standardization

Standards have been described and related to each other by means of level models. In the following discussion, five different models are presented in order to illustrate different approaches to categorizing e-business standards. Based on these approaches, a general typology is developed.

Communication Model by Voigtmann and Zeller

Voigtmann and Zeller (2002; 2003) analyze the requirements of an automated communication between systems. Based on the communication model by Shannon and Weaver (Shannon 1948), they subdivide a communication link into four hierarchical levels. Each of these areas can be understood as a level of integration. The basis of any integration is the realization of interoperability. Accordingly, on each level different integration requirements arise. Integration on a higher level can only be realized after it is fully achieved on the level below. A superior level uses the services implemented on the levels underneath.

The use of standards is proposed as a solution for the integration needs of the four communication levels. For each level, specific standards are available. As a result, several standards are used at the same time in order to achieve complete integration across all communication levels. Figure 3.1 shows the model (based on Voigtmann and Zeller 2002; 2003).

Communication Level	Requirement	Role of a Standard
4 Pragmatic Level	The reaction to a message is correct	Action and reaction rules
3 Semantic Level	A message is interpreted correctly	Regulating the meaning of the exchanged data
2 Syntactic Level	A message is read correctly	Formatting the data exchanged
1 Technical Level	A message is correctly transferred	Standardization of the technical transmission

Fig. 3.1. Role of standards on the communication levels

On the first level, a channel in the sense of the technical medium of communication is established. This medium can be described by means of the ISO/OSI Reference Model which specifics several layers of vendor-independent network protocols for open system connections (Zimmermann 1980).

A message is structured and formatted using standards on the syntactic level. The meaning of the message is addressed on the semantic level. The respective semantic standards can be divided into standards for classifying products and services, for structuring product catalogs and for structuring business transaction documents. On the pragmatic level, standards allow formulating rules on how to express the intention of a message. The fundamental objective on this level is to control and manage actions and their expected reactions.

EDI-level Model by Müller-Lankenau and Klein

Based on the EDI architecture model by Kubicek (1993), Müller-Lankenau and Klein (2004) develop an extended EDI level model, further detailing the focus of standards on the semantic level. All model levels are hierarchical. If the standardization requirements on at least the four lowermost sublevels are fulfilled, digital documents can be processed electronically. Figure 3.2 shows the respective model (based on Müller-Lankenau and Klein 2004).

EDI Level	Requirement	Role of a Standard
3 Integration	Technical Integration	Provision of interfaces and support of exchange formats
	Organizational Integration	Process Integration
2 Business Language	Pragmatic	Definition of exchange agreements and action/reaction patterns
	Semantic	Specification of the meaning of field contents through definition of data elements, value ranges, codes
		Definition of data-field formats
	Syntax	Specification of the the data-exchange format by definition of document structures
1 Data Transmission	Transmission Services	Provision of transmission services
	Transport Systems	Provision of technical transport infrastructure and security

Fig. 3.2. Role of standards on the EDI levels

With respect to the first level, the authors describe the message transport, which is executed as described in the ISO/OSI Reference Model. For the definition of business languages, the concept of semiotics is applied. Thus, on the second level, we find the respective three sublevels: syntax, semantics, and pragmatics. On the syntactic sublevel, the document structure is defined with regard to order, size and type of the data fields used. On the semantic sublevel, the meaning of the contents of the data fields is specified. On the pragmatic sublevel, rules for appropriate reactions are set through the definition of action-reaction patterns for the application systems concerned. Following Müller-Lankenau and Klein, rules for integrating processes organizationally and technically build on top of integrating the business language.

Interoperability Model by Hofreiter and Huemer

Moving beyond the scope of semiotics, Hofreiter and Huemer (2002) define an interoperability model with six hierarchical integration levels. To achieve full B2B integration, interoperability needs to be realized on each of those levels. Mutual consent between the communicating parties is needed about either the format to be used or how to map one format to another. The facilitation of interoperability can be measured by the degree to which it is realized on each of the levels. Figure 3.3 shows the levels (based on Hofreiter and Huemer 2002).

Interoperability Level	Requirement	Role of a Standard
6 Business Process Semantics	Defining business activity flows w.r.t. to content	Definition of unambiguous business transactions
5 Document Semantics	Provision of mutual understanding of document content	Agreement about semantics used
4 E-Business Vocabulary	Coding content in business documents	Sorted collection of business data
3 Transfer Syntax	Structuring of business documents	Metadata format
2 Transmission Protocol	Document transport	Message format
1 Transport Protocol		Transmission mechanism

Fig. 3.3. Role of standards on the interoperability levels

The transport protocol on the first level enables the technical transmission. In the case of utilization of message-oriented middleware on the second level, reliable transmission protocols are needed for distributing and delivering messages. But this does not guarantee interoperability, since incompatible protocol variants could be in use. Transfer formats structure the syntax of business documents and set the order of the data fields contained. On this level the semantics cannot yet be matched, since a document structure does not add a predefined meaning to the content of the data fields. The content meaning of a document can be individually defined at the time of its creation. This possibility of creating e-business vocabularies leads to the development of various languages. They can be seen as word collections and, along with this, as term-definition collections. A common agreement about the semantics used is necessary to achieve interoperability on this level. Finally, well-defined business process semantics that define business activities including their context-specific content enables interoperability on the highest level.

Standardization Model by Schmitz and Leukel

According to Schmitz and Leukel (2003), e-business standards are generally a prerequisite for efficient B2B transaction processing. Out of the abundance of standards available, suitable standards have to be chosen and, if necessary, adapted. The level model shows a hierarchical standardization order, but in contrast to the previously described approaches, the authors here separate between formatting metadata, technical data and business information by encapsulating business data into a domain-independent technical framework. Classifying a standard according to the model cannot always be done definitively, because allocating a standard to a specific task is not clearly distinct in all cases. A standard may fulfill more than one role, even across several levels. Figure 3.4 shows the model (based on Schmitz and Leukel 2003).

Standardization Level	Requirement	Role of a Standard
6 Metamodel	Abstraction of business communication	Generic model for description of the lower levels
5 Framework	Transmission of documents	Regulations for control and management of the transmission process
4 Processes	Evocation of correct responses to received documents	Content related sequencing of document types
3 Documents	Linking related terms	Definition of business document types
2 Vocabulary	Specification of business-specific terms	Definition of data elements
1 Data Types	Typing data elements	Definition of permitted codable data values

Fig. 3.4. Role of standards on the standardization levels

Data types define the information contained in a data element and set the possible values. A set of data elements makes up a vocabulary. It represents the business language between communication partners, since, by following naming conventions, identical issues are designated with the same terms. Data elements may occur in atomic or compound forms, e.g., a string may represent a single product description or an address as composition of street name, postal code and city.

Document types are created by putting together vocabulary elements, whereas a document is a possible instance of the corresponding document type. A document is a logical unit containing data elements related by content and is the basis for any business communication. It is sent from a sender to a receiver and contains commercially relevant information. The intention is to prompt a reaction by the receiver. Thus, the document itself carries a pragmatic aspect.

A succession of documents and their underlying logic specify the business transaction taking place, as depicted on the fourth model level called "processes". This business logic results from the business content. The sequence of documents to be sent and the prompted reactions in the form of documents returned is regulated by the intra- and interorganizational business processes concerned.

The standards of the framework level, which is the fifth level, regulate the transmission execution and the security. This level encompasses the first four levels and covers the technical aspects of communication, such as transport protocols, transmission services, message enveloping, and delivery. These formats are independent of the business-related contents of the document transmission. In the previously described models, this technically oriented level focuses on the same tasks, but is regarded as the bottom layer and thereby the foundation.

On the metamodel level, by use of a generic model, all underlying levels and their relation are represented. Specific application models represent the scope of the processes, as they are specified for an industry or typical scenarios on the process level.

Integration Model by Chari and Seshadri

Chari and Seshadri (2004) propose a different approach by extending the basic idea of hierarchically ordered levels for technology, data formatting and process definitions. They systemize standards by means of a three-dimensional framework that distinguishes between the standards according to objectives and scope. When deciding for or against adopting one or more standards, this integration framework should show potential gaps in coverage.

The application architecture includes three functional components. The data logic enables data management by transferring them into a format that allows further processing. The business logic comprises the business applications' process logic. The presentation logic facilitates the interaction between an application and the various interfaces, such as web browser, voice recognition, mobile devices and terminals.

Upon integration of applications, one or more components are affected and need to be integrated on one or more levels. On the transport level, data is transferred between applications. For this, the infrastructure and the abstraction required are provided with the aid of communication protocols. Consistent data representation is sought on the data format level. The data elements of various systems are combined into formatted messages. Typical tasks on this level are data encoding, formatting, ontology-based specification of data fields and message composition. The messages contain the data, together with the metainformation about encoding, message content, security and message transmission. The interaction of applications for realizing business transactions is organized on the process level. Figure 3.5 shows the levels and functional areas (based on Chari and Seshadri 2004).

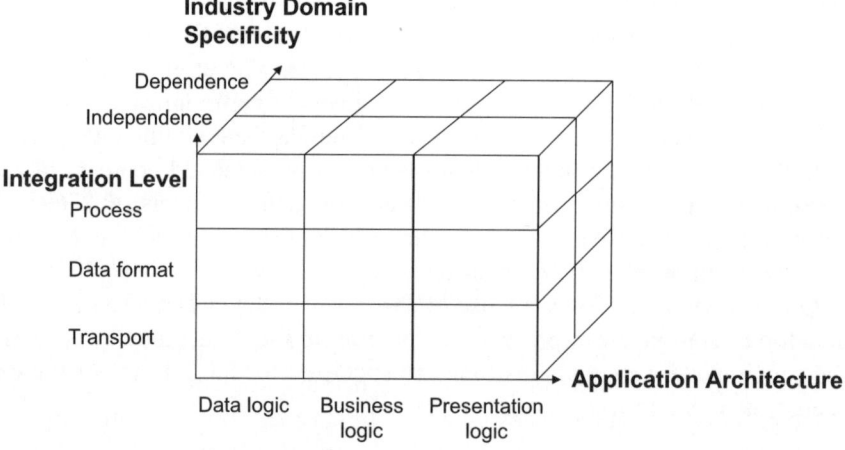

Fig. 3.5. Integration framework

Collaborations are coordinated according to process flows defined in advance. The dimension of the industry domain specificity expresses the scope of the intended standardization. Industry-independent standards are mostly generic, while dependent standards are used specifically for a particular industry.

3.2.3 Standards Typology Model

The five models introduced above all use a document-oriented approach and describe the requirements and achievements of e-business standards in various focus areas. Although there are differences in the details, a comparison of the models shows general similarities. All models assume hierarchical analysis levels and foresee the provision of a technical channel for data exchange aside from the formatting of business information and the representation of the interorganizational business processes. Even though the levels differ in number, positioning and naming, through their aggregation, the scope of standards for e-business integration can be harmonized with regard to the main features.

Accordingly, three major types of standards can be distinguished: *technical*, *business information* and *security* standards.

Technical standards for the creation of an interoperable communication infrastructure are independent of standards for formatting business-relevant information. Once the technical means for communicating have been set up, business information may be transmitted. To this end, the main questions about the standardization are in regard to the structure and content of documents as well as their exchange sequence. These requirements for standardizing business information can be sufficiently described according to the semiotic model already introduced. Additionally, in business conversations, security needs have to be considered.

The critical importance of security is mainly due to the fact that e-business connectivity and the functioning of business processes are increasingly dependent on reliable public information and communication technology (ICT) infrastructure, namely the Internet (EC 2005c). Security issues can arise for several aspects of a communication (Vlachakis et al. 2003; Daum and Mertens 2003, Rebstock and Tafreschi 2002):

- *Integrity* of data and messages requires protection against manipulations such as modifications or corruption of message content.
- *Confidentiality* and privacy need to be assured by preventing eavesdropping or access to information by unauthorized persons.
- *Authentication* and authorization can be assured by means of access control in order to establish the origin of data and the identity of communication partners and avoid message interception by unauthorized third parties.
- *Verifiability* and non-repudiation allows for the verification of genuine data and messages and prevents later denial of ownership of a message or data modifications, so that legally binding contracts can be transmitted.

Such risks can be reduced through the use of the different types of security standards. General security standards can be applied to e-business conversation, for example, the secure socket layers (SSL) technology (Daum and Mertens 2003). For providing security on a more functional level, standards for protecting message content, such as encryption of data or the use of digital watermarks, can be applied and incorporated into secure message exchange protocols (Rebstock and Tafreschi 2002).

In consideration of all the aspects discussed, Figure 3.6 describes a general typology of e-business standards.

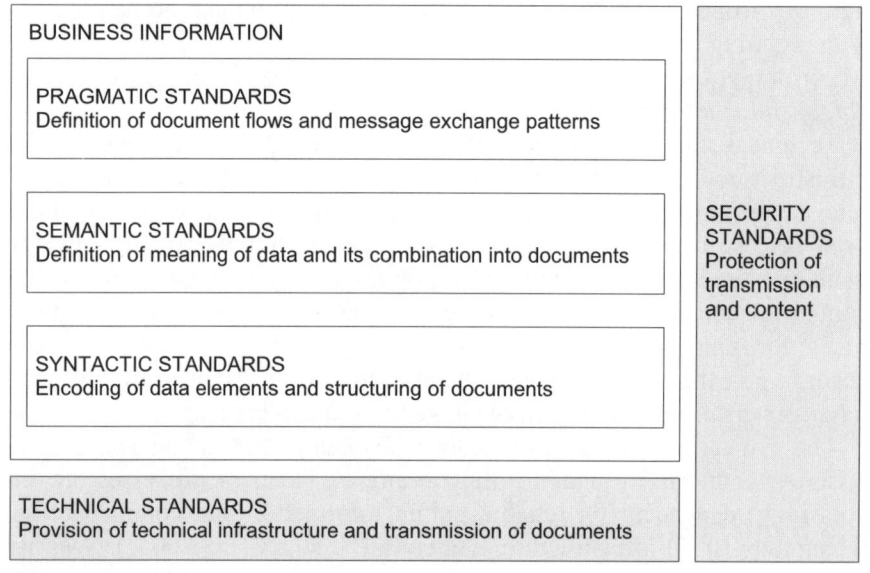

Fig. 3.6. General e-business standards typology

Technical standards provide the transmission infrastructure for delivering the business information payload. Concerning the payload itself, the semiotic stack of syntax, semantics and pragmatics can be applied. Standards can be attributed to the respective levels depending on their focus. Additionally, for a reliable dialogue, all information exchange services have to address the security issues introduced above. Security standards supply the necessary framework.

3.3 Technical Standards

Classical *transmission standards* used for the still most important type of electronic document transfer – EDI – were specialized protocols such as X.400, a non-Internet message handling format, or the File Transfer Access and Management (FTAM) protocol. With the growth of the Internet and its increased utilization for business purposes, standards based on the Transmission Control Protocol/Internet Protocol (TCP/IP) became popular for business communication use (Tanenbaum 1996). Very common today are the Hypertext Transport Protocol (HTTP), Post Office Protocol Version 3 (POP3), the Internet Message Access Protocol (IMAP) and the File Transfer Protocol (FTP).

Functional standards serve for complementing business data with additional technical information. Such standards, mostly for unformatted data, exist in different industries. Examples are construction data from Computer Aided Design (CAD) and Computer Aided Engineering (CAE) systems, formatted according to the Initial Graphics Exchange Specification (IGES) or the ISO standard 10303-21 Standard for the Exchange of Product Model Data (STEP) or the German formats VDAFS and CAD-I for exchanging geometrical production data for CAD systems (Wigand et al. 1997). Information formatted according to such standards may be added to business content as multimedia information, e.g., a Multipurpose Internet Mail Extension (MIME) added to an electronic product description.

3.4 Syntactic Standards

For classical e-business communication, well-known syntactic standards are ASCII-based EDI-formats such as UN/EDIFACT or ASC X12. They serve for the interorganizational exchange of structured information. Besides recent XML-based standards (discussed in more detail below), a number of *de facto* standards such as the Intermediate Document (IDoc) by SAP, the comma separated values (CSV) format, rich text format (RTF) or MS-Excel or MS-Access formats are also used for structured business documents. While formats like IDoc or CSV have been conceptualized for generic usage, EDI formats have been developed specifically for B2B data exchange (Bussler 2001).

EDI standards define the sequence, length and data types of elements grouped together in segments and thereby set the message layout (Bussler 2001). Additional bilateral agreements usually regulate the customizing of standard document types according to the partner-specific requirements

(Hofreiter et al. 2004). As a consequence, business partners have to comply with those presettings and amend their import and export procedures accordingly for further processing in their internal systems.

Figure 3.7 illustrates the data stream of an EDI transmission, using an order document as an example.

```
UNB+UNOC:3+1234567890123:14+9876543210987:
14+070101:1000UNH+785+ORDERS:D:93A:UN:EAN0
07BGM+220+678901234567DTM+137:20070101:102
NAD+BY+4909090909991::9++ABCD AG+Frankfurt
er Str 12+Darmstadt+64295++DE`NAD+SU+49999
99123123::9++XYZ Chemicals+10 Nin Chang Rd
. Lin Hang District+Shanghai+220245++CNCUX
+2:EUR:9LIN+1++4934635645623:ENQTY+21:50PR
I+AAA:28.9::LIUPRI+AAB:54.9::SRPLIN+2++493
4563567675:ENQTY+21:20PRI+AAA:48.9::LIUPRI
+AAB:84.9::SRPUNS+SUNT+25+785UNZ+1+525
```

Fig. 3.7. EDI transmission (example)

Traditionally, EDI systems employed specialized communication networks, mostly in the form of private VANs. In the late 1990s, Internet-based EDI became popular, as it offered easier network installation using the Internet and its technologies, as well as lower management and use costs (EC 2005b). The adoption of the Internet, and with it the use of XML, promised easier definition and implementation of data exchange as well as lower deployment and transmission costs (Bussler 2001).

XML – eXtensible Markup Language – is a general format on which various e-business standards are based. It serves as a *metastandard* for formatting and structuring information logically and thus preparing it for transmission via the Internet, in particular the World Wide Web (WWW) (W3C 2006a). Using XML, arbitrary data and document formats can be specified (W3C 2006a). XML documents are represented as a tree structure that is supposed to be readable by machines as well as by humans. Document structures are specified by using markup tags. Such formatting labels are supposed to be independent of vendor, programming language or operating systems used (Obasanjo 2003). Markup encodes a description of the document's layout and associates attribute name and value pairs with its logical structure (W3C 2006a). Applying this method, rules are created that define the logical structure and succession of data in a document. Still, XML does not specify a tag set or any semantics. Structural elements and their position in a specific XML document type can and have to be assigned individually – making document specification flexible and extensible, but also potentially unclear. Still, with XML, some shortcomings of traditional EDI are expected to be overcome since it provides implicit means for the representation of terminologies and explicit naming facilities for document elements (Omelayenko 2002).

As an extension of XML, various XML-based technologies have emerged, e.g., the Document Type Definition (DTD) (W3C 1998) and XML Schema (W3C 2004b). With the aid of these structure guides and schema languages, valid fields and hierarchical and quantitative relations within an XML document can be set. As a result, XML offers the possibility of creating structured data formats with unambiguous labels for the data fields. But even by doing so, the semantics of such fields and their possible values may still not be defined unambiguously (Hepp 2003). For an illustration, Figure 3.8 shows two different examples of an address setup using XML.

```
<NameAddress>                         <ADDRESS>
  <Name1>University of Applied          <NAME>Hochschule Darmstadt</NAME>
  Sciences</Name1>                      <NAME2>University of Applied Sciences</NAME2>
  <POBox></POBox>                       <DEPARTMENT>Faculty of Business
  <PostalCode>D-64295</PostalCode>      Administration</DEPARTMENT>
  <City>Darmstadt</City>                <CONTACT>
  <Region>                                <CONTACT_NAME>Fengel</CONTACT_NAME>
    <RegionCode>Germany</RegionCode>      <PHONE type="office">+49 6151 16
  </Region>                                    9458</PHONE>
</NameAddress>                            <FAX></FAX>
                                          <URL>http://www.fbw.h-da.de</URL>
                                        </CONTACT>
                                        <STREET>Haardtring 100</STREET>
                                        <ZIP>64295</ZIP>
                                        <CITY>Darmstadt</CITY>
                                        <COUNTRY>DE</COUNTRY>
                                        <VAT_ID></VAT_ID>
                                        <URL></URL>
                                      </ADDRESS>
```

Fig. 3.8. Examples of address representation in XML

As can be seen, some elements with the same information are present, but they are named differently, e.g., <NameAddress> and <ADDRESS>. Furthermore, different levels of granularity are foreseen, as demonstrated by the additional supplements of <NAME2> and <DEPARTMENT> on the right and the provision of a coding possibility for the country where the business partner is located. Also, the example on the right provides the possibility of entering a contact, which would need to be done in another section of the document for the example on the left.

XML itself does not predefine any particular formats for specific document or data types. Those are specified in further XML-based standards or vocabularies, since XML allows a simple representation of nested structures and dependencies. By using constraints, such as setting element names or defining attributes and document structure, XML languages can be configured. The resulting XML Schemas express shared vocabularies and can be used for defining the structure, content and semantics of XML documents (W3C 2004b). The customizing of markup languages brought forward various application-domain-specific semantics. These XML-derived standards all show a common data format, so that data can be exchanged between different applications without major prior efforts at creating interface specifications and conversions. Over time, this led to the emergence of a multitude of XML-based application standards, sometimes for partially overlapping application domains, and thus to *semantic* standardization problems.

3.5 Semantic Standards

In contrast to syntactic mismatches originating from differences in the naming and structural depths of product catalogs or other business documents, content mismatches are caused by the usage of differing real-world semantics (Fensel et al. 2001). The deployment of semantic standards is intended to disambiguate the meaning of business information content. Such business languages standardize documents *and* their semantics, as well as document fields *and* the meaning of their content.

In looking at business information exchange, two levels of standardization can be distinguished. Semantic ambiguity can occur on the structure – or schema – level and on the content level. Referring to the example introduced earlier, if the data field is labeled "Terms of Delivery" and is filled with the information "FOB Shanghai", then both the meaning of the label ("What does 'Terms of Delivery' mean, i.e., which information does the field carry?") and of the content ("What does 'FOB Shanghai' mean in terms of the logistics of this specific transaction?") may be unclear. Thus misunderstandings may arise when business partners have a different perception of or are unsure about the (exact) meaning of any of the terms in use on either level.

Concerning their focus, *data-oriented* standards provide a basis for uniformly expressing information about business terms and goods, focusing on unambiguous designations for suppliers, products and their attributes. Mostly, they serve for formatting master data. Transaction data is much more dynamic. *Process-oriented* standards focus on a uniform representation of business process structures and supply a standardized form for complex workflows within and between organizations.

Considering this, today's approaches towards systematizing standards can be differentiated into five areas (Quantz and Wichmann 2003a; EC 2005b):

- Identification of goods, organizations and business terms
- Classifications for describing and searching products and services
- Catalog exchange formats for easier automated exchange of catalog data
- Transaction standards for exchanging business documents
- Process standards for the automation of complex courses of action in business flows

Following the e-business standards typology already presented and detailing it further, Figure 3.9 shows the detailed typology of e-business standards.

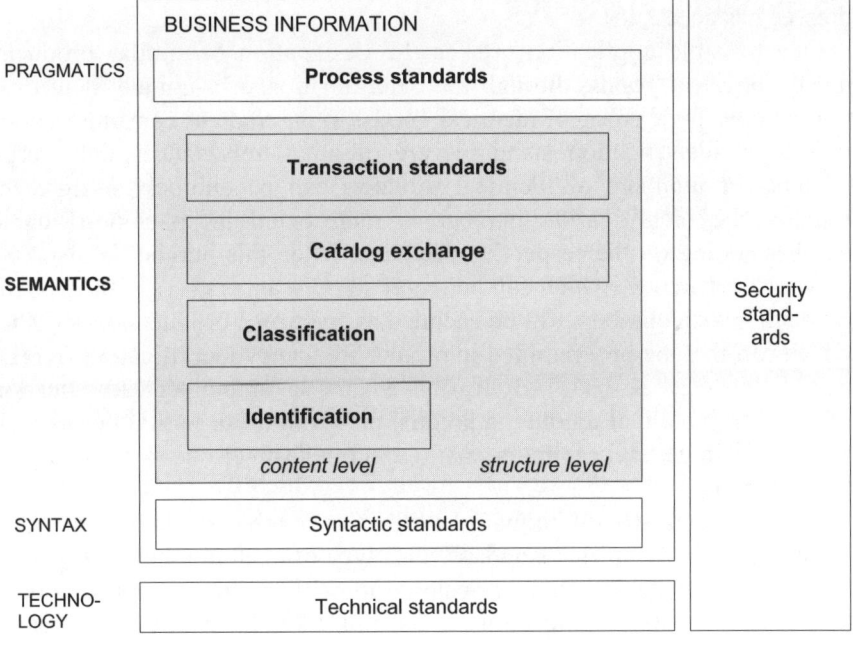

Fig. 3.9. Detailed typology of e-business standards

Some standards – industry-specific or generic, cross-industry standards – cannot be clearly assigned to a particular type because they standardize elements from multiple typological areas. Thus, standards can overlap, complement one another, or compete. Also, they may vary considerably in terms of their usability and the degree to which they fulfill the given requirements of standardization. Presently, there is no comprehensive standard covering all aspects of semantic standardization alike. Due to the increasing complexity of the standardization objectives on the different levels, standards are often utilized in combination.

In the following section, the purpose of semantic standards for each typological area is described and frequently used standards within these areas are introduced.

3.5.1 Identification Standards

Objects and units of all kinds can be identified by means of identification codes. A uniquely assigned code number eliminates the need for transmission of full text addresses, product descriptions or any other details in full length (supplied this information is already persistent in databases the addressee has access to).

One possible application area is the designation of similar products, mostly physical goods, through the determination of a unique identification number for a group of identical goods. In the trade or consumer goods industries, identification standards are of great importance, since large amounts or numbers of identical products can be uniquely designated. Usually the identification number is represented in machine-readable number coding on the respective products. Often this number is also displayed as a barcode, which can be recorded by scanners (GS1 2006a). Additionally, such numbers can be encoded as electronic product codes (EPC) which can then be programmed into radio frequency identification (RFID) tags (Schuster et al. 2007). Both ways enable the automated identification of objects. (Note that unique, individual pieces of art or antiquities as well as services in general cannot be marked in this manner due to their respective nature.)

One of the most well-known identification number systems is the GS1 system, a globally unified standard. This type of open number system provides a worldwide unique and accurate identification of items, products, assets, services and organizations, logistic units, and their location. It is often implemented within supply chain systems. The representation in the form of GS1-barcodes facilitates a basis for easy communication of information about an object. The development was started in 1977 in Europe as the European, later International, Article Number (EAN) system, an association of manufacturers and merchants from twelve European countries.

Another major identification system was the US-American Uniform Product Code (UPC), as provided by the American Uniform Code Council (UCC). In 1992 both systems were combined into the globally usable EAN.UCC system, today called GS1 system (GS1 2006a). The developing initiative is currently present in over 100 member states of the GS1 organization. The development and maintenance of identification systems enables globally non-recurring, non-overlapping designation through the following major key concepts (GS1 2006b):

- Global Location Number (GLN) for identifying organizations and their units in their function as physical locations and legal entities.
- Global Trade Item Number (GTIN) for identifying articles, products and services.
- Serial Shipping Container Code (SSCC) for identifying an item of any composition established for transport and/or storage.
- Global Returnable Asset Identifier (GRAI) for identifying reusable packages or transport equipment.
- Global Document Type Identifier (GDTI) for a document type combined with an optional serial number to access database information required for document control.

The numbers can be displayed in the GS1 barcode symbol for automated reading and are thus protected against mix-ups. This symbol is based on uniquely defined data elements and fields. The symbols can completely display the ASCII-code, include a check digit, and provide good readability and printability while providing a high data density. A plain-text line is provided with each symbol showing a readable translation of the code for humans. Figure 3.10 shows an example of a barcode (GS1 2006a).

(01) 90614141000415 (3202) 000712

Fig. 3.10. Barcode of a GS1 Identification Number

Other well-established identification standards are the International Standard Book Number (ISBN) for identifying books (ISBN 2007) or the D-U-N-S Number, developed by Dun & Bradstreet in the US for identifying organizations by means of a 9-digit company index (DNB 2007).

In addition to numbers, letters may also be used for unique identification. Collecting relevant terms and assigning distinct alphabetic characters leads to term collections in the form of controlled glossaries or dictionaries. A term is understood as the designation of a defined concept in a special language by a linguistic expression (Leukel et al. 2005). The International Chamber of Commerce published the International Commercial Terms, known as INCOTERMS, as early as 1936 to assist business partners in different countries in understanding one another when negotiating sales contracts (ICC 2007). These thirteen standard trade definitions are to be used in international contracts to provide legal certainty regarding the buyers' and sellers' responsibilities concerning the transport, cost and risk sharing for the delivery of merchandise. Among the best-known terms are "Free on Board" (FOB), which is followed by the name of the port of shipment, and "Cost, Insurance and Freight" (CIF), which is followed by the name of the port of destination. These terms are applicable independent of the means of transportation; i.e., they are usable for sea as well as air freight.

Various other international industrial and commercial norms and standards intended for identification purposes have been published by ISO, including the following:

- ISO 639 defines codes for the representation of names of languages, such as "eng" for English or "jpn" for Japanese.
- ISO 3166 defines codes for country and dependent area names, such as "us" for the USA or "de" for Germany, used as the basis for the Internet country code top-level domains or in ISO 9362, which is the code standard for bank identifier codes within the Society for Worldwide Interbank Financial Telecommunication (SWIFT) code, also known as Bank Identifier Code (BIC).
- ISO 4217 defines the names of currencies in three-letter codes, such as "USD" for US Dollars or "CHF" for Swiss Francs.
- ISO 13584, the Industrial automation systems and integration - Parts library (PLIB), developed in cooperation with the International Electrotechnical Commission (IEC), publishing the IEC 61360 Component Data Dictionary provides definitions for the standardization of electrical equipment.
- ISO 10303 Industrial automation systems and integration – Product data representation and exchange, known as STEP STandard for the Exchange of Product data, defines an exchange format for product information.

More complex standards often incorporate identifications. For example, a number of classification standards, catalog exchange standards and transactional standards include data fields in which standardized identification numbers, e.g., GS1, can be stored.

3.5.2 Classification Standards

A classification is a system for sorting objects. Like a taxonomy, it provides a method for grouping objects into categories, but with the additional capability of systemizing them into a hierarchical order (Merriam-Webster's Online Dictionary 2007a). A set of items or business objects such as products, materials, services, packages or industries may be divided into subsets according to differences in certain predetermined characteristics (Leukel et al. 2005). A class is a set of objects grouped together following common features. For a more detailed description, classified objects may be extended through the use of further property descriptions and associated property values. For the purpose of minimizing the number of attributes and asserting their non-redundancy, classification systems often include a defined attribute pool (Leukel et al. 2002a). This way, products not only become clearly identifiable, but can also have unique, universally valid descriptions associated with them. Furthermore, by using a classification, product lines may be organized according to standardized hierarchies by grouping products and services into categories, commodity groups and classes, respectively. Thus, subclass and superclass relations are definable.

The purpose of creating names or codes for commodities and sorting them into a particular order is to facilitate easier searches for products to be purchased, the processing of expenditure analysis and general uniformity across the company. The process also allows for channeling and distribution of product and marketing information, and multiple language use (Granada 2001).

In order to enable the comparison of products of different origin, these products need to be named, described and classified consistently, so they can be clearly related and their unique identification is enabled independently of the document syntax used (Otto et al. 2002). Since products can be further described with different properties and attributes respectively, those can be combined into supplemental attribute lists for further detailing a search (Quantz and Wichmann 2003a). To enable information exchange regarding products without any limitations, product descriptions have to be modeled according to a consistent method and a consistent semantic data model. Presently, the standards available do not possess a common data model. Most of the models presently available only provide the representation of basic products like indirect goods, articles for maintenance, repair and operation (MRO), which do not possess interdependent properties, as is the case with configurable and non-standardized goods (Beckmann et al. 2004). The only internationally standardized formal data models for product descriptions and classification are the identical normative standards ISO 13584-42 and IEC 61360-2, which use the same data model (Beckmann et al. 2004).

Various factors have led to the differences in the structure and wording of classification standards for similar or identical products. Some reasons include industry-specific requirements or the particular internal needs of enterprises. Classifications, and their respective description by properties, may be shaped differently, and thus may not be unambiguously interpretable. The definition of a property called "color" may serve as an example: As a property value, a simple declaration like "light blue" or "green" may be chosen. Yet a more advertising-oriented naming, like "cool blue" or "papyrus," or a more technical classification, according to color scales such as RAL, RGB, HKS or Pantone, may also be used (Quantz and Wichmann 2003b). In Germany, for instance, an industry-wide online dictionary of standardized product properties has been set up by the National German Institute for Standardization. This is called DINsml.net and is based on the formal information models ISO 13584, IEC 61360 and DIN 4002. In the dictionary, normative product properties are collected together with their standardized definitions in order to enable information exchanges about cataloged products and parts in various industries (DINsml.net 2007). Thus, vendor- and manufacturer-spanning comparability of product information, and its further usage in computer aided design (CAD), computer aided engineering (CAE) or product lifecycle management (PLM) systems, can be provided.

Furthermore, standards differ with regard to their orientation towards specific industries. Horizontal standards provide a rather high-level classification of products across industries, often describing general demand or MRO goods. In contrast, vertical standards focus on one specific industry and provide a narrow, in-depth classification within the limits of their domain. Basically, a vertical standard could extend some of the bottom-level categories of a horizontal standard, thus complementing it (Omelayenko and Fensel 2001).

When using a particular classification system, it may occur that not all products produced by an organization are unambiguously classifiable. The reasons may be the particular specificity of the products or general technological progress. Therefore, some classifications allow for the creation of proprietary classes. Alternatively, the product properties may be used to describe a product for which no appropriate class can be found in the classification (Hepp 2006b). Unfortunately, this steady semantic extension and variation can lead to different versions of the same system. Similarly, the particular terminologies and operational requirements of markets and industry sectors have brought forth the development of specific classifications without one prevailing across industries (Leukel et al. 2002a). In consequence, various horizontal and vertical classification systems have been developed – as of recently, there are more than thirty-five (CEN 2006). An extensive overview is provided by Eurostat (Eurostat 2007b). Some of the most well-known horizontal systems for classifying goods and services are:

- UNSPSC – United Nations Standard Products and Services Code – is an open, global multi-sector standard for the classification of products and services. It is administered by members' initiative (UNSPSC 2007).
- CPC – Central Product Classification – is a comprehensive classification of goods and services. It is administered by the United Nations Statistics Division (UNSD) (UNSD 2007a).
- GPC – Global Product Classification – is a part of the GS1 System, providing a common language for category management with a set of common categories to group products globally. It is administered by GS1 (GS1 2006c).
- NAICS – North American Industry Classification System – is a product and services classification system developed jointly by the U.S., Canada, and Mexico to provide comparability in statistics about business activity across North America. It is administered by the U.S. Census Bureau (U.S. Census Bureau 2007).
- eClass is an internationally oriented standard for the classification and description of products (materials and services). It is administered by the eClass association in Germany (eClass 2005).
- CPV – Common Procurement Vocabulary – is a classification system for European public procurement. It is administered by SIMAP, the Système d'Information des Marchés Publiques, i.e., European Electronic Procurement Service (SIMAP 2007).
- ePDC Global Multilingual Product Description and Classification for eCommerce and eBusiness is a European CEN initiative for harmonizing the various differently modeled systems in classifications and multilingual electronic catalogs and their respective data modeling (CEN 2006).
- NATO Codification System is managed by a North Atlantic Treaty Organization Cadre Group as a uniform and common system for identification, classification and stock numbering of items of supply in order to

improve logistics systems and operations for participating nations and facilitate global logistics operations (NATO 2007).

- eOTD – ECCMA Open Technical Dictionary – is an international open-standard descriptive language for cataloging individuals, organizations, locations, goods and services. It is administered by the Electronic Commerce Code Management Association (ECCMA) in the US (ECCMA 2007).
- BEC – Classification by Broad Economic Categories - defined in terms of SITC, Rev.3, (BEC Rev.3) – is intended for categorizing trade statistics into large economic classes of commodities. It is administered by the United Nations Statistics Division (UNSD) (UNSD 2007b).
- A classification with a more economic focus is the NACE – the Nomenclature générale des activités économiques dans les Communautés Européennes (Eurostat 2007a) – which is based on and amended from the ISIC – International Standard Industrial Classification of All Economic Activities, Third Revision, (ISIC, Rev.3) – for classifying industrial sectors (UNSD 2007c).

Some of these standards, e.g., GPC, can be used for interlinking and synchronizing with master data pools like SINFOS (SINFOS 2006) or Transora (Transora 2007). These master data pools are central collection points for multilateral exchange of item data between business partners.

Well-known vertical standards include the following:

- RNTD – RosettaNet Technical Directory – contains common properties for defining products for inclusion in a RosettaNet Partner Interface Process (PIP) that defines business processes between trading partners in the electronics and telecommunications industry (RosettaNet 2007c).
- Proficlass is a German classification for the building industry, which is working together with comparable initiatives to assure compatibility (proficlass 2004).
- PIDX – Petroleum Industry Data Exchange – is used for formatting eCommerce messages in XML and EDI and a product classification and service component standard with defined nomenclature and attributes. It is administered by the American Petroleum Institute's (API) committee on Electronic Business Standards and Processes (API 2007).
- SNITEM – Syndicat National de l'Industrie des Technologies Médicales – focuses on the medical technology industry on an international level. It is administered in France (SNITEM 2007).
- HS Harmonized Commodity Description and Coding System by the World Customs Organization (WCO) is a nomenclature used as a basis

for trade facilitation, the collection of customs duties and international trade statistics worldwide (WCO 2007).

Besides these internationally oriented approaches, there are many local, regional or national initiatives creating specific standards or considering regional, national, sector-specific or administrative and official regulatory aspects, such as, for example, customs tariffs.

Taking writing paper as an example, the following analysis of two of the most common classification standards demonstrates some key issues of classification system design.

Internationally, especially in the English-speaking parts of the world, UNSPSC is a widespread cross-industry hierarchical classification for products and services. It was developed in 1998 by the United Nations Development Programme (UNDP) and Dun & Bradstreet Corporation (D&B). A UNSPSC code includes four hierarchical levels to which a fifth company-specific level for further detailing may be added. Each level is coded with a two-digit numerical value, so that the code notation is an eight or ten digit number, respectively. Table 3.1 depicts the structure for writing paper with the UNSPSC code 14111511.

Table 3.1. Classification structure of UNSPSC

Segment	Family	Class	Commodity	Business Function
14000000 Paper Materials and Products				
	14100000 Paper materials			
		14101501 Paper pulp		
	14110000 Paper products			
		14111500 Printing and writing paper		
			14111501 Onion skin paper	
			14111507 Printing paper	
			...	
			14111511 Writing paper	
			...	
		14111600 Novelty paper		
			14111601 Gift wrapping paper or bags or boxes	
			...	
		14111700 Personal paper products		
			14111703 Paper towels	
			...	
		14111800 Business use papers		
			14111818 Thermal paper	
	14120000 Industrial use papers			
		14121500 Paperboard and packaging papers		
		...		

Within this standard, the levels are called "segments" for logically grouping "families" for analytical purposes. A family describes a commonly recognized interrelated group of product and commodities categories. A "class" is a group of goods sharing a common use or function, while a "commodity" is a group of substitutable products or services. A "business function" is defined as an organization in support of the commodity for specific labeling (Granada 2001). UNSPSC does not provide a property list.

In Europe, next to UNSPCS and GPC, eClass is also very popular (CEN 2006). It is an international cross-industry standard for classifying and describing products, materials and services along the value chain. Table 3.2 shows the structure for writing paper with the eClass code 24-34-03-03.

Table 3.2. Classification structure of eClass

Segment	Main group	Group	Commodity class	Property set	Key words

24 Office products, facilities and technics, papeterie
    24-20 Office supplies
        24-20-01 Inkjetprinter and inkjetfax-supplies
           24-20-01-01 Ink and inkjetprint heads

        ...
        24-20-02 Laser printer- and laserfax-supplies
      ...

  ...
    24-34 Fancy goods, gift, party articles
      ...
        24-34-03 Writing paper, greetings card
          ...
        24-34-03-03 Writing paper

Property	Key words
BAA059001- Article number	Airmail paper,
BAA351002- Color	Colourless,
BAE967001- Description of noteworthy features	Loose paper, Handmade notepaper, Luminous
BAF591001- Design of ruling	notepaper, Pri
BAA271001- EAN code	vate notepaper,
BAA001001- Manufacturer's name	Transparent note
BAB664002- Material	paper
BAE455001- Paper size	
BAA316001- Product name	
BAA002001- Product type description	
BAF821001- Square measure of paper	
BAG653001- Watermark (Y/N)	

        ...
    24-34-04 Album
  ...

This standard is available in several languages and enables the structuring of commodities according to a logical schema with detailing descriptions defined by normative properties. Products and services can be classified along a hierarchical numerical class structure with four levels, each expressed by two-digit values. The actual version consists of 25 segments on the first level, 514 main groups on the second, 4,658 groups on the third and 25,083 commodity classes on the fourth. Additionally, enumerations of standardized properties with defined value ranges facilitate an accurate description and subsequently identification of products and services. For efficient product searches more than 51,000 keywords are available (eClass 2007b).

As can be seen from the example, not only the hierarchical categorization of an item – here, writing paper – in any two standards may differ substantially concerning both content and structure of the category tree. Moreover, underlying the design of the category tree, the actual perception of what the nature of a specific item mostly is, is not harmonized between standards.

3.5.3 Catalog Exchange Formats

Information about an organization's products and services is often compiled into an electronic catalog. For an automated exchange of such catalog information with business partners, standards for describing the catalog content are required. The information exchanged includes master data such as product designations, product descriptions, prices and delivery terms. An extract of a company's product database could be generated, e.g., in the form of a CSV file, an MS Excel sheet, an MS Access report or an XML file. By means of catalog systems, the extracted data can be converted into another format. Catalogs may also contain multimedia data such as pictures, graphics, technical documents or videos. Often, the catalog data provided by a supplier are combined with data from other applications. Thus, the rather static product information is transmitted in the same format together with current dynamic data such as price or availability (Quantz and Wichmann 2003a).

A jointly used catalog exchange format eases the integration of several catalogs into a multisupplier catalog, since no efforts at transformation or integration arise. However, even when using those standards, the content of non-standardized data fields, for example the properties of classifications, could be incompatible. The combination of product information with variable details like prices or delivery terms necessitates further definitions within the catalog exchange format. As the specification of a price information could, in some cases, depend on framework contracts or quantities ordered, information about such constraints would also be desirable and should be included in a uniform manner (Quantz and Wichmann 2003b).

In most electronic catalog documents, three different sections can be distinguished (Segev et al. 1995). A header contains control information as well as specifications about customer and supplier, framework contracts and standard values. In the second section, the product data may include (BME 2006):

- Identification, by company-specific article numbers or standardized identifiers like EAN/GTIN,
- Description,
- Classification details, e.g., ERP commodity class numbers,
- Properties, e.g., weight and color,
- Order information, e.g., order unit or minimum order size,
- Price information, e.g., customer price or list price,
- Multimedia information, e.g., images or PDF files,
- Markings, e.g., as special offer or discontinued model,
- Reference to other products like accessories or alternative products,
- Any further user-defined data.

The third section comprises the information about the document structure. For a standardized transmission of catalogs, catalog exchange formats are used. The existing standards can be differentiated into three groups:

- CSV files for importing the data into databases or spreadsheets,
- XML-based formats,
- Formats for traditional EDI for catalog data exchange,
- Industry-specific exchange formats.

Often, formats for catalog exchange are part of broader standards for the exchange of a number of different business documents (Leukel et al. 2002b). Their primary purpose therefore often is not the formatting of master data according to a classification, but rather to facilitate its transmission into a business partner's application system. An example for such formats is UN/EDIFACT (UNECE 2006). Besides many others, UN/EDIFACT includes message types called PRICAT and PRODAT. PRICAT is the price/sales catalog message that enables the transmission of information regarding pricing and catalog details for goods and services. PRODAT is the product data message and is used for the submission of master data. It contains product descriptions together with price and delivery specifications. Figure 3.11 shows one of the segments of the PRODAT message (UNECE 2007a).

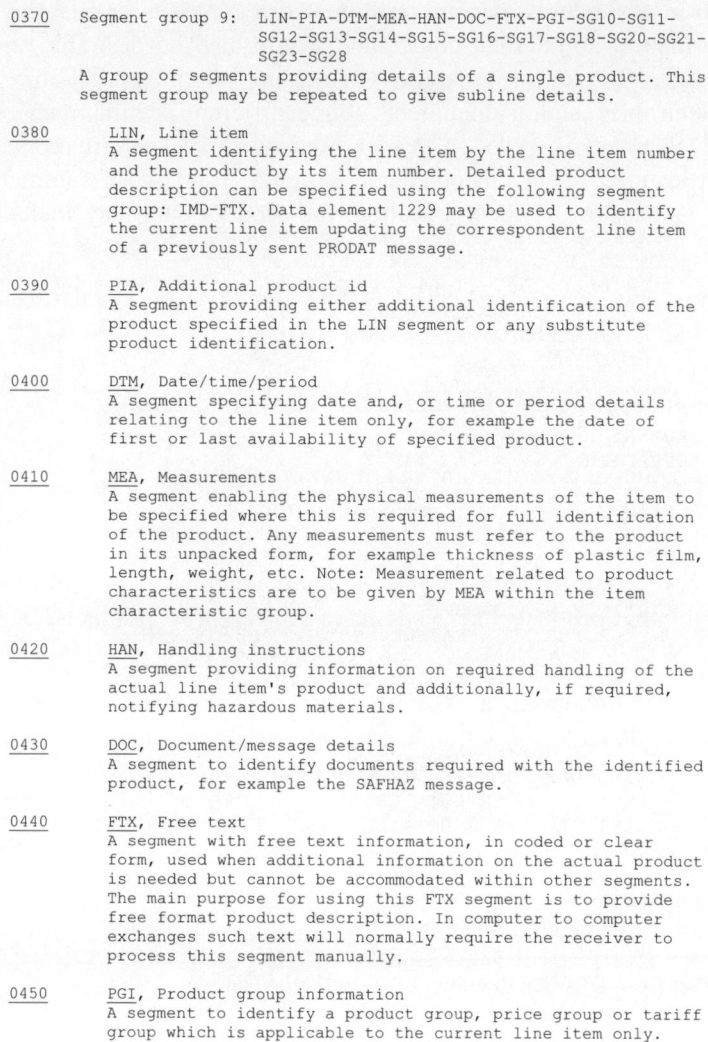

```
0370    Segment group 9:   LIN-PIA-DTM-MEA-HAN-DOC-FTX-PGI-SG10-SG11-
                           SG12-SG13-SG14-SG15-SG16-SG17-SG18-SG20-SG21-
                           SG23-SG28
        A group of segments providing details of a single product. This
        segment group may be repeated to give subline details.

0380        LIN, Line item
            A segment identifying the line item by the line item number
            and the product by its item number. Detailed product
            description can be specified using the following segment
            group: IMD-FTX. Data element 1229 may be used to identify
            the current line item updating the correspondent line item
            of a previously sent PRODAT message.

0390        PIA, Additional product id
            A segment providing either additional identification of the
            product specified in the LIN segment or any substitute
            product identification.

0400        DTM, Date/time/period
            A segment specifying date and, or time or period details
            relating to the line item only, for example the date of
            first or last availability of specified product.

0410        MEA, Measurements
            A segment enabling the physical measurements of the item to
            be specified where this is required for full identification
            of the product. Any measurements must refer to the product
            in its unpacked form, for example thickness of plastic film,
            length, weight, etc. Note: Measurement related to product
            characteristics are to be given by MEA within the item
            characteristic group.

0420        HAN, Handling instructions
            A segment providing information on required handling of the
            actual line item's product and additionally, if required,
            notifying hazardous materials.

0430        DOC, Document/message details
            A segment to identify documents required with the identified
            product, for example the SAFHAZ message.

0440        FTX, Free text
            A segment with free text information, in coded or clear
            form, used when additional information on the actual product
            is needed but cannot be accommodated within other segments.
            The main purpose for using this FTX segment is to provide
            free format product description. In computer to computer
            exchanges such text will normally require the receiver to
            process this segment manually.

0450        PGI, Product group information
            A segment to identify a product group, price group or tariff
            group which is applicable to the current line item only.
```

Fig. 3.11. Extract from EDIFACT message for catalog data

In the German speaking countries, the XML-based standard BMEcat is in use. It is a universal, platform- and vendor-independent data format for exchanging electronic multimedia product and catalog data between suppliers and buyers. It was initiated in 1999 by a committee of a federal association with partners from academia and industry. For the most part, BMEcat is used to provide master data about MRO goods in electronic procurement systems (BME 2006). Figure 3.12 shows an extract from an example document.

```
<?xml version="1.0" encoding="ISO-8859-1"?>
<!DOCTYPE BMECAT SYSTEM "bmecat_new_catalog_1_2.dtd">
<BMECAT version="1.2"
xmlns="http://www.bmecat.org/bmecat/1.2/bmecat_new_catalog">
    <HEADER>
        <CATALOG>
            <LANGUAGE>English</LANGUAGE>
            <CATALOG_ID>QA_CAT_002</CATALOG_ID>
            <CATALOG_VERSION>001.002</CATALOG_VERSION>
            <CATALOG_NAME>Office Supply</CATALOG_NAME>
            <DATETIME type="generation_date">
                <DATE>2007-01-01</DATE>
                <TIME>10:59:54</TIME>
                <TIMEZONE>-02:00</TIMEZONE>
            </DATETIME>
            <CURRENCY>EUR</CURRENCY>
        </CATALOG>
        + <BUYER>
        + <SUPPLIER>
    </HEADER>
    <T_NEW_CATALOG>
        <ARTICLE mode="new">
            <SUPPLIER_AID>Q20-P09</SUPPLIER_AID>
            + <ARTICLE_DETAILS>
            <ARTICLE_FEATURES>
                <REFERENCE_FEATURE_SYSTEM_NAME>UNSPSC-
                5.02</REFERENCE_FEATURE_SYSTEM_NAME>
                <REFERENCE_FEATURE_GROUP_ID>14111511
                </REFERENCE_FEATURE_GROUP_ID>
            </ARTICLE_FEATURES>
            <ARTICLE_ORDER_DETAILS>
                <ORDER_UNIT>1</ORDER_UNIT>
            </ARTICLE_ORDER_DETAILS>
            + <ARTICLE_PRICE_DETAILS>
            + <MIME_INFO>
        </ARTICLE>
    </T_NEW_CATALOG>
</BMECAT>
```

Fig. 3.12. Extract from BMEcat document for catalog exchange

BMEcat can ingest various classification structures such as UNSPSC, eClass or a proprietary in-house standard. For transmitting a catalog, three transactions are available: one is for transferring the complete catalog, one is for updating product information only and one is for price information.

3.5.4 Transaction Standards

The processing of business transactions is realized by means of exchanging business documents. The transmission sequence, or transaction, has traditionally been executed paper-based. But increasingly, document exchange is executed paperless. Basically, business documents fulfill the same purpose in all organizations and can be understood as forms. By standardizing and structuring those forms uniformly, the data exchange can be processed electronically. Generally, a document invokes an action on the part of the recipient and enables the execution of a transaction. Transaction standards provide templates for business documents, which can be used during the phases of executing a business transaction. A specific document is a collection of properties of several business domain objects grouped together for a particular operation. For example, a purchase order specifies some properties of a supplier, such as his name, but possibly not the bank information, as this is done in the invoice (Omelayenko 2002).

In the general EDI scenario, the sender and receiver of a message are application systems. The transmission is processed without human intervention. As a framework for this, an agreement between business partners is necessary in order to customize the document type according to the partner-specific requirements. The document types to be exchanged and the order of the exchange have to be defined. Based on this document flow, the internal structure for each document type has to be agreed upon as well. It is necessary to specify which information needs to be included, how it is designated and which values are allowed (Quantz and Wichmann 2003b).

The most encompassing transaction standard developed today is the UN/EDIFACT standard. It is developed by the UN Centre for Trade Facilitation and Electronic Business (UN/CEFACT) as an international cross-industry standard (UNECE 2006) and today contains more than 200 message types. Examples for EDIFACT message types are:

- PRICAT Price/sales catalogue message
- PRODAT Product data message
- ORDERS Purchase order message
- DELJIT Delivery just in time message
- INVOIC Invoice message
- PAYORD Payment order message

Of the more than 200 message types, less than ten are used in over 90% of all messages exchanged (DEDIG 2004). UN/EDIFACT message types have been customized according to the specific needs of an industry or user group. Such customization is done by omitting optional data elements or segments or by not using certain message types at all. The emerging *EDIFACT subsets* take into account industry-specific requirements and focus on special individual needs in particular. Being EDIFACTconforming, they contain mandatory data elements together with relevant optional elements for the given industry. Thus, message size is reduced by 50% to 80% (DEDIG 2004). Examples include:

- EANCOM, named by combining EAN with Communication in the consumer goods industry containing 44 out of the 200 message types possible (GS1 Germany 2007a)
- ODETTE in the automotive industry (ODETTE 2007)
- SWIFT by the Society for Worldwide Interbank Financial Telecommunications (SWIFT 2007)
- EDIFICE in the electrical industry (EDIFICE 2007)
- EDITEX in the textile industry (EDIFrance 2007)
- SEDAS formerly used in the German consumer goods industry (GS1 Germany 2007)
- TRADACOMS, the Trading Data Communications Standard, formerly used in the UK and Ireland

In the US, Canada and Australia, ASC X12 is the counterpart commonly used. It was developed by the American National Standards Institute Accredited Standards Committee X12 (ASCX12 2006). An example for a subset based on X12 is Health Level Seven (HL7), which is used in healthcare (HL7 2007).

The open standard Commerce XML (cXML) was developed under the lead management of Ariba Inc. in the USA and can be used across industries. It describes business transactions and offers specifications for XML-based document exchange through the provision of formats for common business transactions as DTDs. The focus lies on catalog-based procurement through a streamlined protocol for consistent communication between procurement applications, e-commerce hubs and suppliers (cXML 2006).

XML Common Business Library (xCBL) is an open XML-based standard maintained by Commerce One since 1997. XML Schema specifications are provided as a document framework and a set of XML building blocks as a component library for creating trade documents to facilitate global trading (xCBL 2006).

The Universal Business Language (UBL) is a globally usable free-of-charge standard library of various basic XML business documents, with a description of the underlying processes and a library of XML data elements based on the Core Components Technical Specification ISO 15000-5 (OASIS 2006). It is developed and maintained by the Organization for the Advancement of Structured Information Standards (OASIS), in cooperation with other standardization initiatives like ebXML and UN/CE-

FACT, as an interchange format that can be extended to meet particular needs.

A very recent approach is the development of the United Nations electronic Trade Documents (UNeDOCS). It is a generic approach at developing a set of aligned, internationally usable trade documents, which can be rendered in paper and electronically in XML or EDI format as individually required. The building blocks available for putting together documents are based on a common data model, so that the same data can be used across many documents. The foundation is the UN/CEFACT Core Component Technical Specification (CCTS) and the United Nations Trade Data Element Directory (UNTDED), building the UNeDocs Data Model (UNECE 2007b).

In Germany the open standard openTRANS has been developed as a complement to the catalog exchange format BMEcat. Standardized business documents can serve as the basis for interorganizational system-to-system communication. Combining BMEcat and openTRANS provides a consistent standardization similar to UN/EDIFACT, xCBL, xCML or RosettaNet (Quantz and Wichmann 2003b). Figure 3.13 illustrates the process of exchanging documents, using the openTRANS documents as an example. This standard gives no statement as to the process design. It is up to the business partners to choose from the documents available for their specific needs (openTRANS 2002).

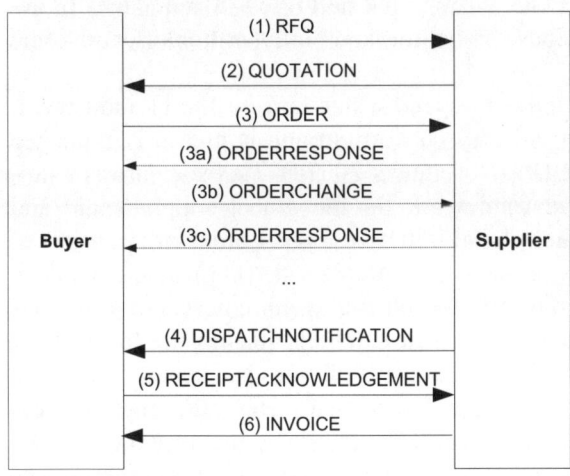

Fig. 3.13. Possible document flow in openTRANS

Consensus on the structure of transaction documents does not provide an appropriate document flow. Organizations may have different roles within supply chains and expect different documents at different points in time. For example, not all organizations involved in a transaction may expect an acknowledgment as a reply to a purchase order. Also, different documents may contain different obligatory information (Omelayenko 2002). Therefore, the composition of document flows reflects internal business procedures and shows basic aspects of process design.

3.6 Process Standards

For structuring the document flow as required, processes between communicating partners need to be agreed upon. Standardizing processes is carried out at the highest level of communication, the pragmatic level. Defined processes set the conditions for exchanging documents. To automate cross-company business processes, conditions as well as documents need to be reconciled and agreed upon, so that they lead to the appropriate reactions within the process flow.

An approach towards business process integration is the use of meta-models or business frameworks describing processes. Such frameworks can regulate workflows by controlling the actions and reactions invoked by messages coming from application systems of transaction partners (Voigtmann and Zeller 2003). They generally provide tools for machine-readable modeling of processes through the definition of sequences of actions, pre- and post conditions, branching and authorizations (Quantz and Wichmann 2003a).

RosettaNet is a vertical industry-specific standard for the IT industry. It was created in 1998 by an industry consortium and is presently managed by the GS1 initiative in the US (RosettaNet 2007d). This standard is a universally usable XML-based framework for the global supply chain and seeks convergence with other global initiatives. The framework consists of specifications for business-process definitions and technical elements in order to achieve interoperability and enable communication. It defines message formats for products and business transactions in the form of the Partner Interface Processes (PIPs). Each PIP defines the specification and interfacing of two business partners' processes, including the business logic, message flow, and message contents, to enable the alignment of the two processes. It builds on the RosettaNet dictionaries with common sets of properties for the PIPs (RosettaNet 2007b; 2007c):

- RosettaNet Business Dictionary, designating the properties used in basic business activities;

- RosettaNet Technical Dictionaries, providing properties for describing products;
- RosettaNet Implementation Framework (RNIF) Core Specification for the technical aspects of the PIP messages.

As a second comprehensive initiative, the Electronic Business eXtensible Markup Language (ebXML) has been developed by OASIS and UN/CEFACT, starting in 1999. This business framework is a modular set of specifications that should enable organizations of any size and in any geographical location to conduct business electronically. It provides a method for exchanging XML-based business messages, communicating data in common terms and defining and registering business processes (ebXML 2007). It consists of five main specifications, most of them certified as ISO standard 15000 (OASIS 2006b):

- ebXML Business Process Specification Schema (ebBPSS) defines business processes by means of a generic metamodel and a standard language in order to configure systems for business collaboration execution between partners.
- Core Components Technical Specification (CCTS) presents a methodology for developing semantic building blocks to represent the general business data types in use and thus communicate data in common terms.
- ebXML Registry Services (ebRS) and ebXML Registry Information Model (ebRIM) register, locate and access e-business artifacts and services in a distributed environment.
- Collaboration Protocol Profile (CPP) and Collaboration Profile Agreements (CPA) configure partner profiles and technical parameters between business partners. The agreement contains two matched partner profiles and defines the particularities in order to establish an aligned business collaboration.
- ebXML Messaging Service (ebMS) defines a communications-protocol-neutral method for exchanging business messages.

These specifications are used during four different steps. First, at design time, all processes need to be modeled. To do so, the United Nations Modeling Methodology (UMM) can be used for describing the collaboration between organizations. Based on the model developed, organizations can set up profiles about themselves, including information regarding processes and data supplied, and register them for public availability. After searching for a potential partner's profile, both profiles can be matched and combined into an agreement. Governed by this agreement, the business transaction can be executed. Overall, the provision of an open XML-based infrastructure should enable the global use of e-business information in an interoperable, secure and consistent manner for all participants, especially SME. To achieve this, not all components need to be implemented as a complete system. They may be used independently of each other. (An in-depth look into this standard and its development is given in the case study about the work of UN/CEFACT in the next chapter.)

Both approaches presented here have the idea in common to enable an organization to publish information about its processes and the respective documents required. Using process standards in this way allows for systems to be more loosely coupled within open, distributed environments (EC 2005b).

3.7 Semantic Variety

At the present time, besides the e-business standards introduced here, numerous others, less prevalent ones, exist and are used in parallel. In a survey conducted by the European Standardization Committee, more than forty classification standards were counted (CEN 2006). For document formatting, more than twenty-six EDI subsets are widely used (EDIZone 2006) and twenty-five vertical XML-based formats are available (Barry & Associates, Inc. 2006). In total, in the beginning of 2000, 124 business vocabularies, either already existent or under development, had been counted (Kotok 2000). Five years later, approximately 600 such vocabularies were known (Coverpages 2006).

3.7.1 Application Scope of E-Business Semantics

All of the various standards fulfill different functions in the area of semantic and pragmatic definition and partly cover several application areas at the same time. Table 3.3 provides an overview of some major standards (based on Quantz and Wichmann 2003b).

Table 3.3. Application areas covered by semantics

Standard	Identification	Classification	Catalog Exchange	Transactions	Processes
EAN.UCC	**main**				
ETIM		**main**			
eClass		**main**			
UNSPSC		**main**			
proficlass		**main**			
BMEcat			**main**		

Table 3.3. continued

DATANORM	**main**			
EDIFACT	not central	**main**		
EANCOM	not central	**main**		
RosettaNet	not central	not central	**main**	
ANSI ASC X12	not central	**main**		
xCBL	not central	**main**		
openTRANS		**main**		
UBL		**main**	not central	
ebXML			**main**	

(Note that this overview includes only major standards and denotes their respective main focus.)

3.7.2 Semantic Heterogeneity

Standards differ not only due to their partly overlapping application scopes, but also with regard to their concentration onto specific domains. Sometimes industry-specific approaches are conceived as being superior to cross-industry approaches, since they tend to be more detailed and cover the requirements of an industry more completely and precisely (Hepp 2003). Also, cross-industry classifications differ depending on the focus of the developer. A comparison of eClass and UNSPSC shows both to be rather vertically oriented, as in each of them most of the classes can be found on only a few categories. More than 30% of the items included are located in three major sections of the total twenty-five top-level classes in eClass and the total fifty-five top-level classes in UNSPSC (Hepp et al. 2005). Furthermore, the availability of the property pool in eClass adds to incompatibility with UNSPSC descriptions (CEN 2006). However, both standards are continuously developed further, with a monthly average of about 200 new classes. Other standards do not show such a high rate of evolution and adaptation to technological progress and thereby require less maintenance and demonstrate less advancement. Nevertheless, differences can be seen with regard to the balance of these factors (Hepp et al. 2005). Besides their speed of evolution, standards vary in their structure and ori-entation. The structure of eClass is market oriented and focused on the similarity of objects, while UNSPSC is more functionally oriented. This leads to principally different systematizations (Fensel 2001). Thus, a com-parison and relating of the objects between the two standards is rather complicated. The comparison for the term "writing paper", as depicted in Tables 3.1 and 3.2., has already shown the differences in the naming of terms and the detailing of scope and meaning. The example clearly demonstrates the structural and terminological differences in standards' methodologies (Fensel et al. 2001; Bergamaschi et al. 2002; Schulten et al. 2001). Picking up this example, Figure 3.14 (adapted from Fensel et al. 2001; Bergamaschi et al. 2002) illustrates attempts at relating the standards' elements.

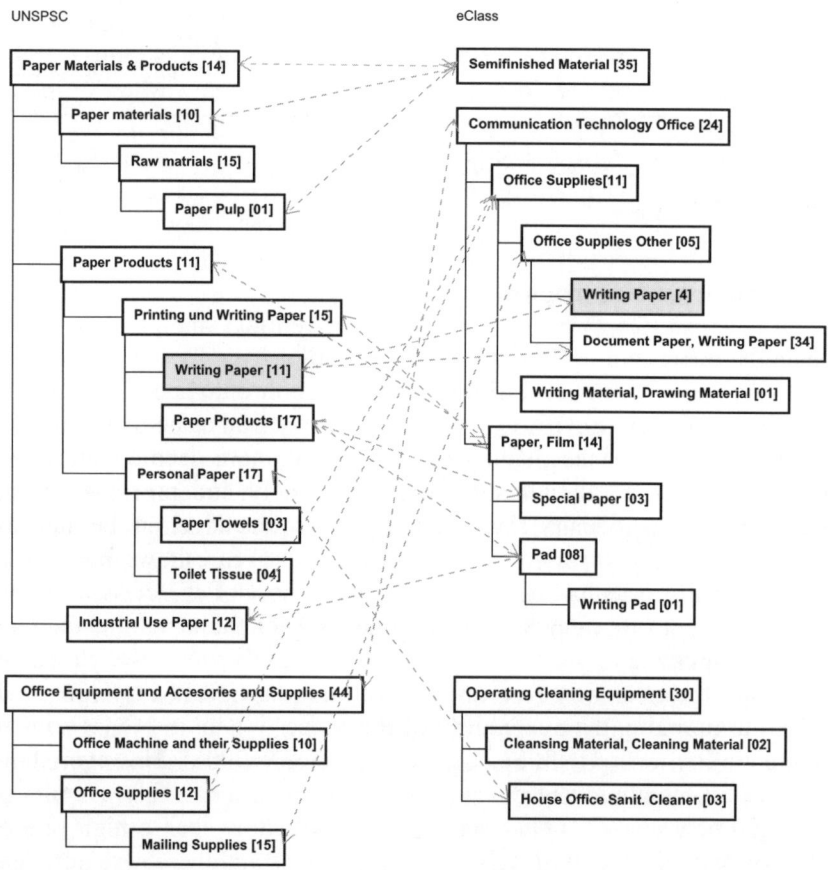

Fig. 3.14. Comparison of UNSPSC and eClass

Relating objects or looking for comparable expressions in the two standards leads to insufficient reflections of scope and positioning of a term. Since categories have different subclasses and belong to different levels in the hierarchies, it is not clear if the intended meaning of terms is really equal or, at least, similar.

Internationally, in the area of classifications, the additional challenge of multilingualism arises. During a recent Europe-wide survey, 46% of the interviewed organizations stated that they exchange multilingual product information with their business partners in the targeted markets within the European Union. For creating and exchanging catalogs, 26% of those interviewed use multilingual catalogs. However, 53% plan on future use of multilingual catalogs (Beckmann et al. 2004). To accommodate these needs, CEN has developed a global multilingual product description and classification (Beckmann et al. 2004; CEN 2006). In doing so, differences in content need to be considered, as they occur not only when different terminologies or languages are used, but also when cultural differences exist. Depending on a business partner's geographic or cultural background, the same term may have a different meaning or describe an object with different features and thus lead to different expectations about an item. Examples include the positioning of steering wheels in automobiles for left- or right-hand traffic or the length of table legs in Central Europe in comparison to Japan (Hepp 2003). Also, local conventions and procedures influence the expression of information; for example, the inclusions and positioning of the different elements required for correctly composing addresses in business documents for cross-country usage, the use of different currencies and the use of the metric system in contrast to a non-metric system. In the end, this can lead to different views on structuring standards for information formatting. However, the scope of the developer influences the level of detailing information considerably. Figure 3.15 provides a structural comparison of extracts from the data model of two transaction standards as an example of the different ways a purchase-order document can be composed.

Looking at the setup for composing information about a contract, the probability of recognizing information as non-ambiguous is low, as trying to relate the various possibilities for expressing and describing the intention of such a data field leads to several conflicting alternatives.

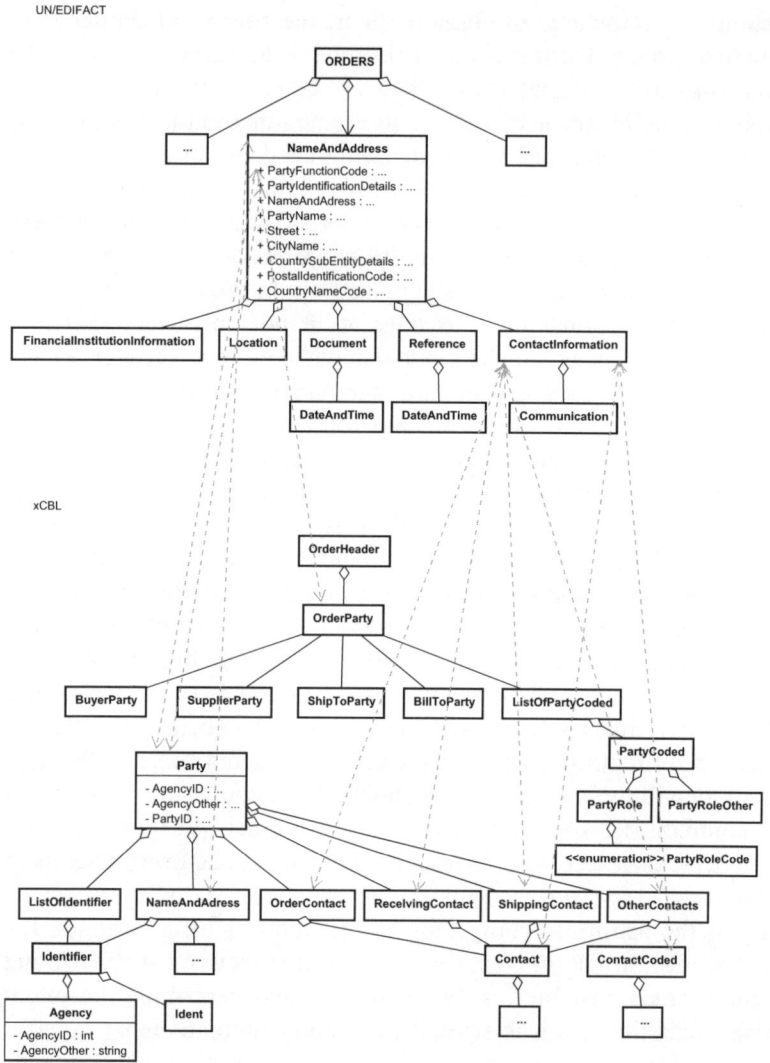

Fig. 3.15. Comparison of UN/EDIFACT and xCBL (based on Huemer 2001)

3.7.3 Criteria for Standards Selection

As previously shown, functional aspects need to be considered when choosing a standard for data exchange. The possibilities of a standard for formatting product information need to cover and describe an organization's portfolio as precisely as possible. A transaction standard needs to fulfill the requirements for the business documents to be exchanged in the most possible detail.

Nevertheless, the choice of one or more standards is not only affected by functional aspects, but also by non-functional considerations, such as the market penetration of a standard, the investments necessary for its implementation, the cost and scope of the usage license, the usage cost and the standard's future guarantee (Kelkar and Mucha 2004). The degree of autonomy possible in developing and maintaining a standard depends on the consortium responsible for it. Normative standards by organizations such as ISO or UN/CEFACT have the status of being published by a legal authority. Standards by consortia, mostly from an industry, need to be analyzed regarding their independence from platforms, systems or vendors. In selecting a standard, it is critical to know if the developer can propagate a standard, i.e., that general usage can be achieved and the critical mass of users can be obtained. Furthermore, the possibility for participating in a standard's development through placing suggestions for further development can also be important (Beckmmann et al. 2004). Another crucial decision factor can be the scope of usage and access. For example, for eClass the general conditions of usage do not permit the standard to be combined or mixed with other classifications (eClass 2007a). These regulations permit only limited usage, as relating or reconciling of information between business partners for electronic data exchange is hindered.

When deciding on the adoption of a standard, the affiliation to an industry is an important decision factor. An enterprise has to verify whether or not the deployment of an industry-wide standard would lead to problems in the execution of cross-industry transactions, as is the case when procuring office supplies or fulfilling demand for the car and truck pool (EC 2004). Where different industry-specific standards also format those goods and service in a different manner, a supplier would have to deal with different designations for the same product. Hence, it can be assumed that organizations with a focus across industries adopt several standards. This can be concluded from the usage of standards for electronic catalog formats by European enterprises; 60% of all enterprises use up to five different formats concurrently, and 10% use up to ten formats at the same time. Next to the open standards, 80% of all enterprises deploy proprietary in-house standards, mostly their own (Beckmann et al. 2004).

3.7.4 E-Business Diffusion and Standard Adoption

The Information Economy Report 2006 by the United Nations Conference on Trade and Development (UNCTAD) examines the extent of the use of information and communication technologies (ICT) and e-business (UNCTAD 2006). One of the indicators for assessing the application of ICT to enterprise activities, and thus realizing e-business, is usage of the Internet. Thus, this may be used for measuring the degree of e-business realization, as it represents one of the core factors and may be considered an imperative prerequisite. In large enterprises in most developed countries Internet access is almost universally given with nearly 100% diffusion, even though this adoption rate varies depending on the sector (UNCTAD 2006). The nature of the business determines intensity, focus and impact of e-business adoption, next to regional factors such as access cost, missing security and uncertainty about legal aspects in closing trade agreements (EC 2007). The structure of an economy in combination with the particulars of an enterprise sector may result in differing aptness towards e-business realization and the use of the Internet. In general, organizations focusing on more knowledge-intensive activities, as well as larger enterprises, seem to use the Internet more frequently (UNCATD 2006). Access to the Internet is strongest in the financial sector, wholesale trade, real estate and the renting and business services industries. In contrast, in the developing countries Internet access by enterprises varies broadly. The percentage of enterprises with Internet access that are also setting up a website varies from over 90% to just over 10%, whereas a higher ratio is to be found in the developed countries; in Europe, for example, it is 75% (UNCTAD 2006; EC 2007).

E-business is realized in all sectors of enterprises for integrating business processes internally and externally with suppliers, customers and business partners. For internal process integration, the provision of an intranet and the use of applications for managing integration across business functions are common (UNCTAD 2006). The establishment of an intranet can be taken as a technical basis for executing internal business processes online. In 2005, 34% of all European enterprises had an intranet and 15% an extranet. Setting up an extranet allows online interaction with external users and may be regarded as a more improved e-business capability due to the higher complexity (UNCTAD 2006). The degree of adoption of advanced e-business applications in European enterprises increases in relation to their size. Table 3.4 gives an overview of the diffusion of e-business applications aimed at internal business integration in selected sectors from 10 European countries in 2006 (EC 2007).

Table 3.4. Diffusion of applications for internal e-business in Europe

Proportion of enterprises using…	an intranet	ERP systems	Accounting software	CRM systems
Total (10 sectors, EU-10)	23%	11%	57%	10%
By Sector				
Food & beverages	16%	10%	58%	5%
Footwear	11%	7%	58%	5%
Pulp & paper	24%	16%	66%	9%
ICT manufacturing	38%	16%	63%	14%
Consumer electronics	21%	12%	53%	11%
Shipbuilding and repair	50%	17%	78%	9%
Construction	22%	11%	58%	5%
Tourism	20%	7%	46%	11%
Telecommunications	41%	11%	61%	24%
Hospital activities	55%	21%	77%	8%
By Size (EU10)				
1-9 employees	19%	7%	50%	7%
10-49 employees	28%	16%	70%	12%
50-249 employees	43%	25%	85%	16%
over 250 employees	76%	45%	88%	28%
By Country (EU10)				
Czech Republic	24%	10%	54%	3%
Germany	23%	8%	62%	11%
Spain	24%	17%	71%	19%
France	19%	16%	58%	9%
Italy	36%	14%	59%	8%
Hungary	22%	6%	33%	3%
Netherlands	18%	8%	59%	16%
Poland	31%	10%	68%	10%
Finland	16%	8%	58%	11%
United Kingdom	25%	2%	76%	5%

In 45% of the large enterprises in the European Union, ERP systems are widespread, but they are noticeably less evident in SME. Instead, here the adoption of accounting software is the method of choice for accounting and planning purposes by up to 70% of small enterprises, even though this offers much less functionality for integration and process automation (EC 2007). Similarly, the use of CRM systems is mainly seen in medium-sized and large enterprises. Also, there is a similar difference with regard to the adoption of specific applications for sales and marketing; it is more common for large enterprises to link sales processes with integrated systems, while SME often adopt simpler means such as online orders from a website or by e-mail (EC 2005a). For the integration of cooperative and collaborative processes across company borders, e-procurement is part of daily business operation and one of the most frequently used e-business applications (UNCTAD 2006). It is a fundamental activity in the manufacturing and trade industries (EC 2007; UNCTAD 2006). Placing and receiving orders online can be summarized as e-commerce; the medium used is not only the Internet, but also other networks such as EDI.

The biggest portion of worldwide e-commerce concerns business-to-business transactions. Overall, this sector of the world economy continues to grow (UNCTAD 2006). In the developed countries e-commerce has become commonplace, with differing adoption rates in the various countries and industries. In the OECD countries in 2004, between 20% and 60% of all enterprises placed orders online, whereas only 10% to 20% received orders online. For example, in 2005, nearly 30% of European enterprises procured at least 5% of their demand online. However, only 10% sold at least 5% of their offerings online (EC 2006). This has been called the "e-commerce paradox". It seems that many enterprises in the developed countries procure electronically without selling electronically as well, particularly when the e-procurement activities are limited to sourcing office supplies and MRO articles (EC 2004). Another reason could be a lower number of suppliers than of buyers of such goods. The e-commerce activities of European enterprises are not showing great variations in the adoptions rate by company size, with an overall average of 44%. However, the use of specific application systems for e-procurement or online sales is more common in medium-sized and, in particular, large enterprises (EC 2005a).

In some developing and transitioning countries the situation regarding the ratio of more online purchasing than selling appears to be the opposite, since online selling exceeds online procuring. This may be explained in part by different local value chains (UNCTAD 2006).

In order to provide an impression of the extent of electronically executed external business integration, the volume of global e-commerce can be drawn upon. Even if comparisons are somewhat difficult due to the usage of differing statistical methodologies, a roughly consistent basic overview can be compiled. Figure 3.16 shows the percentage of enterprises in selected countries from around the world selling and procuring over computer-mediated networks such as the Internet and EDI networks in 2005.

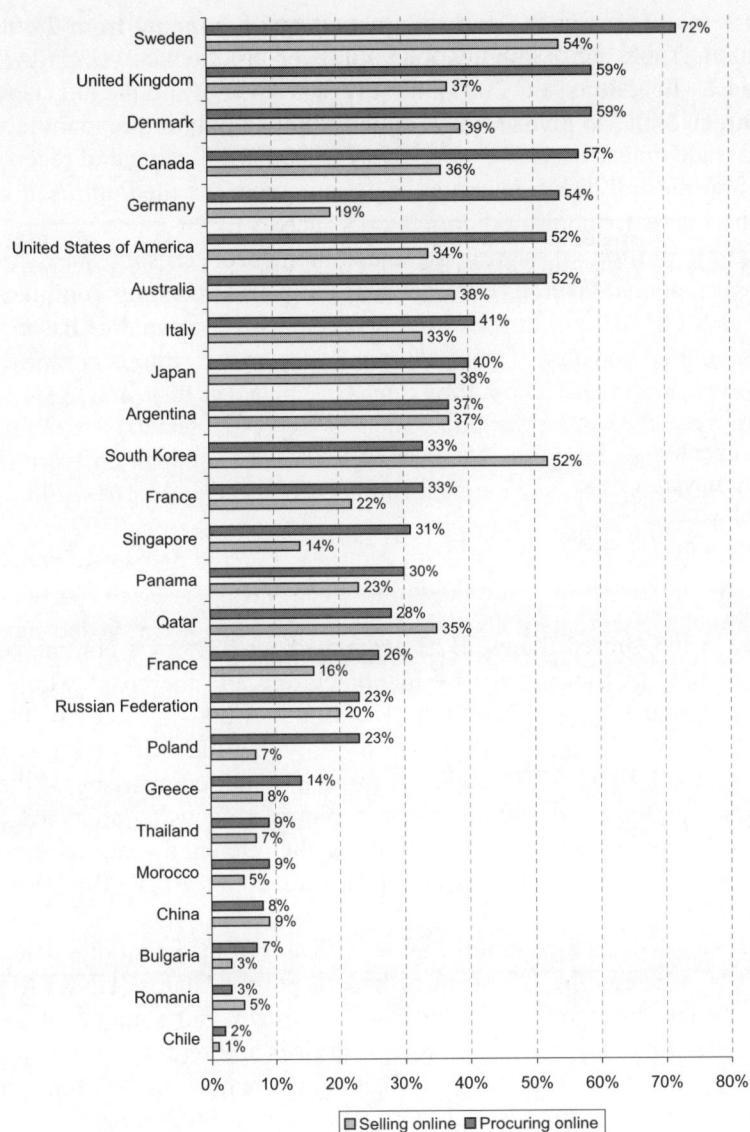

Fig. 3.16. Extent of e-commerce in percentage of enterprises in 2005 (based on
UNCTAD 2006; EC 2005a; BITKOM 2007)

In Australia, Canada and the US, between 50% and 60% of all enterprises placed purchase orders online; in Europe the average was 35% for
all enterprises (UNCTAD 2006; EC 2005a; EC 2007). To assess the economic value of extending business activities into the realm of e-commerce,
a look at the turnover portions generated by e-commerce reveals compara-

ble amounts in enterprises in the developed countries, ranging from 7% to 12% in 2004. Table 3.5 combines data surveyed by the UN (UNCTAD 2006), the EC (EC 2005a; EC 2007), EITO (EITO 2005), and the US (U.S. Census Bureau 2006) to give an impression of these amounts.

Table 3.5. Volume of B2B E-Commerce

	Australia	Canada	Japan	Korea	USA	EU (25)
Market volume (= e-transaction volume)	AUD 33 b (€ 20 b)	CAD 26.4 b (€ 16.4) b	JPY 91 mill (€ 104 b)	KRW 235 b (€ 176 b)	US$ 2,051 b (€ 1,641 b)	€ 1,069 b (EU 15+N, CH 2005)
Reference year	2003/04	2004	2004	2003	2004	2004
Proportion of country total turnover	2%	< 1%	n/a	n/a	10% (4 sectors)	2,5% (2005)
Percentage of enterprise total turnover from e-commerce	7%	n/a	12%	n/a	10%	9%
B2B portion of e-commerce	n/a	75%	86%	88%	92%	88%

In 2005, in the United States, B2B accounted for 92% of e-commerce turnover (defined as transactions by manufacturers and merchant wholesalers) and totaled US$ 1,892 billion (1 billion = 1,000 million). In the European Union the B2B proportion was 88%, with a turnover of € 943.1 billion (UNCTAD 2006; EITO 2006). A more in-depth comparison of the trade volumes in 2004 and 2005 is given in Figure 3.17, using an average currency exchange rate of € 0.8 to the US$ for the reference years covered and showing billion Euro (U.S. Census Bureau 2006; BITKOM 2005; BITKOM 2004).

The UN regards B2B e-commerce as an indicator of the economic value of e-business, whereas the US seem to have a pioneer status (UNCTAD 2004). In Western Europe in 2004 and 2005, Germany had a market share of 30% for electronically traded goods and services and with this the highest percentage. With this, Germany was leading in conduction e-commerce in Western Europe. In comparison, France was the next biggest market and had a market share of 14% (BITKOM 2004; BITKOM 2005). An explanation may be a rather extensive use of established technologies such as EDI next to Internet-based activities by large, but also small and medium-sized enterprises in Germany (König et al. 2006).

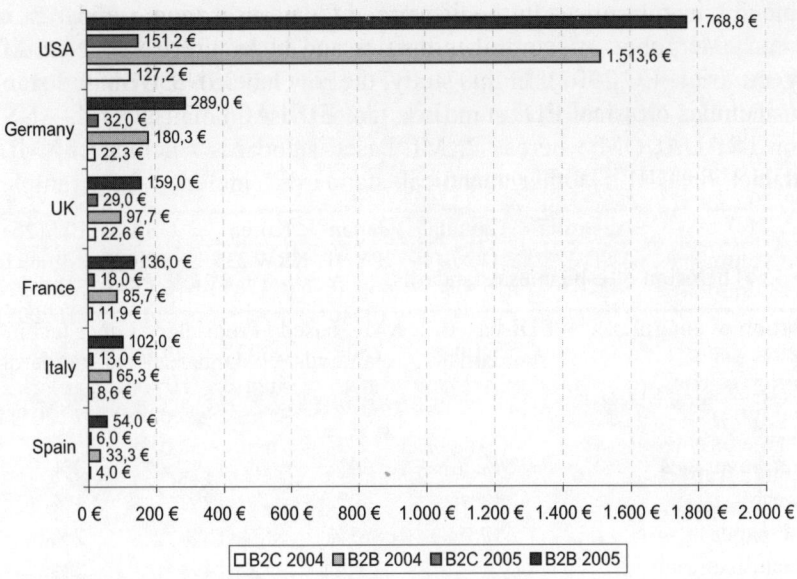

Fig. 3.17. E-Commerce trade volumes (in billion €)

The activities in e-commerce constitute the exchange of data between business partners. Its standardization is increasingly recognized as important for e-business (EC 2005a). Some major facts about structured data exchange and use of standards may be summarized as follows (EC 2005b; U.S. Census Bureau 2006; EC 2007):

- As a result of the still rather low level of B2B turnover, relatively few enterprises have adopted standards yet.
- The proportion of enterprises exchanging standardized data increases with enterprise size, with up to 60% of the large enterprises doing so.
- EDI-based standards are mainly used in the manufacturing, wholesale and retail sectors, which may be reluctant to switch to other standards due this legacy.
- XML-based standards appear to be quite widely used. Meanwhile, they have become nearly as similarly widespread as traditional EDI standards. It seems that awareness of XML is higher among the knowledge-intensive sub-sectors of business services and in the high-tech sectors of electronics and ICT services.
- The use of proprietary formats is significantly higher than the use of open standards for traditional EDI or open XML-based standards, thus enabling data exchange between a only limited number of companies operating in the same supply chain.

Table 3.6 shows the actual diffusion of data-exchange standards in European enterprises in selected industries and by enterprise size, in different countries (EC 2007). In this study, the row labeled "EDI-based standards" includes classical EDI standards like EDIFACT, EANCOM, ANSI X12 or TRADACOM whereas "XML-based standards" include ebXML, RosettaNet or UBL. "Other technical standards" include, for example, STEP.

Table 3.6. Diffusion of e-business standards

Proportion of enterprises using …	EDI-based standards	XML-based standards	Proprietary standards	Other technical standards
Total (10 sectors, EU-10)	3%	5%	12%	2%
By Sector				
Food & beverages	6%	4%	11%	3%
Footwear	2%	2%	12%	1%
Pulp & paper	6%	5%	15%	2%
ICT manufacturing	3%	10%	14%	3%
Consumer electronics	4%	6%	17%	5%
Shipbuilding and repair	2%	2%	19%	8%
Construction	2%	4%	10%	2%
Tourism	2%	6%	10%	1%
Telecommunications	5%	14%	23%	4%
Hospital activities	19%	21%	30%	4%
By Size (EU10)				
1-9 employees	2%	6%	10%	1%
10-49 employees	4%	5%	13%	2%
50-249 employees	10%	10%	24%	2%
over 250 employees	29%	27%	31%	7%
By Country (EU10)				
Czech Republic	2%	2%	7%	1%
Germany	5%	4%	17%	1%
Spain	6%	11%	15%	4%
France	4%	3%	16%	2%
Italy	1%	4%	11%	1%
Hungary	3%	2%	10%	3%
Netherlands	3%	6%	2%	0%
Poland	5%	10%	27%	2%
Finland	5%	6%	8%	1%
United Kingdom	3%	4%	7%	3%

A closer look at the use of EDI-based standards allows for examination of the distinction between the usage of the Internet and the usage of other networks by European enterprises (EC 2007), as shown in Table 3.7.

Table 3.7. Media usage for EDI

Proportion of enterprises…	Using Standard EDI over private networks	Using Internet-based EDI	Using Both (standard and Internet-based)	Planning to migrate from EDI to XML
Total (10 sectors, EU-10)	3%	71%	26%	3%
By Size (EU10)				
1-9 employees	1%	87%	12%	2%
10-49 employees	8%	58%	34%	5%
50-249 employees	25%	39%	36%	8%
over 250 employees	31%	22%	48%	17%

As seen above, the use of EDI-based standards is more common in large enterprises. However, it is not exclusively concentrated in private networks, but rather is adapted to a large extent for exploiting the possibilities of the Internet. Accordingly, in total only 3% of all enterprises are planning to migrate from traditional EDI formats to XML-based standards for electronic data exchange within the coming year (EC 2007).

For a more detailed look at the use of e-business standards, Germany may be taken as an example, since it conducts a rather high proportion of Western Europe's e-commerce. An international comparison shows, that the German e-business diffusion rate displays a similar development as in Denmark or the US and may thus serve as an illustration of a "fast follower of e-commerce" (König et al. 2006). Surveys conducted over the last years show the adoption of various standards (Pols et al. 2004; Fricke et al. 2006). Figure 3.18 illustrates the findings in percentages of enterprises.

Next to the classical diffusion of UN/EDIFACT and EANCOM, an equally balanced usage of standards of German origin such as BMEcat, along with standards from the US such as cXML and xCBL, can be found. Noteworthy is the high usage rate of proprietary standards. In the area of classification standards, eClass dominates over UNSPSC, which might be explained by the German origin of eClass. During the surveys, increasing importance of some standards was assumed. These are not only the younger XML-based standards, but also the already established UN/EDIFACT format. Presumably, the XML-based standards cover areas not covered by the classic EDI-based standards. The limited usage of XML-based standards is explained in the studies as being due to their rather low profile, since about half of the interviewed enterprises did not know them (Pols et al 2004; Fricke et al. 2006). UN/EDIFACT and EANCOM are well established. For 2006, GS1 reports 7,400 active users of EANCOM (GS1 2007b).

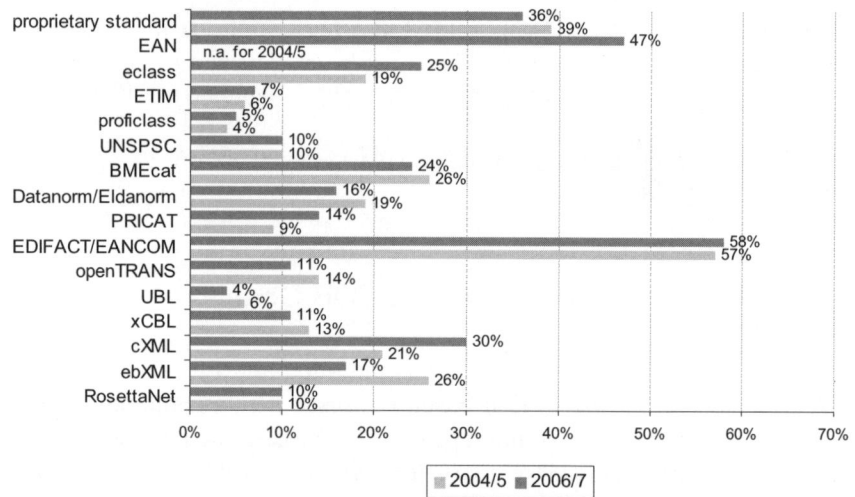

Fig. 3.18. Adoption rate of e-business standards in German enterprises

The above analysis reveals huge amounts in absolute value of B2B turnover; however, in relation to national gross products, the amounts are not so big. Even though the proportion of B2B trading is very small, the UN assumes large potential for growth (UNCTAD 2006).

The adoption rates of individual standards show a rather fragmented growth. The affiliation to an industry or the size of an enterprise is not the only factor that seems to influence the selection of a certain standard. Instead, since standards cover various requirements in different ways, this also leads to further disunity. Presently, the non-availability of universal standards and thus the missing semantic interoperability prevent technological progress and further diffusion of e-business, thereby increasing the risk in e-business investments (EC 2005b).

As a consequence, the semantic heterogeneity at hand needs to be managed and a fruitful coexistence of e-business standards needs to be facilitated. In the next chapters, after a case study about standardization work, we develop a methodology for semantic synchronization that provides this capability.

4 Case Study: Designing ebXML – The Work of UN/CEFACT

by Klaus-Dieter Naujok with Christian Huemer

4.1 Background – UN/CEFACT's B2B Goal

The United Nations Centre for Trade Facilitation and Electronic Business (UN/CEFACT) is a standardization organization that became well known for creating and maintaining the UN/EDIFACT standards (Berge 1994) for EDI (Hill and Ferguson 1989). In 1999, due to the growing popularity of XML, UN/CEFACT also started to look for an XML solution which should be compatible with existing UN/EDIFACT to protect the huge investments already made worldwide. UN/CEFACT's Techniques and Methodology Working Group (TMWG) was responsible for doing a feasibility study on using XML for B2B information transfer. The TMWG report on this subject rejected the idea of creating 'Yet Another XML Solution' by converting EDIFACT to XML. This decision was mainly based on the fact that a syntactical transformation would hardly solve any EDI problem, but would just add another e-business vocabulary to the XML world (Li 2000).

Instead, TMWG recommended starting an initiative aimed at developing a B2B solution that would utilize Business Process and Information Modeling (BPIM), Object Oriented Technology, Common Business Objects, Unified Modeling Language (UML) (Booch et al. 2005), UN/CEFACT's Modeling Methodology (UMM) and XML. This recommendation resulted in the commencement of the ebXML initiative. Accordingly, UN/CEFACT's vision for ebXML was as follows:

The initiative will develop a 'framework' that utilizes BPIM, UML and UMM in such a way that any industry group or standards body, including UN/CEFACT, can create models that identify every possible activity to achieve a specific business goal. These models will be registered and stored in a global 'virtual' repository. Trading partners will register 'their' particular path/paths through the model so that others who want to engage with that trading partner can determine if they share at least one scenario. To ensure that the models not only follow the UMM but also are interoperable, the ebXML initiative will provide the most common objects (Common Business Objects) that will be used by the modelers as they document a particular business process. In addition, ebXML will define the XML messaging format, packaging and routing and the metamodel for the repository.

4.1.1 The ebXML Vision à la UN/CEFACT

To fully understand UN/CEFACT's original vision summarized above, let's expand it to provide more detail. Before ebXML parties can engage with each other, they need to find each other. In order to do so, any business or organization that is ebXML capable will need to store information about its ebXML capabilities in an ebXML registry. This information will include which transport options are available, such as SMTP or HTTP, and, further, which security features one can invoke, such as encryption, non-repudiation and digital signatures. Last but not least, it will identify, which business activities are available for engagement. Is it just order placement, or the full supply chain? Are there various scenarios for the same business process? This registry will not be hosted by a single party but may be distributed over many hosts. Possible hosts could be industry user groups/consortiums, standard bodies, major market creators/enablers or software solution providers. However, regardless of who will host the registry, they are all linked together to create a single virtual registry.

Once the registry is set up, anyone who is ebXML enabled can access the information in order to find businesses that offer the services one is looking for. This could be a search for a particular product, such as red women's shoes, or a very specific item, such as a Number 2 pencil, or less specific for any hardware vendor. The ebXML Trading Partner Profile Specification will allow parties to provide as much detail as they are willing to publicly disclose. Some parties may provide a link to their complete product catalog; others will only provide high-level product categories or services. However, in order to engage in an ebXML business process, the parties will need to identify at least one business process model scenario they are capable of executing.

After a party has searched the registry for a list of businesses that can provide the product or service, the next step, in addition to selecting a business that fits the requirement from the product and/or service point, is to determine if the business processes available can be handled by the searching party's own ebXML application/system. Depending on the software, this could be as simple as matching predefined processes against the available ones or performing an internal analysis in order to determine whether the system can dynamically adopt itself to any of them. Once the party wishing to engage with the selected party in one of the business scenarios, a Trading Partner Agreement (TPA) will be sent. The TPA will outline which of the available options will be utilized in the engagement. This includes the transport and security option and the selected business scenario. The selected party will then either accept the TPA by sending a positive acknowledgment or reject it with a negative acknowledgment and the reason for the rejection. After receiving a positive acknowledgment, the selected business scenario will be initiated by the appropriate party, which sends the first business information message. Depending on the result, the rest of the scenario will be executed with the resulting messages being exchanged. This could be the normal (positive) flow of information or exceptions as identified in the business process model. Regardless, sooner or later there will be an end to that particular engagement. To engage with that particular party again in a new exchange, a TPA will need to be sent again.

4.1.2 The ebXML Scenario

UN/CEFACT's vision results in the typical ebXML scenario between a large corporation (Company A) and an SME (Company B) that became part of the ebXML architecture (Walsh 2001). This scenario is depicted in Figure 4.1.

In the typical ebXML scenario, Company A requests business details from the ebXML registry (step 1) and decides to implement its role in the requested ebXML business process (step 2). Company A submits its own business profile information to the ebXML registry (step 3). This profile describes the company's ebXML capabilities and constraints, as well as its supported business scenarios. Company B, which uses an ebXML-compliant shrink-wrapped application, discovers the business scenarios supported by Company A in the registry (step 4). Company B sends a request to Company A stating that they would like to engage in a business scenario (step 5). Before engaging in the scenario, company B submits a proposed business arrangement directly to Company A's ebXML-compliant software interface. The proposed business arrangement outlines the mutually agreed upon business scenarios and specific agreements. Company A then accepts the business agreement. Company A and B are now ready to engage in e-business using ebXML (step 6).

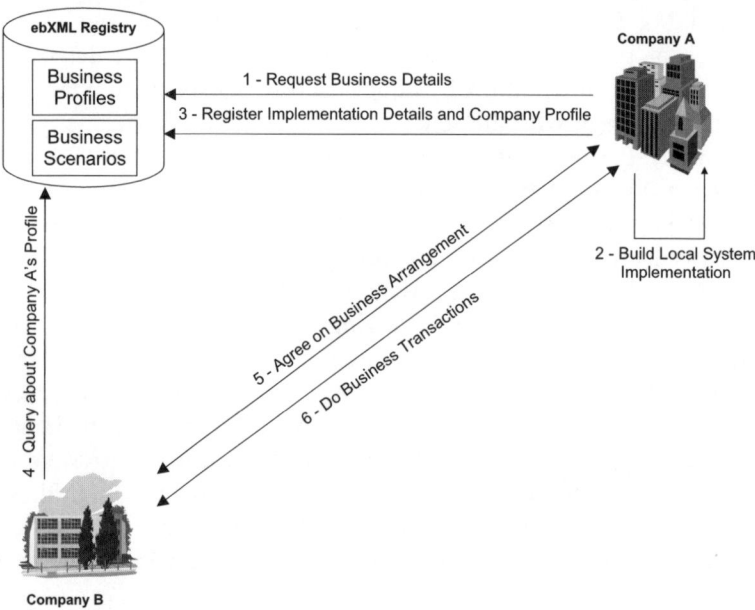

Fig. 4.1. Typical ebXML scenario

4.1.3 The Role of Large Companies/Organizations/Industries

Following the scenario described above, it becomes evident that the success of ebXML depends on businesses registering and storing their business scenarios in the repository. Instead of individual organizations modeling their respective views of how they think a particular business goal should be achieved, it is envisioned that standards organizations such as UN/CEFACT and user groups such as SWIFT create the models. These models would contain all the possible activities that pertain to a particular business goal. In other words, if there is more than one way to accomplish a certain step in the process, they all are included. There is no prejudging regarding which way is best.

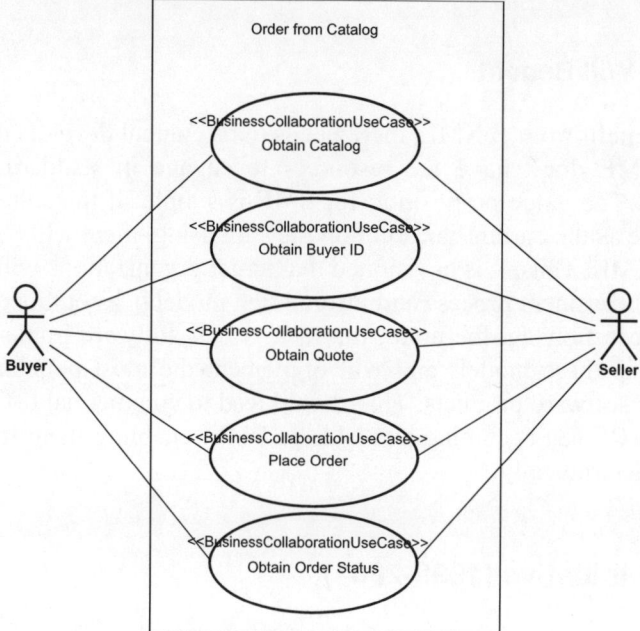

Fig. 4.2. Use case diagram: order from catalog

As an example, Figure 4.2 shows a UML use case diagram that follows the UMM and outlines the high-level activities that may be executed in a catalog order. Only two out of the five use cases shown in the figure are mandatory: obtaining a buyer ID and placing an order. The other three are optional: getting a copy of the catalog, requesting a quote and enquiring about the order status. Because of this, there are a number of different scenarios available for executing this business process:

• Registration to obtain a buyer ID
• Order (after previous registration)
• Request for catalog (with or without registration)
• Quote (after registration)
• Status (after order placement)

The first two activities are the minimum requirement for any party to be able to execute the process. Depending on their own internal systems, some companies may register any or all of the other three activities and, thereby, related scenarios.

This is a simple example. In more complex business processes there may be more than one way to place an order, in which case there would be more available scenarios.

4.1.4 How SMEs Will Benefit

Before SME can benefit from ebXML, there needs to be content developed on their behalf. SME don't have the resources to engage in standard-development work. The value proposition for SME is simple: if the solution is not as simple as the current fax solution they are using, there will be no adoption of ebXML. Thus, it is envisioned that larger organizations will develop the content (business process and information models), as outlined in the previous subsection. Furthermore, the idea is that software implementers will take up these models and will implement the most popular scenarios into their software products. This should lead to commercial off-the-shelf software (COTS) becoming available to SME, enabling them to conduct business electronically.

4.2 The ebXML Initiative (1999-2001)

It all began in the summer of 1999. The United Nations Center for Trade Facilitation and eBusiness (UN/CEFACT) and the international technology business consortium called Organization for the Advancement of Structured Information Standards (OASIS) joined forces to produce a global XML framework for e-business called "Electronic Business with XML" (ebXML). At the beginning more than 120 companies and standards bodies signed up for the "ebXML Initiative". Over the following eighteen months, more than 2,500 participants across the globe worked on the development of several interrelated specifications. At the final ebXML meeting in May 2001 in Vienna, the participants ratified the first generation of ebXML specifications, delivering the ebXML infrastructure.

The reason for the successful creation and approval of the ebXML infrastructure specifications was because nothing new was invented. The project teams evaluated proven technology, which was to be used as the baseline for all specifications. The editing teams leveraged as much existing technology as possible, including the World Wide Web Consortium's XML Schema, XML Linking Language (XLINK), and the XML Signature Syntax and Processing (XMLDsig) specifications. In addition, several references from the Internet Engineering Task Force's Request for Comments were considered. This was not all. New initiatives that were launched well after the ebXML project started were carefully examined, including Security Services Markup Language (SSML), Simple Object Access Protocol (SOAP) and Universal Description, Discovery and Integration (UDDI). SOAP was successfully incorporated into the ebXML Message Servicing Specification.

The ebXML infrastructure as documented in the suite of approved specifications (Walsh 2001) provides the only open, out-of-the-box, standards-based solution ready for use. So what sets ebXML's solution apart from the rest? Some solutions are available, however, none of them simultaneously support all the business verticals. Enterprises electing to use one of these commercial solutions may not be able to participate in a truly global business environment.

The ebXML framework (Hofreiter et al. 2002, Kotok and Webber 2001; Nickull et al. 2001) comprises five major work areas as shown in Figure 4.3.

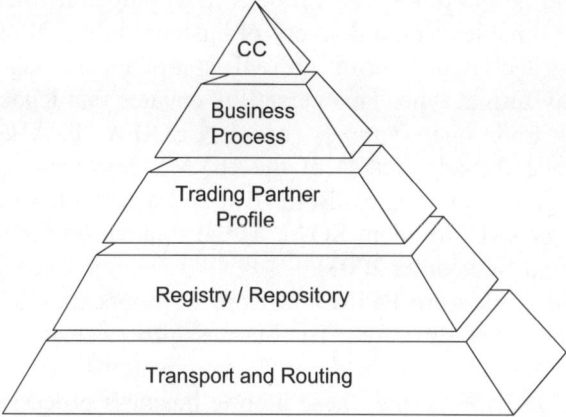

Fig. 4.3. ebXML protocol stack

The Registry and Repository component supports all of the above functions, making it a major piece of the infrastructure. The ebXML registry provides a set of distributed services that enable the sharing of information. This simplifies business process integration between business parties. The registry provides the interfacing access services by means of the registry information model and reference system implementation, while a repository provides the physical back-end information storage. For example, an ebXML registry may retrieve configuration information for a particular business entity from the repository in response to a query, or an ebXML repository may contain document type definitions or schemas that are retrieved by a registry query.

Collaboration Protocol Profiles (CPP) are another key element of the infrastructure. The CPP specification is based on the Trading Partner Agreement Markup Language (tpaML) work begun by IBM (Dan et al. 2001). The IBM work was enhanced through the efforts of the ebXML Trading Partner Agreement project team to produce a method for defining the transport, messaging and security environment of a specific business entity. Also, the team defined methods for dynamically exchanging the CPP data between business entities and for negotiating message exchange agreements – called Collaboration Protocol Agreements (CPA) – between the parties. These profiles may be maintained by the individual business entities within the ebXML business domain or may be stored within an ebXML repository.

Information packaging and transport mechanisms, specified in the ebXML Message Service Specification, are the third critical component of the ebXML infrastructure. A protocol-neutral method for exchanging the e-business messages is defined in this specification. Enveloping constructs are specified that support reliable, secure delivery of business information. These flexible enveloping techniques permit ebXML-compliant messages to contain payloads of any format type. This versatility ensures that legacy e-business systems using traditional syntaxes (i.e., UN/EDIFACT, ANSI X12 or HL7) can leverage the advantages of the ebXML infrastructure along with users of emerging technologies. Both IBM and Microsoft were instrumental in pursuing ebXML to adopt SOAP as the foundation for its Message Services (Patil and Newcomer 2003).

The other two areas of work were BPIM and Core Components (CC), both related to the content and context area. The business process team defined a metamodel that described business transaction patterns used to achieve business goals. In simple terms, these atomic business processes prescribe the detailed interaction of business documents and business signals among parties, called choreographies. ebXML processes define activities such as "order goods" or "deliver goods," as compared with traditional EDI documents that are electronic versions of paper documents such as purchase order or ship notice.

When UN/CEFACT presented its proposal for the business semantics portion of the work at the first ebXML meeting, it was mostly envisioned in terms of a library of common business objects (CBOs). These CBOs would be the building blocks linked to the relevant business process in the associated BPIM model notated in UML. This would ultimately yield to schemas for XML messages. However, right from the start, the participants in this work rejected the application of an objected-oriented approach in lieu of a document-centric solution. The argument for the change in direction was their knowledge – reinforced by years of experience with EDI –

that a piece of information might mean different things or have different component parts in different business contexts. The counterargument by the business process people was, and still is, that any model in itself will always be in context with the business process and its related information. However, due to the lack of enough business process experts, who could have helped with the CBO work, the end outcome was the creation of the core component concepts. As a result, the core component approach serves as the semantic foundation for ebXML business document exchanges.

Core components are reusable data elements found in business documents. They are semantically neutral objects; their actual meaning in business documents depends on their context, provided by the business domain and industry in which they are applied. Core components can be single elements or aggregates, defined as natural collections of core elements. A telephone number, for example, may contain a country code, city or area code and a number, which, when strung together, constitute an aggregate. Core components provide the means for industries to continue using their own terminology in business documents and, at the same time, relate their terminology to common business processes and neutral identifiers provided by ebXML. As long as trading partners can relate their own terminology to neutral ebXML core components, businesses have a basis for achieving interoperability.

4.3 The Transition Period (2001-2004)

After the completion of the infrastructure specification in May 2001, UN/CEFACT and OASIS signed an agreement to continue the ebXML work. Infrastructure support services were assigned to OASIS, and the business components were placed within UN/CEFACT. The reason for doing this was to allow each organization to proceed with the work within its own area of expertise in order to ensure continuing rapid progress.

UN/CEFACT continued the work started under ebXML phase one; advancing development as related to business processes, core components and e-business architecture.

UN/CEFACT adopted a business process and information modeling methodology, referred to as the UN/CEFACT Modeling Methodology (Hofreiter et al. 2006), that provides the framework under which its project teams concurrently develop technical specifications that fit seamlessly together.

A business process and information model draws from reusable common business process models as provided for in reference libraries (imported from various levels of business process models, i.e., transactions, collaborations and processes), simple "best in class" business collaboration patterns as determined from industry examples, pieces of collaboration patterns, e.g., patterns of how commitment categories are specified, resources are described, etc. and business transaction patterns as already established in the UMM, business entities, defined as business information objects that each have a life cycle that transitions through defined states in the fulfillment of the commitments in a collaboration, and core components specialized for business contexts.

The business process and information modeling and the core components work carried over from the initial ebXML initiative and have come into fruition with the benefit of several iterations, revisions and comments. The modeling of information required to enter and determine successful execution of a business collaboration or transaction, i.e., states of business entities, is benefiting from the core components library as a reference for conceptual information entities. Business entities are then elaborated in the model of "on-the-wire" business documents as normalized business information entities.

4.4 A Critical Evaluation of ebXML

As with any standard, the success of ebXML is measured by its acceptance and the number of implementations based upon it. In order to succeed, CEFACT needed to complete the work and not get sidetracked by other activities that may have seemed like they were competing. One should remember that with respect to CEFACT's responsibility on the content and context side, there is no dependency on technology. This technology- and protocol-neutral work will survive many different infrastructure solutions. However, to be accepted as such, the work has to be completed and implementers must have the necessary vision and patience. Rushing the work will lead to failure. It takes extra time to develop a framework and its details that are "future proof" because they are not tied to any specific technology. The past has shown that it is simpler and quicker to develop proprietary solutions based on a single technology. However, as technology changes, technology-specific specifications become obsolete, and implementers are faced with migrating to new solutions. It took UN/CEFACT until the summer of 2004 to advance its content and context work (BPIM and CC) specification to the first version that could be implemented. Now that it is 2007, one can – no, must – ask: Has ebXML fulfilled its promise?

4.4.1 Did ebXML Fulfill Its Promise?

There can be no question that the original ebXML project was a milestone of close cooperation, which proved that people from around the world could come together and agree on a set of technical specifications in a short time with a minimum of overhead. In retrospect, the eighteen-month success has to be credited to the fact that the initiative lived outside the highly formal standards bureaucracy. Yet, in a way, the eighteen months of work demonstrated how global standards should be like:

• Clear and focused on a single idea,
• quickly developed,
• decisive, with a strong bias for action over politics.

When the eighteen-month effort started in late 1999, the original goal was to enable anyone, anywhere to conduct business, without prior agreement, using the Internet. Now, after eight years, one can ask if the project achieved this goal in the real world.

Based on current market penetration, ebXML did not fulfill its promise; nor did it come close to its original goal. The failure of ebXML really has nothing to do with the original technical merits. It simply failed to stay with the business and technology times and gain the critical mass that was hoped for in Vienna. There may be those within the still existent and loyal ebXML community who would disagree with this statement and would point to a number of ebXML implementations. However, a close examination of those implementations shows that most of them are government-sponsored initiatives that supply the client software as well. In other words, there is no real "off-the-shelf" software allowing anyone to engage with anybody else anywhere else "out of the blue". These implementations can solely be found within specific application areas where, literally speaking, the "500 lb gorillas" use the ebXML infrastructure to lock their clients/customers into their closed systems.

The failure is not because ebXML started with the wrong ideas or was an invalid solution. Compared to the early web service work six years ago, ebXML had some better technical qualities; for instance, a more reliable and secure messaging solution for B2B integration and a more mature Registry and Repository model. But what ebXML didn't have after its completion six years ago was the support from the major technology vendors. Even though IBM was one of the main contributors to ebXML, they based their products on web services (Ferris and Farrell 2003), which was started by them, Microsoft, and others some months after the ebXML kick-off.

In all fairness, ebXML was an eighteen-month effort, and it was only at the end of eighteen months that there was any notion of continuing on with the project after the initial initiative. Vienna was a deciding moment where some people decided to continue and others didn't. We now know that the web services vision was to address much more than B2B, and today we can see web services used on devices, inside internal company applications and also to some degree for B2B. We now know that web services were driven by the need for distributed computing on the Internet.

At an ebXML meeting before Vienna, Microsoft was instrumental in helping to resolve a technical impasse regarding the fundamental question of whether the ebXML messaging solution should be based on SOAP or not; what we now know as ebXML Messaging Service (ebMS) was originally based on MIME types. There was much hope within the ebXML community that Microsoft would come to support ebXML, showing the world that the big three, Microsoft, IBM and Sun, were on the same page. Sadly, we now see that that was optimistic thinking, but they and other technology vendors like SAP and Oracle are now all working together in the area of web services. So maybe ebXML contributed a little to increased collaboration in that industry.

Accordingly, the world of software companies had already moved onto another track called web services. In consequence, because of the lack of commercially available solutions for ebXML, any early implementers would have had to pay large sums to roll out their own solutions. Commercial ebXML just never happened. It should be noted that Open Source ebXML does exist today. However, compared to the market adoption of web services and what is called service oriented architecture (SOA) solutions today – the Open Source ebXML market numbers aren't grossly overwhelming. To be fair, implementing any ebXML Open Source solution is not an easy task, and is definitely not what the vision of ebXML hoped for: "off-the-shelf" software for SMEs that required no technical know-how to set up and use.

4.4.2 The Successful Elements of ebXML

Its messaging service is probably the most popular specification of ebXML, with a number of successful implementations around the world. But relative to web services or EDI, one is still not looking at a very large installed base. ebMS always offered a payload agnostic solution that is superior to AS2 of the Internet Society (RFC 4130), with reliable and secure messaging. One observation, though: it appears that each year the work on ebMS is taking on more of the web service specifications. At this pace ebMS is almost becoming just another web services profile; this is nothing new because web services provide a set of protocols that can be assembled in a number of different ways for different purposes.

Next in terms of popularity is ebXML's Registry/Repository (Reg/Rep) specification. There may even be more Reg/Rep implementations than there are ebMS ones. However, it appears that most of the Registry implementations are not used as originally envisioned from Vienna: to store ebXML Collaboration Profiles and Business Process Specification Schemas (BPSS). Instead, Reg/Rep seems to be more frequently used to store other types of online data for public access. It should also be noted that before the start of ebXML, work on web services' UDDI had started and continued in parallel during the development of Reg/Rep with the support of major contributors of ebXML.

As for the rest of the ebXML specifications, one has to conclude that there aren't really any major community implementations. It follows that the specifications concerning the business content did not start off as expected. Interestingly, web services do not offer competing standards in this area. Accordingly, we still have to wait for a standard on business semantics that is well accepted by industry.

4.4.3 Why Didn't the ebXML Elements Dealing with Business Semantics Succeed?

Due to the political wrangling over the BPSS, which were originally the responsibility of UN/CEFACT but were finally published by OASIS, potential implementers of that specification were left in limbo for some years, not knowing who was truly in charge. Furthermore, it should be noted that after Vienna the web services community released the Business Process Execution Language (BPEL), which got a lot of attraction from industry. Thus, it is seen as the winner among all business process related XML standards (Mendling and Nüttgens 2006). However, BPEL is still not able to express a global choreography, as BPSS does, in order to describe the commitments and agreements between trading partners from a neutral perspective.

Also, the core components standard did not meet expectations. The idea behind the core component architecture is to address the lack of semantic interoperability by a combination of structured information and the use of context. This structure uses a series of layers, designed to take into account commonality across industry business processes. Further, the structure is designed to support specialization based on the specific use of contexts. Context is the description of the environment within which use will occur.

Overall, the concept of a core component library is not a bad one, but again, six years later, the component structure is not only being used to change the structure of the EDI messages in use today, but also serves as the basis of UBL, OAGi BODs and a number of industry-specific electronic XML documents. Instead of being based on its business usage, the information structure is now based on harmonized semantic structures that are not only different from normalized data but are also not anywhere close to lexical structures.

Regrettably, it took three years after Vienna before, in 2004, the first CCTS specification was formally finalized. It seems, however, that instead of having a stable CCTS for CEFACT to start populating a CC library that would allow implementers to test the usability of the concepts, controversy is surfacing again with the release of a new CCTS version. Unfortunately, this new version is not backwards compatible with the existing version. Consequently, early adopters are left in limbo, not knowing if their current application will be able to migrate over to the new version; CEFACT has not issued any plans regarding how to deal with major differences between the two versions and how to migrate the existing core components library.

The fallout from all that is that UN/CEFACT lacks any business-centric XML payload that is 100% based on the CCTS. However, some of the key CCTS people were also active in OASIS. While UN/CEFACT didn't have a formal CCTS available, those same people, and others from OASIS, went out and started gaining support for OASIS's own Universal Business Language (UBL) solution, which was loosely based on UN/CEFACT's Core Component and Simpl-EDI message work. To be complete, established industry communities such as OAGi, RosettaNet, SWIFT and EAN/UCC (now GS1) were all going to be converting to CCTS. Now, one might think that the resulting solutions of these different organizations are interoperable because they are based on the same semantic foundation of core components. However, this is not the case. They share parts of the meta-level concepts defined in the CCTS, but they all develop their own schema level concepts. For example, an address defined by one organization is not the same as one defined by another organization.

4.5 Conclusion

The original ebXML vision, as concluded in Vienna, failed to reach its goals because it failed to recognize (and embrace) the coming market trends and adapt to changing perceptions in both business and technology. Today, talk is about services architecture such as SOA. And about Web

2.0, so not just about the next generation of businesses but about living in the digital world.

The failure of ebXML really had nothing to do with the original technical merits; ebXML was simply overtaken by web services due to the support of the software industry. ebXML was a first attempt to use XML in the area of connecting autonomous applications, and many of the ideas were later incorporated into web services. In this respect, ebXML may be seen as a "spin doctor" for web services. Apart from its purely technological elements, ebXML also focused on solutions concerning the business content – which have not been absorbed by web services. Maybe UN/CEFACT's ebXML work on business semantics will become a kind of "spin doctor" for a yet-to-be-developed global business semantics framework.

Part II

Knowledge Management Technologies

5 Ontology Engineering

Over recent years, methods developed in the field of artificial intelligence have become the subject of increasing attention. Capturing knowledge in ontologies and thereby formalizing fact collections in well-defined semantics promises to facilitate the interpretation of the meaning of terms by humans and, also, by machines. In this chapter we discuss methods of ontology engineering, focusing on approaches for establishing semantic interoperability.

5.1 Ontologies in Computer Science

The notion of *"ontology"* emanates from philosophy. It denotes the science of being and, with this, of descriptions for the organization, designation and categorization of existence (Gruber 1993b). Thus, ontology aims to explain the nature of the world. Carried over to computer science, *"an ontology"* is the capture of the recognized and conceived in a knowledge domain for the purpose of their representation and communication. In informatics, this led to the formation of "ontologies" – the plural of what was originally used in philosophy solely as the singular "ontology" – since in many knowledge domains several representations can coexist side by side (Hesse 2005). Hence, in this context an ontology is a precise description of knowledge in a usually logic-based language with well-defined semantics allowing for machine processing and logical deducting (Uschold and Gruninger 2004). Having originated in the discipline of artificial intelligence as a means of sharing and reusing knowledge, ontologies link human understanding of signs, symbols and scripture to machine processability (Davies et al. 2003). Through the assignation of names terms receive a formal meaning, making them machine interpretable (de Bruijn 2004). With this, reuse of knowledge and automated reasoning for the discovery of tacitly inherent knowledge can be achieved (Uschold and Gruninger 2004).

5.1.1 Structure

In principle, an ontology is the content specification of a particular domain. The domain can be of any kind. Thus, an ontology is often described as "an explicit specification of a conceptualization" (Gruber 1993b) or "a shared explicit formal specification of domains of knowledge," respectively, in the form $(C_1..C_j, I_1..I_k, R_1..R_m, A_1..A_n)$ (de Bruijn 2004; Bouquet et al. 2005; Martin-Recuerda et al. 2004, Gómez-Pérez et al. 2004). Conceptualization denotes the abstraction of ideas into concepts and the relations between them (Mizoguchi 2003). Thereby, an ontology provides a simplified abstract view of the world formally described by representational vocabulary for a shared domain of discourse (Gruber 1993b). It can thus be understood as a conceptual schema, similar to database schemas (Antoniou et al. 2005). An ontology's elements, the entities, are as follows:

- C_i = class or concept, $1 \le i \ge j$, representing a set of objects with common properties
- I_i = instance, $1 \le i \ge k$, representing the individual objects
- R_i = relation in terms of property or slot, $1 \le i \ge m$, which are functions
- A_i = axiom, $1 \le i \ge n$, which is a formalized statement or assertion assumed to be true without having to be proved for modeling non-deducible knowledge

These elements are specified in a formal language as modeling elements, the primitives. This data modeling is different from the modeling of objects. Object models specify the encapsulation of data and methods; the goal is the provision of executable software where the object behavior is embodied in the code fragments and the physical representation of data is provided. An ontology model specifies knowledge and structures concepts of a certain domain. No execution mechanism is required for this, since it is provided by the application systems working with the ontologies. In this way, object modeling and ontology modeling can complement each other (Polikoff and Allemang 2004). Table 5.1 shows the differences between the two types of modeling.

Table 5.1. Comparison of object model and ontology model (based on Polikoff and Allemang 2004)

	Object Model	Ontology Model
Attribute	Local with each class	Exists independently of classes; can be united with other attributes or reused in several classes; reasoning is possible across classes and instances.
Relation between attributes	Limited semantics, shows only the relation	Possibility of creating subclasses of relations for describing different attributes, e.g., transitive relations.
Relation between classes	Can be described between two classes	Validity for several different classes can be defined.
Class	Is a specification of instance behavior	Can be a specification of the allocation of instances to classes. Instances may have several attributes, making them assignable to different classes at the same time. Class affiliation is dynamic and depends on attribute values.

In an ontology, individual designations are modeled instead of software classes. Conceptually, ontologies and database schemas resemble each other. For example, the entities of an entity-relationship model (ERM) correspond to the classes of an ontology and the attributes and relationships of an ERM correspond to the relations or properties in most ontology languages. In ontologies constraints are formalized as axioms, which provide the machine-readable meaning as the basis for automated reasoning. In database schemas the constraints serve mostly to provide data integrity (Uschold and Gruninger 2004).

Ontologies provide the meaning of notions for enabling information exchange between humans and heterogeneous, decentralized applications. They can be understood as logical theories and, by means of algebra, can be expressed as pairs (Kalfoglou and Schorlemmer 2005), as shown in Eq. 5.1:

$$O = (S,A) \tag{5.1}$$

where

- S = ontological signature for describing the vocabulary, and
- A = set of ontological axioms for specifying the intended interpretation of the vocabulary.

This structured knowledge about a particular domain is explicit, since it is clearly and uniquely stated and can be communicated. In contrast to implicit knowledge, it does not have to be inferred by logical deduction.

5.1.2 Types of Ontologies

Structured and, also, semi-structured knowledge can exist in different forms, as the extent of formalizing may differ. The simplest form of an ontology is as a collection and description of terms in natural language intended for aggregating the facts about a certain domain of discourse. A first step towards formalization is presetting a default structure for this description, for example in XML, by defining the terms contained and their hierarchical order. To assign semantic disambiguity and define the intended meaning of these definitions, a formal semantics can be employed as a next step. The most powerful forms are strictly formalized descriptions derived according to first-order logic, as this allows for quantified statements of objects and relations (Russell and Norvig 2003).

Furthermore, ontologies vary regarding the extent of explication provided (Stuckenschmidt and van Harmelen 2005). So-called lightweight ontologies are hierarchically structured in the form of identification systems, vocabularies, glossaries, thesauri, classifications and taxonomies. They describe concepts and their relations and attributes and form a network of relations. The so-called heavyweight ontologies contain additional interlinking through relations of the concepts, stated as axioms and constraints in terms of predefined conditions. Thereby the meaning of ontologies' entities can be described non-ambiguously (Gómez-Pérez et al. 2004).

What is common to all these types of ontologies is that they are vocabularies of application domains as well as specifications of the meaning of terms and concepts (Uschold and Gruninger 2004). They are expressed as systems of concepts and relations by a logical theory that describes the relations between the included terms while at the same time restricting the number of possible interpretations (Devedzic 2002). Figure 5.1 shows the range of ontologies according the degree of the formalization and thus semantic precision of the specification, adapted from McGuinness (2003), Uschold and Gruninger (2004) and Euzenat and Shvaiko (2007).

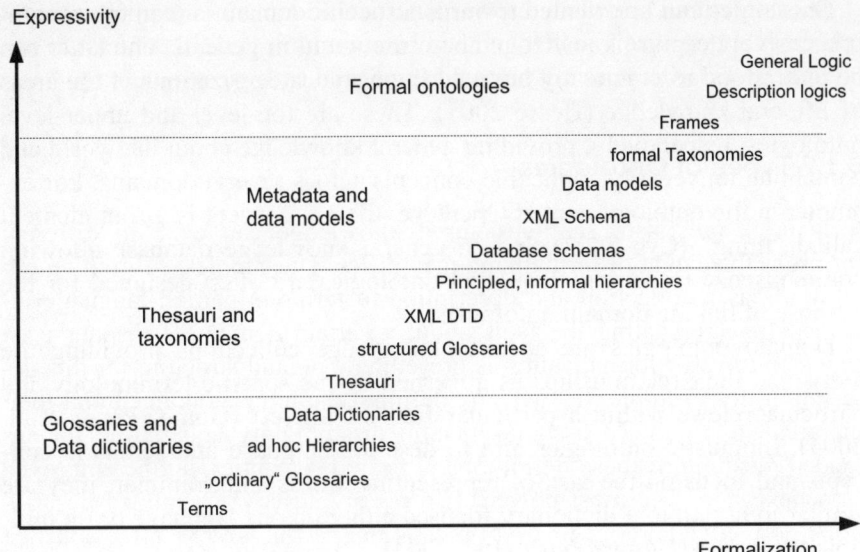

Fig. 5.1. Types of ontologies

The simplest ontologies are controlled vocabularies with a restricted list of terms, such as catalogs or identification systems, similar to dictionaries that are systematically arranged collections of words of a certain domain (NISO 2007). Another form of specification are glossaries, i.e., a list of little-known terms with their meaning description in natural language. Taxonomies are classifications of a particular subject field, i.e., a hierarchically organized controlled vocabulary. Thesauri offer additional semantic information regarding the relations between the terms, as they describe related classes as abstractions of objects and instances with identical properties, respectively. For doing so, basic term hierarchies use the idea of generalization and specialization by describing them as relations. Schemas define abstract record structures and thus organize them in accordance to conceptual models of the data to be represented. In formal ontologies the relation between super- and subclasses is strictly observed. Additional formalization is achieved, first, by including instances in the classification schemas and, second, by defining value constraints for the describing properties. The highest degree of expressivity is achieved by defining the properties by means of mathematical equations containing values of other properties or by logical statements in first-order logic, such as disjoint or inverse classes or part-of relations (McGuinness 2003; Uschold and Gruninger 2004).

Ontologies can be oriented towards a specific domain or can try to comprehensively capture knowledge about the world in general. The latter can be understood as practically oriented linguistic categorizations of the areas of life and knowledge (Hesse 2005). These are top-level and upper-level ontologies, respectively, providing general knowledge about the world and containing universally applicable concepts across several domains. For example, in the ontology named OpenCyc, the top concept is a root element called "thing" (Cyc 2002). It is a general knowledge database allowing commonsense reasoning. Top-level ontologies are often designed for the purpose of linking domain ontologies.

Domain ontologies are specific knowledge collections providing the terms and their relationships as governed by the specific terminology and particular views within a particular field of interest (Gómez-Pérez et al. 2004). Linguistic ontologies aim to describe language and semantic concepts and focus on the task of representing words and grammar; they are similar in notion to a dictionary focused either on one language or on multiple languages (Gómez-Pérez et al. 2004).

5.2 Representation

Information contained in ontologies can be specified by means of logical languages. Ontology languages allow for machine-interpretable coding, programming and description of knowledge. Through logical modeling of a particular domain, a certain part of the real world is reconstructed by means of logic. For this, the representation system, which is the ontology language, has to provide adequacy of expressivity and efficiency of notation. Thus, from a collection of single facts knowledge can be generated by means of terminological abstraction, generalization, classification and representation of the underlying rules. The meaning of ontology content is contained entirely in its structure and the formal semantics, and thus is interpretable by both humans and machines (de Bruijn 2004).

5.2.1 Logical Representation

Logical languages facilitate accurate and distinct representations in the form of ontologies. They are specifications on an abstract level for describing what holds true in a certain domain through the definition of constraints that express what is supposed to be valid for all possible instances (Antoniou et al. 2005). The goal is to dissolve multiple meaning interpretations and thereby disambiguate semantically. The steps required are:

- terminological *standardization* through the definition of relevant terms, which are the classes, relations and objects of a domain;
- hierarchical *structuring* of the system of concepts and the object relations;
- *determination* of the restrictions for interpreting the terms;
- *authorization* of automated deduction of various characteristics of the terminology from the definitions and restrictions, e.g., synonymy or subsumption.

The use of first-order logic extends the possibilities of propositional logic. The latter is a formal language providing symbols for elementary statements used to describe states by assigning logical values. Through logical composition they can be combined into sentences (Russell and Norvig 2003). First-order logic extends this vocabulary of logical expressions. Individuals, features and relations are regarded as predicates. A predicate is the linguistic expression or term for describing a statement about something. Single-digit predicates with one argument express a property, for example, a statement like "fish swim." Multi-digit predicates describe a relationship between their arguments, such as, for example, "John eats fish." Usually, nouns and properties are represented by single-digit predicates, verbs and relationships by multi-digit predicates. Knowledge can be made accessible by composing phrases in the form of non-logical axioms (Russell and Norvig 2003).

When the implicit knowledge contained in ontologies is made available and new knowledge is deduced, the use of first-order-logic-based languages leads to the problem of non-determinability or semi-determinability. Languages are determinable if their characteristic function can be calculated fully or, at least, partly. Therefore, for knowledge management, determinable, sufficiently expressive first-order-logic subsets are used: the description logics. They provide well-defined formal semantics without variables in the formalism of predicates. Concepts, roles and individuals, as existent in the real world, can be described independently of each other (de Bruijn 2004).

A description-logic-based language consists of two parts. The TBox, the terminological box, defines the terminology of a domain's concepts and with this all predicates and relations. The ABox, the assertional box, describes facts and assertions, respectively, regarding the defining properties of entities or concept instances and their relations. This corresponds to the representation of the state of the modeled part of the real world. Thus, new concepts may be automatically classified into the hierarchy and instances may be automatically classified as well. Of central importance in description logic is the subsumption relation and complex general terms (Russell and Norvig 2003).

5.2.2 Ontology Languages

The existing logical languages can be distinguished into traditional and markup, or web-based, languages (Gómez-Pérez et al. 2004).

Traditional ontology languages were mainly developed in the early 1990s in the field of artificial intelligence. Figure 5.2 provides an overview.

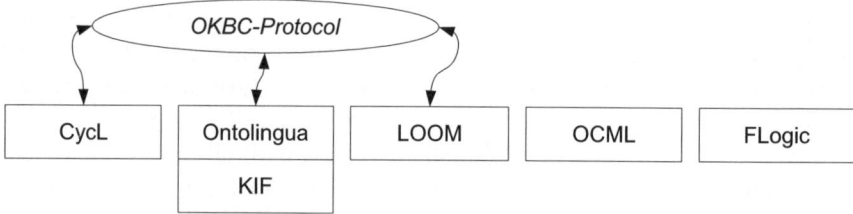

Fig. 5.2. Traditional ontology languages (Gómez-Pérez et al. 2004)

The first language was CycL, which is based on frames and first-order logic. A frame is a data network with nodes and relations representing a stereotyped situation that can be adapted to reflect changes over time and combined with other frame systems (Minsky 1975). Shortly after CycL, the Knowledge Interchange Format (KIF) was developed, also based on first-order logic. To simplify the building of ontologies in KIF, Ontolingua was built on top. LOOM is based on description logics. Operational Conceptual Modelling Language (OCML) was developed in 1990 to be in the same style as Ontolingua. FLogic is a language combining frames and first-order logic. However, it does not show a syntax similar to the programming language List Processing (LISP), which utilizes linked lists, as had been common so far (Gómez-Pérez et al. 2004). By means of the Open Knowledge Base Connectivity (OKBC) protocol, knowledge bases can be accessed in a standardized manner, analogous to the idea of the Open Database Connectivity (ODBC) protocol in the field of databases.

Web-based ontology languages generally build on XML. They vary in terms of the degree of expressiveness. Figure 5.3 provides an overview.

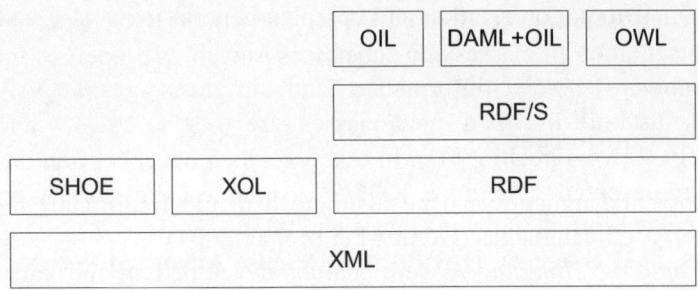

Fig. 5.3. Web-based ontology languages (Gómez-Pérez et al. 2004)

SHOE – Simple HTML Ontology Extensions – is a frame-and-rule-based language that offers an HTML-extension for the semantic annotation of webpages (Gómez-Pérez et al. 2004). Rules are specifications of system behavior according to preset assertions, which are predicates stating something is true and can be tested for (Norvig and Russel 2003). The XML-based Ontology Language (XOL) includes a subset of language elements based on the OKBC protocol. It was developed for exchanging formal knowledge models in bioinformatics and influenced by the ideas of frame-based representation languages (Antoniou et al. 2005).

A language often used for basic ontologies is the Resource Description Framework (RDF) (W3C 2004c). This is a specification for information – the resources on the Web. Resources can be described by attributes and their values, and also with the help of links to other resources (Hesse 2005). Metadata is described in triples, similar to elementary sentences in the form subject, verb and object (Berners-Lee et al. 2001). A triple contains `<object, attribute, value>`, whereas the attribute links the object (which is representing a resource) to the value. The latter are nodes, so that an RDF model forms a semantic network (Mizoguchi 2003). An example for an RDF triple is shown in Figure 5.4. It depicts that a certain web page, represented by its URL, has a title and states it.

```
<rdf:Description rdf:about=http://www.w3.org/TR/rdf-syntax-grammar">
        <dc:title>RDF/XML Syntax Specification  (Revised)</dc:title>
<rdf:Description>
```

Fig. 5.4. Example for RDF notation (W3C 2004c)

Most widespread is the serialization of RDF in XML. The Resource Description Framework can serve as a fundamental general-purpose format for representing lightweight ontologies (Mizoguchi 2003). With RDF-Schema (RDF/S), the formal vocabulary for describing the semantics of the RDF elements used can be defined (W3C 2004d). RDF-Schema includes the representation of classes and subclasses as well as properties for describing relations between information and instances, respectively (OMG 2005). Its built-in main meta-classes are `rdfs:Class` and `rdfs:Property` (Mizoguchi 2003). In this way, the concepts of an ontology can be represented. Therefore, RDF/S is suitable for classification hierarchies (Stuckenschmidt and van Harmelen 2005).

On this basis, the US-agency DARPA, the Defense Advanced Research Projects Agency that also created the Internet's predecessor Arpanet, developed the DARPA Agent Markup Language (DAML) as a communication language for software agents. This was later combined with the Ontology Inference Layer (OIL) (Hesse 2005). OIL was intended to be an ontology language with formal semantics and extensive deduction possibilities (Antoniou et al. 2005). Together, the so-called DAML+OIL provided the basis for developing the Web Ontology Language (OWL). The Web Ontology Language is a W3C specification for creating ontologies with a formal representation language. In principle, it is a semantic markup language. Terms and their relations can be formally described by OWL in such a way that they become machine understandable. Technically, this language builds upon the RDF syntax and also employs the triple model, but it features more powerful possibilities for building expressions than RDF/S. As an extension of RDF and RDF/S, in OWL further language constructs are included, allowing for expressions formulated similarly to those with first-order logic. Vocabulary is added, providing the representation of relations between properties and classes, such as equality, cardinality and basic constraints (W3C 2004a).

The Web Ontology Language exists in three versions of different power which build on top of each other. Each lower and thereby less expressive dialect is a subset of the dialect above it. Accordingly, OWL Lite is the least expressive dialect and OWL Full the most substantial (de Bruijn 2004). These dialects facilitate the definition of constraints to different degrees, thus enabling deductions that are as comprehensive as possible (Gómez-Pérez et al. 2004). OWL Lite offers the functionalities of RDF/S with a few additions, but does not allow for metamodeling. Definitions and axioms can be represented as well as, to a small extent, properties for defining classes (Antoniou et al. 2005). This language serves mostly for creating taxonomies and lightly axiomized ontologies with basic constraints (OMG 2005). OWL-DL, which is OWL with description logic, is the successor of DAML+OIL and adds expressive constructs from the field of description logics, such as transitivity of properties. With this dialect, maximum expressivity is possible while, at the same time, calculative correctness is ensured, which is of importance for automated reasoning (OMG 2005). OWL Full, sometimes also called OWL Heavy, builds on top of OWL-DL without any restrictions and thus provides for metamodeling (Mika and Akkermans 2003). This dialect also offers maximum expressivity, but it has additional potential for syntactical designing, similar to what is possible in RDF. However, due to these possibilities, calculative correctness is not fully ensured (OMG 2005). For the same reason, this dialect can provide for handling classes as instances and vice versa. When coupling ontologies, this feature proves to be helpful (Stuckenschmidt and van Harmelen 2005).

5.2.3 Visualization

The interrelations between terms, their environments and their possible correspondences to other terms can be illustrated and rather intuitively exemplified by visualizing them as a tree structure or in form of a net. A tree structure can be navigated relatively easily, but shows only hierarchical structures. A net structure allows for associative recognition of a term's environment. Such nets are called *semantic nets*. The nodes represent the concepts, i.e., the classes or instances of an ontology, and the directed edges stand for the properties, i.e., associative relation types (Hepp 2003; Miller 2006). In principle, semantic nets are graphs according to graph theory (Hesse 2005). The relations between terms can be visualized as the end point of directive graphs based on distance, weighting and angle. Often, the expressions ontology and semantic net are used synonymously, as they both stand for related semantic information. Figure 5.5 shows a basic visualization of an ontology about videos and the representation of two of its classes in OWL (Bao et al. 2004). The subclasses are expressed as *is-a* relations.

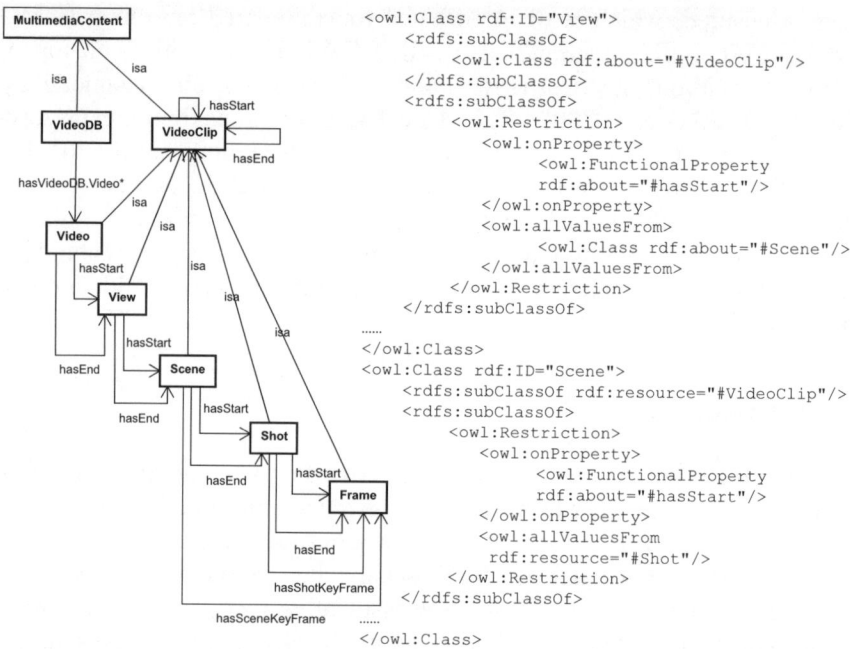

```
<owl:Class rdf:ID="View">
    <rdfs:subClassOf>
        <owl:Class rdf:about="#VideoClip"/>
    </rdfs:subClassOf>
    <rdfs:subClassOf>
        <owl:Restriction>
            <owl:onProperty>
                <owl:FunctionalProperty
                rdf:about="#hasStart"/>
            </owl:onProperty>
            <owl:allValuesFrom>
                <owl:Class rdf:about="#Scene"/>
            </owl:allValuesFrom>
        </owl:Restriction>
    </rdfs:subClassOf>
    ......
</owl:Class>
<owl:Class rdf:ID="Scene">
    <rdfs:subClassOf rdf:resource="#VideoClip"/>
    <rdfs:subClassOf>
        <owl:Restriction>
            <owl:onProperty>
                <owl:FunctionalProperty
                rdf:about="#hasStart"/>
            </owl:onProperty>
            <owl:allValuesFrom
            rdf:resource="#Shot"/>
        </owl:Restriction>
    </rdfs:subClassOf>
    ......
</owl:Class>
```

Fig. 5.5. Representations of an ontology (adapted from Bao et al. 2004)

In the given case, "scene" means the film location and "shot" means the documentation of an action. Applied, for example, to any James Bond movie, an instance of scene would be the place where the MI5 agent meets his opponent for the first time, and an instance of shot would be the famous introduction with the words "...Bond. James Bond".

The visualization of an ontology serves to simplify management of the ontology for humans, especially in case of huge complex nets. For such nets, a possible form for presenting them concisely could be hyper trees, which are based on hypberbolic graphs and show tree structures in geometrical form (Lamping et al. 1995). Huge graphs can be visualized by means of grouping and clustering information. These subgraphs can be visualized in detail upon request (Fluit et al. 2003; Miller 2006). An overall overview of a graph can be visualized in form of a semantic net. As an example of a semantic net, Figure 5.6 shows a fragment from the RosettaNet Business Directory.

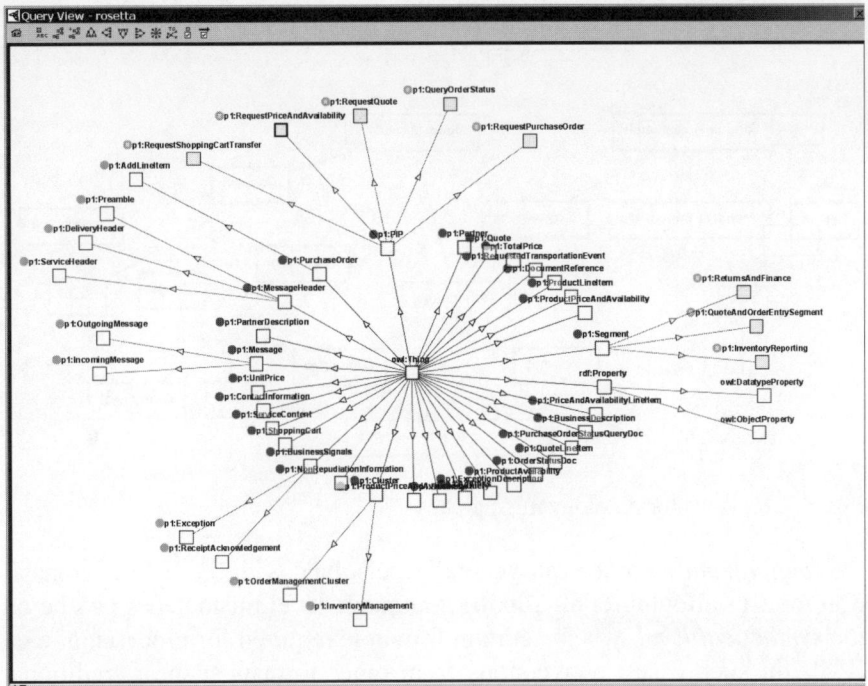

Fig. 5.6. A semantic net

5.3 Ontology Mismatches

Ontologies are developed by different bodies. Therefore, it has to be assumed that they contain differences not only in content, but also in their conceptualization. The resulting ontology mismatches hinder an automated reconciliation of ontologies (Visser et al. 1997; Klein 2001; Klein 2004). Types of mismatch and resolution approaches are discussed in the following.

5.3.1 Types of Mismatch

Ontology mismatches can occur on the language and the model level; both causes can be detailed further. Figure 5.7 provides an overview (adapted from Kalfoglou et al. 2005b)

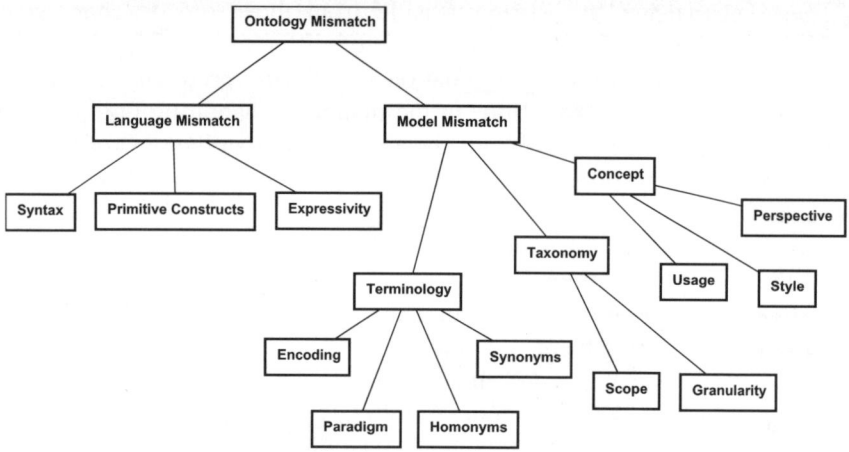

Fig. 5.7. Reasons for ontology mismatches

Language mismatches can generally be solved with the help of translation tools (Kalfoglou et al. 2005b). Language level mismatches can be on the *syntactical level*, when a certain format is required for processing, e.g., XML. In such cases, conversions from other formats such as traditional EDI formats or CSV are required for transformation into the syntax needed. Furthermore, a differing logical representation leads to varying versions of the same statements. For example, when two classes A and B are not connected, in one language this is expressed as (disjoint A B) while in another language the representation would only be possible as a negation in subclasses as (A subclass-of (NOT B)). Thus, a different designation of the *primitive linguistic constructs* leads to different interpretations of the statements composed with them. Note that in this case, transformation rules could remedy these deficiencies (Ehrig 2007). Also, differences in the ontology languages' *expressivity* can prevent the representation of a particular construct in another language.

Model level mismatches are harder to identify and resolve (Kalfoglou et al. 2005b). Concerning *terminology*, non-adequate usage often leads to interpretation difficulties. Diverse ways of *encoding* of dates, measurements or currencies may be in use. More general, different terminology *paradigms*, but also the occurrence of *synonyms* (different terms with the same meaning) or *homonyms* (same term with several meanings) may lead to semantic ambiguity.

On the *taxonomical level*, varying *granularity* or *scope* may lead to different extents in specification depth and width.

These mismatches are distinguishable from those on the *conceptual level*. Differences spring from the *usage* of different concept names for identical classes, or from the assignation of differing properties. Differing modeling *styles* lead to variations in the manner of capturing the meaning to be represented. For example, this becomes evident at the time of modeling properties to be inherited by subclasses. Other sources of conceptual imbalance are inconsistencies and incompleteness that are due to different *perspectives* of the modelers involved.

Furthermore, from an application point of view, license or usage rights guidelines can foresee restrictions in using ontologies, thereby limiting the possibilities of relating them.

Due to the mismatches described, it may be a non-trivial task to find corresponding items in two or more ontologies. A UML model example illustrates this (Malucelli and Oliveira 2004). Figure 5.8 shows a comparison of two simple example ontologies and their terminological and taxonomical mismatches. In this example, standard 1 and standard 2 have different views of the same domain, which is concerned with paper products. The classes "writing paper" correspond, but their attributes describing the product number differ terminologically, i.e., "Article#" and "ProductID" intend to describe the same, but are designated differently. Taxonomically the two standards show different granularity, since standard 2 has a more detailed structuring of the class "paper" into subclasses.

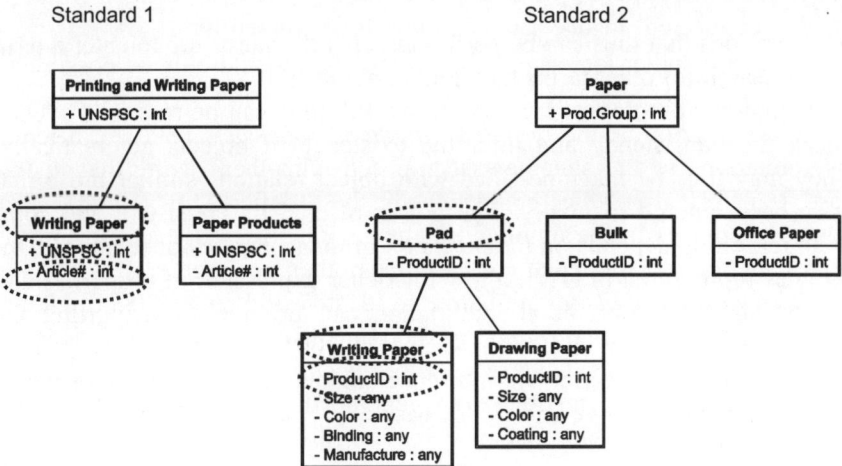

Fig. 5.8. Examples of ontology model mismatches

5.3.2 Basic Resolution Approaches

The use of synonyms and homonyms is an obvious source of ontology mismatch. Often, for solving these semantic problems, approaches based on utilizing thesauri, representing word collections or word nets, are applied. These are systematically ordered, controlled collections of terms from a particular domain with a restricted number of possible relations. Synonyms and some basic relation types can be managed. Hence, a thesaurus is a collection of selected vocabulary (preferred terms or descriptors) with links among synonymous, equivalent, broader, narrower and other related terms. For example, ISO 2788:186 defines the creation of monolingual thesauri and the possible relation types and ISO 5964:1985 defines the creation of multi-lingual thesauri. Table 5.2 shows the standardized relations types used in thesauri (IFLA 2005).

Table 5.2. Relation types in thesauri

Abbreviation	Relation
UF	Used for
USE/SYN	Use synonym
BT	Broader term
NT	Narrower term
RT	Related term
SN	Scope note

Operations that thus can be performed on a thesaurus are to enter a term and to search for other terms that hold relations to it.

In contrast, ontologies are more powerful; they can be reasoned over to check the consistency and infer the existence of objects automatically. They may thus be machine-filled with object relations similar those that have been entered manually. The power offered by consistent and complete reasoning depends on the precision of the semantics of relations. Ontologies represented in OWL allow for richer expression of properties and constraints (Matthews et al. 2004) and can provide for exporting the knowledge onto the Web (Berners-Lee et al. 2001).

In the following section we introduce engineering techniques for working with such expressive knowledge bases.

5.4 Engineering Techniques

Knowledge engineering, focusing on methods and tools for collecting and processing knowledge, is a field that has emerged only in recent years. It has been followed, even more recently, by ontology engineering (Stuckenschmidt and van Harmelen 2005). With ontology engineering, all technologies supporting an ontology's lifecycle are summarized (Hesse 2005). Those technologies include creation, coordination and merging methods, each of which will be detailed further in the following.

5.4.1 Creation

These methods encompass initial building as well as several techniques for the management of specific aspects of a single ontology.

Building

Initial ontology building encompasses representing knowledge and its formation. Ontologies are developed using methods from the field of artificial intelligence in addition to various representation formalisms, like frames and frame-based languages such as F-Logic and predicate logic, in order to analyze the structure of elementary statements in first-order logic, higher-order logic and description logic. In some cases horn clauses are also used; these are of importance to logical programming languages.

The process of building includes modeling all concepts, attributes and relations for their representation. Alternatively, object-oriented techniques from software engineering can be used, for example the UML, for modeling concepts, attributes and relations in combination with the Object Constraint Language (OCL) for complementing the model with axioms. Also, from the field of databases, modeling with the help of ER diagrams can be chosen. These are rather well suited for modeling lightweight ontologies, as they can be translated into the Structured Query Language (SQL) and then extended if necessary (Gómez-Pérez et al. 2004).

Development

Besides building, development describes the design process of an ontology. There exist several methodologies for collecting, retrieving, encoding and evaluating knowledge to be represented. Examples are the Cyc, SENSUS and Kactus methodologies, the methods by Uschold and King or by Gruninger and Fox; Methontology; the On-To-Knowledge methodology for joint development frameworks according to the CO_4-method or the $(KA)^2$-method. Extensive overviews can be found, for example, in Gómez-Pérez et al. (2004) and de Bruijn (2003). The methods vary regarding their maturity, focus and individual process steps, but they have in common the determination of the purpose of the ontology to be developed and the collection of all knowledge of the application domain (Mizoguchi 2003; Sure 2003).

Pruning

The notion of pruning stems from the gardening technique where branches of a tree are grafted onto another tree. Similarly, an ontology can be created by using a core ontology and enriched by learning new concepts from external sources, e.g., business documents. Thus, new knowledge is appended to the base ontology and not needed concepts may be removed afterwards (Gómez-Pérez et al. 2004).

Learning

Learning in this respect denotes the usage of (semi-) automated approaches for the creation of ontologies, applying a combination of assorted machine-learning techniques and inference rules. Processing options include clustering, inductive-logic programming, association rules, frequency-based methods, pattern matching and formal concept analysis as well as information extraction and page ranking next to relation analyzing methods such as concept induction, ABox Mining and data correlation (Maedche and Staab 2004). Because of their importance for the approach developed here, some of those concepts are detailed further in Chapter 6.

Modularization (Extraction)

For subject-related distribution of knowledge, specific parts of ontologies can be extracted. An extraction is "a (partial, directional) projection of the content of one ontology onto another one" (Bouquet cited by Martin-Recuerda et al. 2004).

Following Stuckenschmidt and Klein (2003), "a modular ontology $M = \{M_1, \ldots, M_m\}$ is a set of modules such that for each externally defined concept $C \equiv M_i : Q$, M_i is also a member of M." Thereby Q is the "ontology based query over the signature of M_i" (Martin-Recuerda et al. 2004). By projection, relations between modules are preserved.

By splitting large ontologies into modules their management can be facilitated. Queries may be processed more quickly, since they can be restricted to certain parts of the overall ontology.

Evolution (Versioning)

Ontologies, as other knowledge bases, generally do not remain fixed once they have been created. Changes to the original base establish new versions that have to be managed. Carrying over approaches to database management, Klein (2004) distinguishes *evolution*, i.e., management of continuous development, from *versioning*, i.e., management of discrete development steps. Klein and Noy (2003) combine the tasks of maintaining modifications and versioning advancements into change management and thus do not separate between evolution and versioning. Abecker and Stojanovic (2005) describe evolution as "the timely adaptation of an ontology to the arisen changes (sic)".

Versioning includes recording changes to ontologies for the purpose of traceability, similarly to activities concerned with change- and life-cycle-management for databases. Klein (2001) defines a version as the result of a change, which can exist in parallel to the original. Hence, versioning is a method of maintaining connections between newly created and existing ontologies, in order to keep the data consistent. Since ontologies show distinct differences to database schemata, Klein (2004) combines "ontology evolution and versioning into a single concept defined as the ability to manage ontology changes and their effects by creating and maintaining different variants of the ontology. This ability consists of methods to distinguish and recognize versions, specifications of relationships between versions, update and change procedures for ontologies, and access mechanisms that combine different versions of an ontology and the corresponding data."

5.4.2 Coordination

When working with more than one ontology, methods for their coordinated concurrent use become necessary. Following Bouquet et al. (2005), *ontology coordination* covers all tasks where knowledge from two or more ontologies must be used at the same time in a meaningful way.

Ontologies usually are developed independently of each other for different purposes. For extending the captured specialist knowledge of a certain domain or relating it to other domains, ontologies have to be reconciled. The techniques for doing so include matching, mapping and alignment.

Matching

Ontology matching denotes the search for correspondences between the ontologies' elements. The basic assumption thereby is the existence of flat similarities between the ontology entities, whereby "flat" denotes a missing basis on explicit and precise semantic information, e.g., upon matching strings (Bouquet cited by Martin-Recuerda et al. 2004), similar to matching patterns (Völkel cited by Martin-Recuerda et al. 2004). Basically, all match operators show a similar approach: processing entities of two or more ontologies with the aid of some external information, preset parameters and, if available, already existing matches returns an ontology match set (Euzenat and Shvaiko 2007). Figure 5.9 illustrates the procedure.

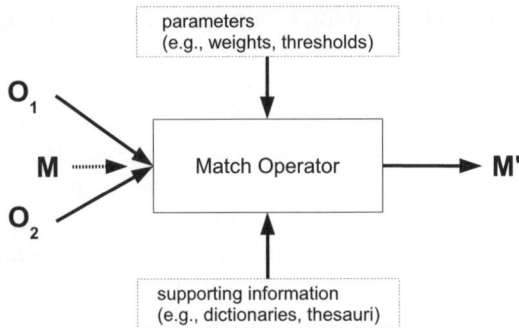

Fig. 5.9. Functioning of a match operator (adapted from Euzenat and Shvaiko 2007)

To facilitate such discoveries of correspondences, existing knowledge can be drawn upon; for finding similarities and subclasses, already existent ontologies can be used (de Bruijn 2004). External information supporting matching processes can be dictionaries, global ontologies, previously performed matchings and, also, user input (Rahm and Bernstein 2001). Usually, such supporting ontologies are (TBox-) ontologies in the sense of knowledge collections (Hepp et al. 2006) and could be top-level ontologies, linguistic ontologies and, depending on the application focus, domain ontologies, for example, e-business standards for relating commercial information. Thus, they may serve as reference ontologies for information integration (Gómez-Pérez et al. 2004; Noy 2004).

Mapping

The correspondences found as a result of the matching procedure can be specified and stored as references, pointers or mappings, respectively, between ontologies. They explicitly specify semantic correspondences or overlaps and can be understood as semantic connections (Maedche et al. 2002). The vocabulary of two ontologies is related without influencing their given structures (Kalfoglou and Schorlemmer 2005). When establishing mappings, the source ontologies are combined but remain unchanged. As is the case with tourist maps, mapping can be denoted as representing and relating connections. Such semantic relations connect decentralized knowledge. A mapping specifies a correspondence discovered at the time of matching. The goal is to determine equivalencies by finding for one ontology entity an entity in another ontology with the same intended meaning. This way, matching and mapping leads to a virtual integration (Klein 2001). The task is to relate "the vocabulary of two ontologies that share the same domain of discourse in such a way that the mathematical structure of ontological signatures and their intended interpretations, as specified by the ontological axioms, are respected. Structure-preserving mappings between mathematical structures are called morphisms" (Kalfoglou and Schorlemmer 2003).

Such a relating of ontologies is put on the same level by de Bruijn (2004) as the creation of mappings whereby the source ontologies are preserved, despite discrepancies, and additional axioms describe the relations. As such, relating is the overall procedure of discovering and mapping concepts and relations of different data sources in the form of a similarity relation or reference (Klein et al. 2003; Dameron et al. 2004). By specifying those references, they can be represented and, thus, preserved and stored (Euzenat 2005; Maedche et al. 2002). Mathematically, a reference is a bridging axiom (Shvaiko and Euzenat 2005) and can be expressed in its simplest form as shown in Eq. 5.2. Thereby, it expresses that two single ontology entities are semantically identical (Ehrig 2004a).

$$map(e_1) = e_2; e_1 \in O_1, e_2 \in O_2 \qquad (5.2)$$

An ontology mapping is the declarative specification of the semantic overlap between two ontologies O_1 and O_2. It may be injective (one-way) or bijective (two-way) and describes the attempt of finding between two given ontologies O_1 and O_2 for each entity C_1, R_1 or I_1 in O_1 a corresponding entity C_2, R_2 or I_2 with the same intended meaning in ontology O_2. Often, in the literature, "articulation", "alignment" or "correspondence" are also used to describe this process.

For discovering similarities, two approaches can be distinguished (Noy 2004; Shvaiko and Euzenat 2005). Heuristic procedures originate mainly from research on ontologies and use metadata such as class names or relations for matching and assuming references. Formal and learning procedures, mostly developed in the area of database management and data warehousing, also employ instance information to be utilized on model theoretic calculations. Basically, a number of different entities can be matched (Noy 2004):

- Concept names and descriptions in natural language
- Class hierarchies with super- and subclasses
- Definitions of properties (ranges, areas, constraints)
- Instances of classes

- Class descriptions in description-logic-based approaches

A match can relate one or several entities. Possible cardinalities are 1:1, 1:n, n:1 and n:m, whereas the latter can often be resolved into several 1:n relations (Maedche et al. 2002).

Various mapping methods have been proposed, employing the various properties of ontologies and using techniques from different fields (Euzenat and Shvaiko 2007). Approaches can basically be differentiated into element level analysis and structure level analysis. Figure 5.10 (adapted from Euzenat and Shvaiko 2007) provides an overview.

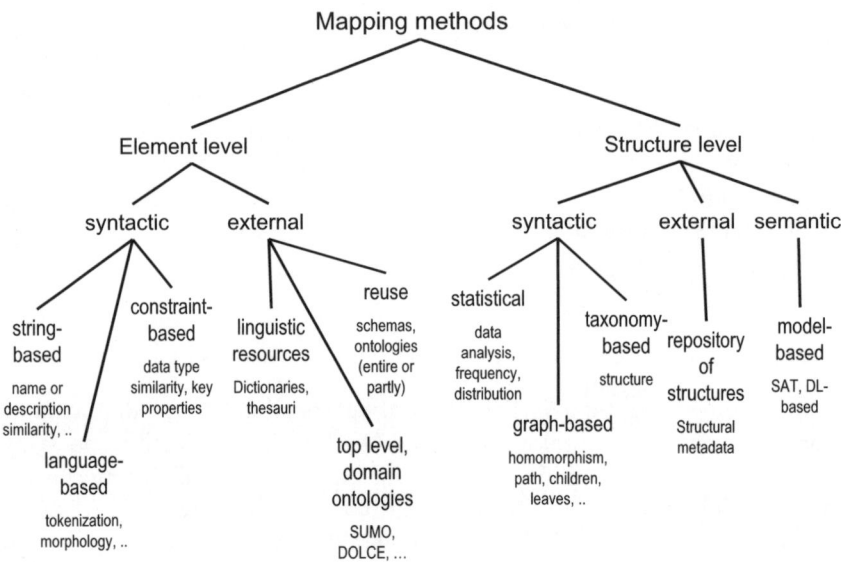

Fig. 5.10. Overview of mapping methods

Element level analysis only considers ontology entities, regardless of their relations and can either including or excluding instance data.

Terminological matches search for similarities of classes and unique re-source identifiers (URIs) by comparing and matching character strings, designations and comments. This can be performed in a string-based man-ner by looking at the sequence of letters and characters to find word simi-larities. Language-based searches use natural language processing (NLP) techniques for discovering correspondences between classes and instances of classes; these techniques can work either intrinsically, when using in-stances' linguistic properties, or extrinsically, through inclusion of external resources such as dictionaries or multilingual methods.

Extensional or instance-based methods examine the set of instances belonging to a class and take them as the basis for matching the associated concepts. Opaque matching does not use the instances' values but rather their statistical attributes, such as distance and frequency. Pattern-based matching uses patterns emerging as a result of analyzing the instances' values in order to compare those to similar patterns.

Purely syntax-based element level analysis methods include:

- String-based techniques that match strings, i.e., letter sequences. Thus, names or descriptions of ontology entities can be matched.
- Language-based techniques that consider names of entities as words in a natural language and use their morphological properties. For doing so, they can split strings into different lexical elements, the tokens, through tokenization or utilize morphology to analyze the grammatical form and structure of words.
- Constraint-based techniques that verify the structure of entities, e.g., the data types or key properties with which unique identification is enabled, for example a product number.

Element level analysis techniques that use additional external resources include:

- Inclusion of linguistic resources for generating words matches, e.g., dictionaries and thesauri.
- Use of top-, upper level or domain ontologies as background knowledge for matching strings and words.
- Reuse of previously found matching results, either as a whole or as customized fragments according to specific interests.

Structure level analysis considers the relations of entities or their instances (Euzenat and Shvaiko 2007). These methods compare ontology structures instead of names or URIs. Internally, criteria such as property value ranges, their cardinality, transitivity or symmetry, are analyzed based on rules. Externally, the position of entities within ontologies can be examined. When two entities of two ontologies correspond to each other, their neighboring entities may be corresponding as well.

A semantics-based method is deductive and set within a model theoretic, such as satisfiability (SAT) and description-logic-based techniques. These types of analysis are suited to discover ontology similarities even when synonyms, hyper- and hyponyms occur. Syntax-based examples of such techniques are:

- Statistical methods for data analysis performing distance-based classification or formal concept analysis as well as frequency distribution.

- Graph-based techniques that regard the ontologies to be matched as labeled graph structures for comparing the similarities of nodes based on their position within the graphs, e.g., finding common subgraphs (homomorphism) or by comparing terms and their positions along paths considering the similarities of children and leaf nodes.
- Taxonomic-based techniques, also graph-based and considering specialization relations, i.e., subclass or is-a relations, respectively.

Structure level approaches that use external resources or models include:

- Inclusion of a repository with similar structures, e.g., the same number of nodes.
- Model-based techniques use model-theoretic semantics and employ propositional and modal ˙SAT techniques as decision procedures for the checking of the possible matches found as well as description-logic-based reasoning.

The different methods shown require different degrees of semantic richness in the expressivity of the ontologies to be matched. Checking for correspondences of character strings demands a low level of semantic expressivity. Semantic richness increases progressively through the utilization of structure-analyzing methods, then context-and-extension-analyzing methods, to the most demanding logic-based methods (Kalfoglou et al. 2005b).

Discovered mappings can be preserved and stored. In order to do so, they must be specified. To specify them, mappings need to be described with a formal specification language. Such an *ontology* or *mapping language* facilitates the representation of mappings, often using a rule-based match operator. To capture relations between ontologies, several requirements need to be fulfilled (de Bruijn 2004):

- Similarities between elements, concepts and relations have to be described for representing synonyms.
- Super- and subclasses have to be described for representing hyper- and hyponyms.
- Specifications for partial mappings for representing non-congruent semantic overlaps need to be made.
- Value transformations for different coding of units, measures, weights, etc. need to be defined.
- Aggregations for capturing disparities in granularity need to be possible.
- Disjointedness needs to be captured.

To represent mappings, again ontologies can be used; in this case the mappings found are the ontologies' instances (Noy 2004). By generating such *mapping ontologies* containing the linked entities of two or more source ontologies to be related, bridges between ontologies can be built and preserved. Therefore, mapping ontologies are also called *semantic bridge ontologies* (SBO) (Klein et al. 2003; Maedche et al. 2002). These can serve to store the mapping structure and, if necessary and desired, the conversion or transformation rules for migrating instances from one ontology to another (Euzenat 2005, Doan et al. 2003).

Articulation denotes the perpetuation of the mapping performed. It preserves the connections found between two aligned ontologies (Klein 2001). This idea corresponds to the notion of articulation in graph theory. Kalfoglou and Schorlemmer (2003) perform the alignment of two ontologies O_1 and O_2 with the aid of mapping pairs contained in an intermediate ontology O_0. This ontology contains the mappings between O_1 and O_2 and is designated as the articulation of two ontologies. It specifies the *possible* procedure for merging the ontologies. Thus, an articulation ontology can be understood as a partial set of the semantic overlap. Figure 5.11 illustrates the principle (adapted from Emery and Hart 2004).

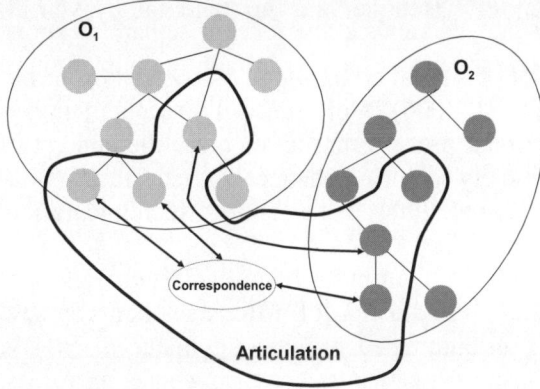

Fig. 5.11. Relation specification in an articulation ontology

Articulation ontologies are specialized ontologies relating concepts between two or more ontologies. The relations could be equivalences, similarities or other types. Thereby, 1:1 relations as well as 1:n- or n:m relations can be both injective or bijective. The strength of relations can vary and can, if required, include conversion rules (Emery and Hart 2004).

Alignment (Mediation)

Following de Bruijn (2004) and Hameed et al. (2004), *ontology alignment* denotes the matching and aligning of ontologies. The source ontologies continue to exist and are related by means of references. This way information can be mutually reused and, in contrast to *ontology merging*, the source ontologies continue to exist (still one may be modified in such a way that it incorporates the correspondences found). Klein (2001) looks at alignment as the task of "bringing two or more ontologies into mutual agreement, making them consistent and coherent." The goal is to establish "a collection of binary relations between the vocabulary of two ontologies" (Kalfoglou and Schorlemmer 2003). Bouquet et al. (2005) define aligning as "a process that produces a set of mappings across ontologies which allow ontology coordination".

Descriptions of relations between entities of different ontologies do not require a new ontology or modified source ontology; only the correspondences are specified as mappings. Martin-Recuerda et al. (2004) quote a statement by Euzenat, who regards "alignment as a second step after mapping[,] looking for deeper analysis of the ontologies to maintain coherence and consistency (noting that it can also imply the modifications of the ontologies to guarantee this mutual agreement)". Such an operation of a "bidirectional projection of two ontologies onto each other' is similar to comparing DNS in molecular biology" (Bouquet and Euzenat cited by Martin-Recuerda et al. 2004).

Ontology alignment has also been called *ontology reconciliation* or *ontology mediation* (de Bruijn et al. 2006). More precisely, reconciliation is considered to be "a bi-directional process that harmonizes the content of two (or more) ontologies, typically requiring changes on both sides" (Bouquet cited by Martin-Recuerda et al. 2004). As a result of such integration, the source ontologies may be modified.

Mediation, in terms of deciding a controversy between ontologies, specifically denotes the balancing and adjusting of differences between several ontologies by means of an automated or semi-automated discovery, and a set of mappings specifying the semantic correspondence, or at least overlap, of terms in heterogeneous ontologies. The goal is to reconcile "differences between inhomogeneous ontologies to achieve inter-operation between data sources annotated ... by discovery and specification of ontology mappings, as well as the use of these mappings for certain tasks, such as query rewriting and instance transformation" (de Bruijn 2004).

In the field of medical informatics, the notion of *ontology synchronization* has been introduced by Oliver et al. (1999) as a periodic routine task of ontology change management. Thereby, jointly used ontologies, such as industry standards, are aligned with locally used, individually amended terminologies. The result has to be understood as a reconciled ontology created from an industry standard and proprietary additions. Updating the local ontology becomes necessary when an industry ontology copy is used, but the original is consecutively changed. In this case, changes in the original ontology have to be carried over into the local copy.

Through *translation*, as the next step after finding mappings, ontologies can be joined and reinterpreted. Thereby, translation foresees "formal inference in a merged ontology" (Dou et al. 2004). The goal is to change "the representation formalism of an ontology while preserving the semantics" (Klein 2001). Mathematically, this can be expressed in "an ontology transformation function t for translating an ontology o written in some language L into another ontology o^0 written in a distinct language L'" (Bouquet et al. 2005). In doing so, the ontology models are unaffected (Euzenat cited by Martin-Recuerda et al. 2004).

A *transformation* occurs when semantic modifications become necessary. This activity is performed through "changing the semantics of an ontology slightly (possibly also changing the representation) to make it suitable for purposes other than the original one" (Klein 2001). Basically, transforming is "a general term for referring to any process which leads to a new ontology o^0 from an ontology o by using a transformation function t" (Bouquet et al. 2005).

5.4.3 Merging

Ontology merging generally denotes the consolidation of two or more ontologies. Often this requires considerable modifications and extensions (de Bruijn 2004). The result is the creation of "a new ontology from two or more existing ontologies with overlapping parts, which can be either virtual or physical" (Klein 2001). The content of the merged ontology is the "minimal union (of) vocabularies S_1 and S_2 and axioms A_1 and A_2 of two ontologies O_1 and O_2 previously aligned through an articulated ontology O_0" (Kalfoglou and Schorlemmer 2003). The goal is the realization of a fusion through the "the creation of a new ontology o_m from two (possibly overlapping) source ontologies o' and o". This concept is closely related to that of integration in the database community (Bouquet et al. 2005).

In contrast to merging, all activities previously mentioned concerning ontology coordination aim at reconciling and reusing ontologies in their original form while establishing and collecting mappings between them. These ontology mappings can be reused and evolve over time, especially when ontology engineering is used in combination with other semantic technologies, as described in the next chapter.

6 Advanced Knowledge Creation Techniques

To use the basic ontological engineering methods presented in the previous chapter for creating real-world applications, it is beneficial to combine them with other techniques to make them more flexible and their results of higher quality. This chapter addresses two areas of advanced ontological engineering techniques for knowledge creation and enhancement. One is constituted by AI methods for deriving new knowledge in ontologies and the other by techniques for dealing with ambiguous ontology mappings.

6.1 Methods from Artificial Intelligence

Several definitions regarding what AI is or what makes a system intelligent exist. According to Russell and Norvig (2003), intelligent systems can be described along two dimensions: as rational vs. human-like systems and as thinking vs. acting systems. The latter are often called "agents" in the literature. Figure 6.1 (adapted from Russell and Norvig 2003) provides an overview of those definitions.

Systems that think like humans	Systems that think rationally
An intelligent system is a system that has a mind built like a human mind, and in which processes similar to human thinking processes are executed.	An intelligent system is a system with decision processes that follow rules of logic. A computational model of thought underlies such systems.
Systems that act like humans	**Systems that act rationally**
An intelligent system is a system that can perform tasks which humans can perform by using human intelligence, at the same or even at a better level than humans.	An intelligent system is a system that perceives its environment, adapts to it, and performs actions that fulfill particular goals.

Fig. 6.1. Different definitions of intelligent systems

From a philosophical point of view, weak and strong AI can be distinguished. *Weak AI* refers to systems that act as if they were thinking (i.e., that simulate thinking processes), while *strong AI* refers to systems that are actually thinking. A detailed discussion of those philosophical questions in AI can be found in Searle (1980). AI research, however, concentrates on weak AI, i.e., on systems that show some form of rational behavior. It ignores whether this behavior comes from real thinking processes in the strong AI sense or not (Russell and Norvig 2003).

The main fields of application of AI are robotics, expert and diagnosis systems, planning, problem solving, theorem proving and reasoning, data mining, machine learning, natural language processing, information retrieval, and games (Russell and Norvig 2003). Ontologies, as such, are a product of AI research, as they are a means of representing knowledge, which is an essential part of building intelligent systems (Fensel 2004). Hence, the methods of inferring and reasoning developed in AI can be used for ontologies (Gómez-Pérez et al. 2004).

6.1.1 Ontology Inference and Ontology Reasoning

Reasoning is the drawing of conclusions or inferences by the use of reason (Merriam Webster's Online Dictionary 2007c). Inference means deriving new facts from known ones. The roots of inference go back to the ancient Greek philosopher Aristotle's works on logic. He defined patterns – so-called "syllogisms" – which can be used to derive facts (Aristotle 1984). One well-known example is: "Socrates is a man. All men are mortal. Therefore, Socrates is mortal" (Russell and Norvig 2003).

Since ontologies can be seen as collections of facts, inference mechanisms can be used on ontologies as well. Depending on the language that an ontology is described with, creating an inference mechanism can vary in difficulty: in general, there is a direct relationship between the language's expressive power and the complexity of an inference mechanism (Gómez-Pérez et al. 2004).

Inference mechanisms can be used on ontologies for several reasons. First of all, the facts that are implicitly contained in an ontology, but not explicitly mentioned, may be of interest to users. Second, the logical integrity of an existing ontology can be validated; that is, it can be confirmed that it contains no contradictions (Calì et al. 2005).

Validating an ontology can find errors such as the following: if invoices are a subclass of business documents and business documents are a subclass of invoices, this is a contradiction because nothing can be a subclass of itself (Conen and Klapsing 2001).

As an example of gathering implicit facts from ontologies, consider the following: an ontology definition states that each business document needs a recipient, and that invoices are a subclass of business documents. Via inference, it can be concluded that an invoice needs a recipient. Inferred facts can also be validated again (Calì et al. 2005). If, in this example, the ontology definition stated that invoices did not have a recipient, validating the ontology against the inferred facts would discover an error.

As ontology mappings can also be seen as a set of facts, inference and reasoning can also be applied to them (Stuckenschmidt et al. 2006). Thus, results of automatic mapping tools can be evaluated and, if inconsistencies are discovered, repaired (Meilicke et al. 2006).

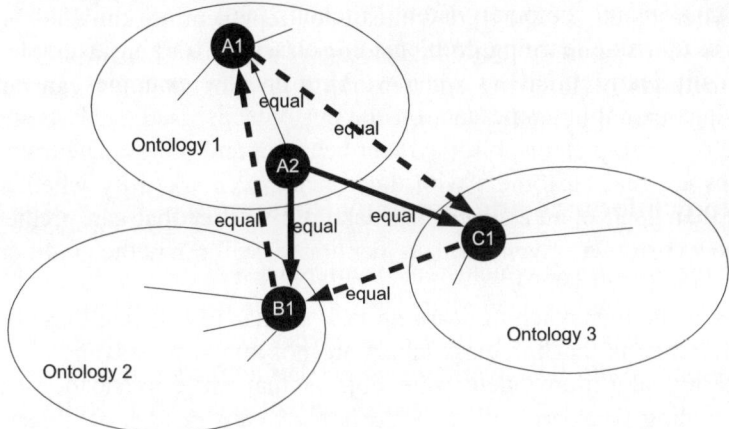

Fig. 6.2. Inferring ontology mappings

Reasoning about mappings may also be used to discover new mappings, by using the facts contained in the mapped ontologies as well as in bridging or upper-level ontologies (Stoimenov et al. 2006). Figure 6.2 shows an example of inferring ontology mappings. Suppose the mappings "A2 equals B1" and "A2 equals C1" are known. Then, the mappings "A1 equals C1", "B1 equals A1" and "C1 equals B1" can be inferred. Thus, ontology reasoning mechanisms can enhance a system relying on ontology mappings.

6.1.2 Machine Learning

Machine learning is another research field in AI which is relevant for ontological engineering. In general, systems using machine learning are able to adapt to given inputs and changes in environment, instead of following hard-wired behaviors. Thus, those systems acquire knowledge from experience with the aim of improving their performance on a given task over time (Langley and Simon 1995). Techniques used in machine learning include decision trees, artificial neural networks, statistical methods and genetic algorithms (Mitchell 1997).

Machine learning can be employed in different fields. Examples include credit decisions, diagnosis systems for mechanical devices, classification of celestial objects observed in astronomy, the forecasting of thunderstorms (Langley and Simon 1995), spam-mail filtering (Sahami et al. 1998; Drucker et al. 1999), predicting customer behavior (Mitchell 1999), medical diagnosis (Peña-Reyes and Sipper 2000; Kononenko 2001), or speech recognition and computer vision (Mitchell 2006).

The typical machine-learning problems use classified training examples to automatically learn classifiers when working on new examples. In the credit decisions example, some data on the customer is used, such as income, home ownership status, bill-payment behavior and others. The training examples are real customers with those features, marked by whether they repaid their loan or not. From that data, a classifier that can predict whether a new customer, given the data mentioned, will repay the credit or not is learned (Mitchell 1999).

Clustering is another machine-learning task similar to learning classifiers. The difference is that the class labels are not known in advance. Instead, clustering algorithms determine objects that are similar to each other, thus finding what are called *conceptual classes*, classes of objects that are similar according to some features. Clustering mechanisms can be used to find for example typical consumer behavior patterns in business or for deriving animal and plant taxonomies in biology (Han and Kamber 2000).

Machine-learning techniques can be used for ontology learning from texts, i.e., from unstructured information, or from instances or schemata (Gómez-Pérez et al. 2004). This means that ontologies may be learned automatically rather than created manually by a group of experts.

Maedche and Staab (2004) propose an architecture for an ontology learning system. That architecture's core is a resource-processing component, responsible for extracting ontologies from different text sources, backed by an algorithm library containing different extraction mechanisms and learning algorithms, as well as mechanisms for combining the results of different extraction techniques. Furthermore, the architecture contains components for storing, browsing, validating, and visualizing ontologies, as well as a user interface for the domain engineer to work with.

According to Maedche and Staab (2004), different machine-learning algorithms can be used in the algorithm library. These include clustering algorithms (finding out which terms often appear near other terms), refining existing classifications, such as WordNet (WordNet 2007), with new terms discovered in the processed source, or using text patterns, e.g., to extract subclass-superclass relations, and thereby taxonomies, as proposed by Hearst (1992). An example of such patterns is "A(n) X, for example a(n) Y". When such a pattern is found in a text, it can be learned that X is a superclass of Y (Hearst 1992). Kavalek and Svatek (2002) use the open directory (ODP 2007) and the webpages contained as training examples for pattern extraction.

Machine-learning algorithms can also be employed to learn ontology mappings. Doan et al. (2004) have developed the GLUE system, which uses instances of concepts described by different ontologies to learn ontology mappings. To this end, the instances are compared according to different similarity measures, and from those instances' similarities, the concepts' similarities are inferred.

6.1.3 Knowledge Evolution

Building intelligent systems requires representation of knowledge; thus, knowledge engineering is a genuine field of research in AI. Representing the knowledge of a given domain requires investigation of the domain, extraction of concepts and relations, and externalization of that knowledge, in a more or less formalized manner (Russell and Norvig 2003). With the recent emergence of terms like "knowledge-based economy" and "knowledge-based society" (David and Fouray 2003), knowledge engineering becomes particularly important.

Knowledge engineering is often considered an iterative, evolutionary process; hence, the term *knowledge evolution* is often used to point this out (Bieber et al. 2001; Hori et al. 2004). Nonaka and Takeuchi (1995) propose a spiral model for knowledge evolution. They distinguish between tacit and explicit knowledge: tacit knowledge is knowledge that a person has in his mind about something, whereas explicit knowledge is knowledge that has been transformed into some encoding, e.g., a text or a diagram. This process of encoding tacit into explicit knowledge is called *externalization*, typically following dialogue, while the transformation of explicit into tacit knowledge is called *internalization*, typically resulting from learning by doing. Tacit knowledge can also be turned into other tacit knowledge by communicating ideas between humans (Nonaka and Takeuchi call this *socialization*), thus building an interaction field for transferring experiences and mental models, and explicit knowledge can be turned into other explicit knowledge by linking existing documents and sources (called *combination* by Nonaka and Takeuchi). During the process, the spiral grows in an outward direction. This movement symbolizes the growth of the overall amount of knowledge, both tacit and explicit. Figure 6.3 illustrates this process.

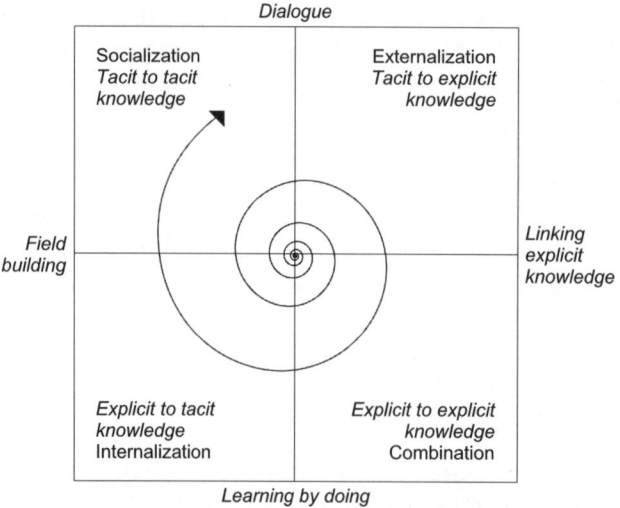

Fig. 6.3. The knowledge spiral (adapted from Nonaka and Takeuchi 1995)

There are three main reasons why knowledge engineering should be regarded as an evolutionary process: First, most issues are too complex to turn them into a perfect model in just one step. Second, a group of experts, rather than one individual, is often required to work on the knowledge representation of a model. Third, the issues which are modeled by explicit knowledge are often evolving themselves (Fischer 1996; Bieber et al. 2001).

Systems have been designed that allow evolutionary knowledge construction (Fischer 1996; Bieber et al. 2001; Hori et al. 2004). The focal points of those systems are:

- Communication and discussion between knowledge engineers (possibly from different domains) and creation of a shared understanding
- Linking and annotating existing knowledge artefacts (e.g., documents)
- Creation and storage of new knowledge artefacts

Hori et al. (2004) discuss the fact that traditional knowledge management techniques, which require a fixed structure of knowledge units, are not feasible for evolutionary knowledge engineering approaches, since the latter require the possibility of processing knowledge in variable structures. Therefore, a model of small knowledge elements is proposed. Knowledge can be *liquidized* into those atomic units, and atomic units can be *crystallized* into new, restructured forms. Depending on a user's context, different units are selected, and they are put together in different ways. By iterative liquidization and crystallization, both the conceptual world (or tacit knowledge in Nonaka and Takeuchi's terminology) and the representational world (or explicit knowledge) evolve, as depicted in Figure 6.4 (based on Hori et al. 2004).

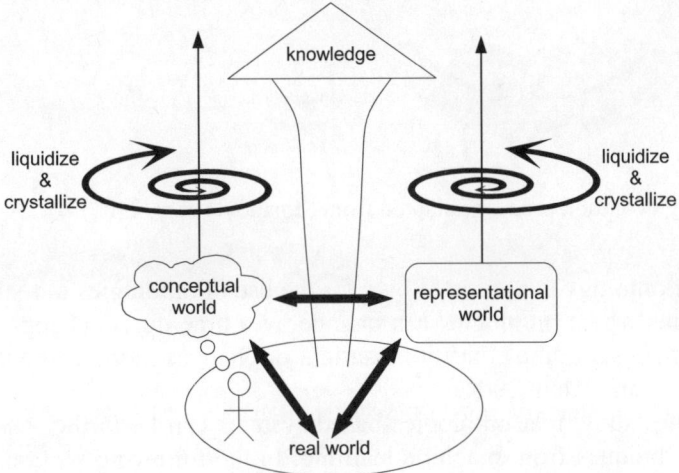

Fig. 6.4. Knowledge evolution by liquidization and crystallization

Because knowledge can be represented by using ontologies (Fensel 2004), research has also been done regarding how ontology evolution can be achieved. Noy and Klein (2004) distinguish between traced and untraced evolution scenarios. In the latter, only different versions of an ontology are available; in the first, the individual changes themselves have been logged.

Stojanovic et al. (2002) propose a six-phase cycle, as depicted in Figure 6.5, for traced evolution. Required changes are captured and represented in a formal way. The semantics of these changes have to be analyzed to avoid inconsistencies when applying them. After this step, the required changes can be carried out on the ontologies, i.e., implemented, and propagated to all of the ontology's instances. Once all the ontologies are up to date, it is possible that validation of applications based on those ontologies will require further changes, causing the cycle to start over again.

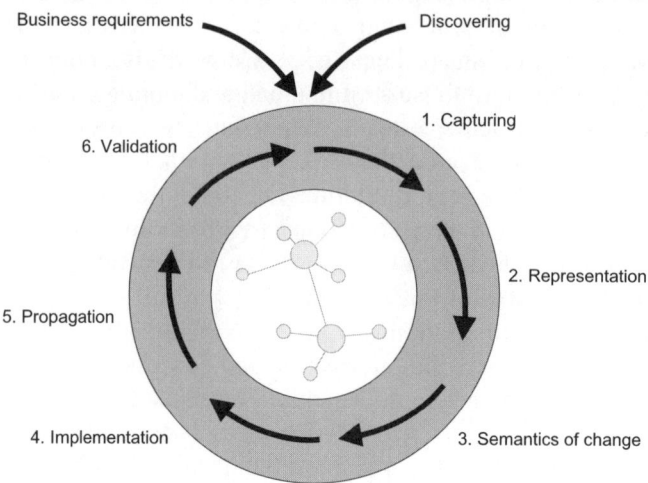

Fig. 6.5. Ontology evolution process (adapted from Stojanovic et al. 2002)

The notion of ontology evolution allows for the use of ontologies in real business scenarios where ontologies can change over time due to changes in the domain, changes in the conceptualization, or changes in the explicit specification (Noy and Klein 2004).

These examples show that ontologies-based systems can be further enhanced using techniques from machine learning. In the following section, we will look at applying AI techniques to a specific problem in ontological engineering.

6.2 Ontology Mapping Disambiguation

As described in the previous chapters, ontology mappings may be ambiguous, while working with them requires non-ambiguity. This raises the need for strategies for disambiguating ontology mappings.

6.2.1 Ratings- and Context-Based Approaches

Ratings are common in e-business: at online stores, users can rate books, CDs, DVDs, etc. Suppliers (private persons or companies) on marketplaces can also be rated, as well as users on private auction platforms (Schafer et al. 1999). Using those ratings, customers can inform themselves about other people's opinions on articles and their experiences with certain vendors.

The simplest possible rating mechanism allows users to give feedback about whether they find something useful or not. More elaborate feedback mechanisms include ratings with number rankings such as one through five stars, comments or combinations of both.

When combined with user profiles, these ratings can be used to provide collaborative or social filtering. Therefore, ratings are often stored together with profile information of the users who gave those ratings. When users with similar profiles search for information, the search results can be ordered in such a way that the information best suited to their profiles is presented in the top positions. The profile information can be gathered explicitly (i.e., the users fill out forms where they expose their likes and dislikes) or implicitly (e.g., by watching which articles users browse and buy) (Buono et al. 2001). The combination of profiles and ratings can also be used to build recommendation systems where customers are presented with articles they might be interested in, based on other users' profiles and ratings (Schafer et al. 1999).

Collaborative or social filtering based on users' ratings is one approach to filtering and ordering information. Malone et al. (1987) identify two other approaches: Content-based or cognitive filtering rates information based on the similarity of its content alone, i.e., by analyzing information such as the products itself. Economic filtering assigns cost values, e.g., real cost of products or object size, to each object and then tries to minimize the overall cost.

While collaborative and content-based approaches are widely used, economic filtering is rarely implemented in actual systems (Specht and Kahabka 2000). The advantages of content-based filtering are that it is easily understandable and that it does not need a critical mass of users to function (Specht and Kahabka 2000). The advantages of collaborative filtering are that it not only filters content but also quality or point of view and that it is also applicable for filtering information that is difficult to analyze directly, such as multimedia content (Shardanand and Maes 1995; Hill et al. 1995). Hybrid approaches combining collaborative and content-based filtering are also possible (Malone et al. 1987; Specht and Kahabka 2000).

Collaborative filtering can also be used to disambiguate ontology mappings. Users can rate the correctness of ontology mappings from their individual point of view. To compute the overall acceptance of an ontology mapping, users' ratings may be summed up and, optionally, weighted according to appropriate criteria. Thus calculating the acceptance for an ontology mapping and ordering the list of mappings by the calculated acceptance is a ranking task. A ranking classifier may be used to order objects (in this case, mappings) according to a certain criterion, e.g., that the best-fitting ones appear first (Provost and Fawcett 2001).

Rankings can be calculated with well-known data-mining approaches, both with lazy methods, such as a Naïve Bayes classifier (Zhang and Su 2004) or the distance-weighted k-nearest-neighbor rule (Dudani 1976), and with eager methods, such as decision trees or rule learning (Mitchell 1997).

For using the latter, a function to compute the similarity between the request's and the ratings' context information is needed. To this end, techniques from information retrieval can be used. Context is described as a vector of context terms, where each term represents a dimension and the vector entries are the context terms' distance values. Other possible description mechanisms are binary vectors and probabilistic models (Baeza-Yates and Ribeiro-Neto 1999). While the use of binary vectors is limited, both vector and probabilistic models are commonly used (Chowdhury 2004), and experts still discuss which one produces better results (Baeza-Yates and Ribeiro-Neto 1999).

While probabilistic approaches define similarity based on conditional probabilities, there are different ways of measuring similarity in the vector model. The most common are the Jaccard coefficient and the cosine coefficient, both having similar characteristics. A comprehensive introduction to similarity measures is given in Chowdhury (2004).

Using context information to disambiguate ontology mappings is similar to a problem in NLP and machine translation, where a word in one language can be translated in different ways into another language, depending on its context. An overview is given in Ide and Véronis (1998) Therefore, a lot of research on how to describe context has been conducted in the field of NLP.

According to Ide and Véronis (1998), context can be described using the *bag-of-words approach*, where only a set of context words is used, or the *relational information approach*, where information on the relation between the word in question and its context words, such as distance or syntactic relation, is used.

These two approaches relate to two main directions in NLP, shallow and deep approaches (Uszkoreit 2005). *Shallow approaches* work only on collections of words, while *deep approaches* also include syntactical and semantic information and world knowledge. Shallow approaches allow more robust and performant computation; therefore, they are more widespread than deep approaches. On the other hand, deep processing is necessary for some problems in NLP that cannot be solved by shallow approaches. For example, sentences in which the names of different persons are found in close proximity can only be correctly decoded by deep approaches (Uszkoreit 2002). Crysmann et al. (2002) showed that an integrated system using both shallow and deep language processing can outperform a purely deep approach.

The crucial point regarding a context-sensitive ontology-mapping disambiguation approach is the question of how to produce (a) the ratings and (b) the context information. In principal, there are two ways of gaining ratings: explicit and implicit (Nichols 1997). *Explicit ratings* are produced by an action made consciously by the user, e.g., by clicking a rating button. *Implicit ratings*, on the other hand, are gathered by observing the user's behavior. For example, at an online bookstore, the ratio of the number of times a book has been ordered and the number of times it has been viewed can be seen as an implicit rating. Other sources of implicit ratings can be the time spent looking at an article, whether an article was saved or printed, or, in the field of scientific publications, the number of times a publication was cited by others (Nichols 1997).

The main advantage of implicit over explicit rating approaches is that no additional effort is imposed on the user. Users just work with a system following their intrinsic aims (e.g., ordering a certain book), and the ratings are generated transparently. Furthermore, when using more fine-grained ratings (such as treating every user action as an implicit rating), more reliable results can be achieved (Claypool et al. 2001).

Like ratings, context information can also be gathered both implicitly and explicitly (Lawrence 2000). Explicit context is provided by the user, in our example, when issuing a query like "I am looking for mappings for the term *paper* in the context of printers, fax, and office supplies." Implicit context, on the other hand, is gathered from the user's activity, such as information entered in other applications, other documents viewed, and so on. With implicit context, the user enters only the search term, and the context information is added to the query automatically (Lawrence 2000).

Generally, both implicit ratings and implicit context are more convenient to the user. A ratings-based system has to rely on a large number of ratings and context information, so it is important that users submit this data. Therefore, gathering it implicitly is possibly a more feasible method. Gathering implicit context data can include several different data sources – browsed webpages, bookmarks, documents on users' computers, and so on (Henrich and Morgenroth 2003). However, most users will have serious concerns in providing such data to a context-sensitive information system. Therefore, one has to find a balance between gathering maximally expressive context data and protecting the privacy of users.

Thus, when employing a system based on implicit ratings, special care needs to be taken regarding user privacy, because some users may object to systems that observe their behavior (Claypool et al. 2001). Privacy policies have to be developed carefully; users have to be able to choose which context data to provide and they need to be sensitized to the need for careful use of those options (Procter and McKinlay 1997). There are also approaches that try to address such privacy concerns, e.g., with cryptographic methods (Canny 2002) or with randomization mechanisms (Zhang et al. 2006).

6.2.2 Community-Based Approaches

In his well-known article about the Web 2.0, O'Reilly mentions the building of communities as one central feature amongst several other characteristics of Web 2.0, such as collective intelligence in wikis, participation instead of consumption, new programming models and others (O'Reilly 2005).

According to Merriam-Webster's Online Dictionary (2007b), a community can be, among other things, a group of "people with common interests living in a particular area"; "a group of people with a common characteristic or interest living together within a larger society"; "a group linked by a common policy"; "a body of persons or nations having a common history or common social, economic, and political interests", or "a body of persons of common and especially professional interests scattered through a larger society". With respect to Web 2.0, the notion of spatial proximity can normally be neglected, but the other characteristics, such as common interests, also hold true for virtual communities. Bieber et al. (2001) define a virtual community as a group of people sharing a particular domain of interest. Early communities in the 1980s were Usenet groups, Bulletin Board Systems (BBSs), and Internet Relay Chat (IRC) channels (Rheingold 2000).

In the Internet, virtual communities often manifest as web portals with different features. Most platforms contain shared information, communication means and personal user profiles. Common parts of community web portals include messaging services, chats, wikis, personal blogs, collaboration and resource sharing facilities, and applications for sharing multimedia content (O' Murchu et al. 2004). There are also social networking platforms, such as Friendster (www.friendster.com), orkut (www.orkut.com) or Xing (www.xing.com, former OpenBC), that allow users to find and manage private or business contacts (O'Murchu et al. 2004).

Zhdanova and Shvaiko (2006) use communities to provide a community-driven ontology-matching service. Using this approach, users can create ontology mappings. Since users belong to communities, mappings can be indirectly associated with communities, thus allowing queries for ontology mappings that are relevant for a certain user, depending on the community he belongs to. Figure 6.6 shows an example of how community-driven mapping disambiguation works.

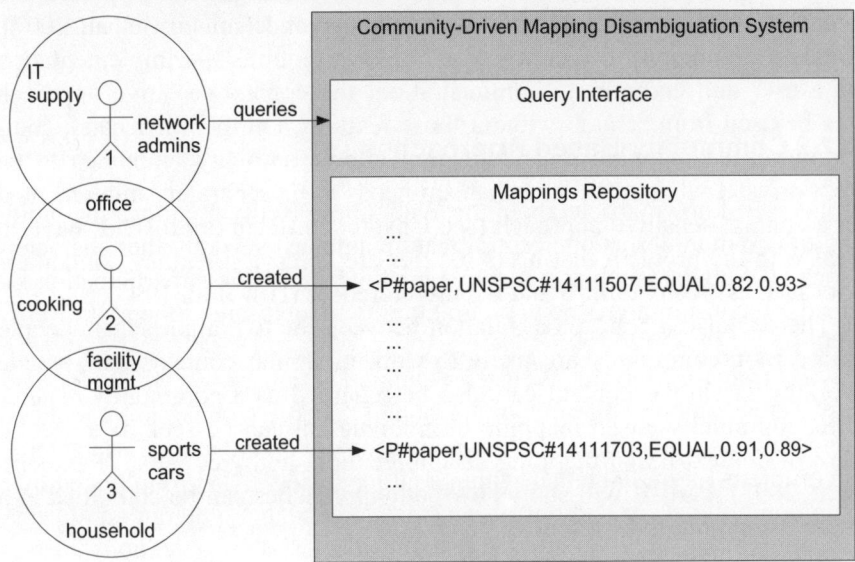

Fig. 6.6. Example of community-driven mapping disambiguation

There is a company using a coarse-grained proprietary standard (named "P"), which has a business partner using UNSPSC. User 3, who works in the communities of household and facility management (and is also member of a sports-car community in her private life), has created a mapping for the term "paper," connecting it to the UNSPSC concept 14111703, namely, "Paper towels". User 2, who works in office and facility management (and is interested in cooking), has also created a mapping for the term "paper," connecting it to the UNSPSC concept 14111507, namely, "Printer or copier paper."

Now User 1, working in IT supply and network administration, wants to order paper at the supplier using UNSPSC. He queries the system to find out the correct UNSPSC number. Since he shares a community with User 2, the system suggests the mapping to printer paper. It does not suggest the mapping to paper towels created by User 3, since Users 1 and 3 do not share any community. Because only one of the two possible mappings for the term "paper" are returned, the two are disambiguated.

Using community-driven ontology matching thus is a feasible approach for dealing with ambiguous references. It is intuitive to use, but it requires the effort of administrating and implementing communities. An approach like this can also be used to ensure the privacy of ontology mappings, because those mappings are filtered by communities.

Both the community-driven approach and the context-sensitive approach have their advantages and disadvantages (Paulheim et al. 2007). While a community-driven approach always requires the implementation of a user and community administration, the context-sensitive approach can be used from scratch without those features. On the other hand, community-based mapping disambiguation allows ontology mappings to be kept private, while such a mechanism needs to be separately implemented in a context-sensitive approach (see Chapter 9). Both approaches have to deal with the problem that users' entries are "noisy," i.e., they contain errors such as wrong ratings and wrong references (Hill et al. 1995).

There is also a conceptual relation between the two approaches: people in a certain community are likely to work in similar contexts, and people working in similar context can also be regarded as a community. Therefore, community-based mapping disambiguation can be seen as a special case of context-based mapping disambiguation, and vice versa (Paulheim et al. 2007). Part III will show how both approaches can be combined in a more comprehensive system.

7 Semantic Web Programming Frameworks

When developing an e-business solution with different ontology-engineering tools, these tools have to be connected by a coherent programming framework. Results provided by different tools often have to be refined and presented to the end user in a simpler form than is the case in the most common, often expert-oriented, user interfaces. In the following, we analyze and discuss such frameworks.

7.1 Rationale

Ontologies, as such, can exist in the form of files. To access and manipulate them with a programming language, which is necessary for building ontology-driven applications, the ontology data needs to be available in the programming language itself. For example, when working with an object-oriented programming language, the data needs to be available in the form of classes and objects (Park and Shon 2005). Frameworks and application programming interfaces (APIs) can provide such a representation. Furthermore, they allow efficient development of high-quality, modular, extendable and reusable software solutions based on Semantic Web technologies (Fayad and Schmidt 1997).

Various frameworks for working with ontologies have been developed. These differ in many respects, including the set of features – such as scalability, expandability and robustness – or the availability of documentation and support (Bechhofer and Carroll 2004; Cardoso and Sheth 2006; Shearer 2007). There are open-source as well as commercial frameworks, platform-independent and platform-specific ones. Implementation of such frameworks is possible in any programming language; however, the most common ones are developed in Java (Cardoso and Sheth 2006). Using a framework can make the development of ontologies-based software substantially more effective (Fayad and Schmidt 1997).

7.2 Basic Framework Features

Even if each ontology framework has a different architecture and a different set of features, some basic features are common to almost all frameworks.

First of all, a framework provides a data model for processing ontology data. For object-oriented programming languages, this is called an object model. Typically, there are classes for all types of ontology information, such as concepts, instances and properties. Those classes have methods for reading ontology data, for instance, by listing all properties of a concept, as well as for manipulating an ontology, for instance, adding a new property to a concept or deleting concepts and instances. Figure 7.1 shows a simplified example data model in UML notation (from the WonderWeb API; cf. Chapter 7.4).

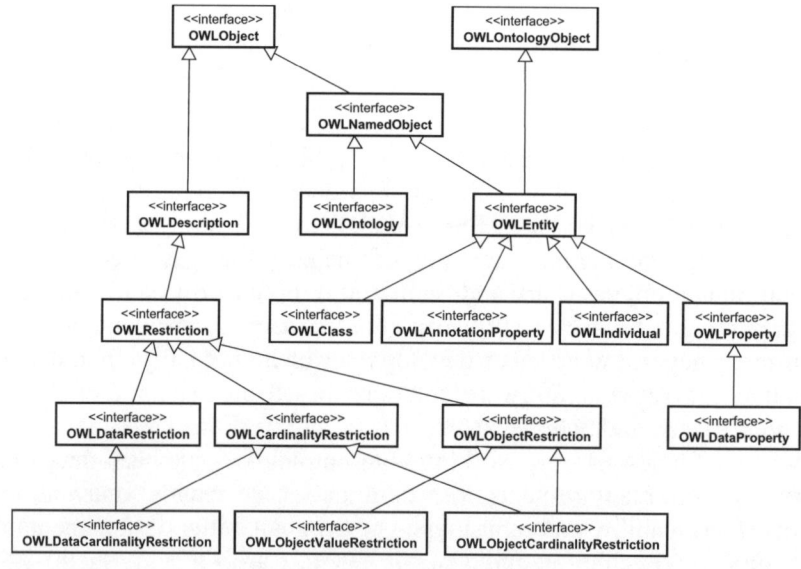

Fig. 7.1. Example data model for an ontology framework

To turn an ontology into an object model and vice versa, frameworks need to provide parsers and serializers (Decker et al. 2000). A parser reads an ontology file (e.g., in OWL or RDF/S format) and turns it into an object model. A serializer, on the other hand, turns the object model into an ontology file again. A parser and a serializer together allow full round-trip engineering of ontologies (Bechhofer et al. 2003). In addition, they provide syntactic interoperability with tools and frameworks that are not compatible with the framework, because as long as both tools and frameworks each have a serializer and a parser, they can exchange data using the serialized format, such as OWL (Decker et al. 2000).

By providing more than one pair of serializers and parsers for different ontology-representation languages and formats, a framework can support multiple ontology representations. In this case, it can also be used to provide a conversion service.

Although serializers and parsers form a sort of a persistence mechanism, most frameworks also allow more generic adapters to different persistence layers. These can include flat-file storage and relational database storage as well as adapters to more sophisticated storage mechanisms, such as OWLIM, the OWLMemSchemaRepository SAIL (Storage and Inference Layer) for Sesame (Kiryakov et al. 2005), which is a repository framework for the storing, inferencing and querying of RDF data (openRDF 2007). If the Semantic Web programming framework provides the possibility of creating proprietary persistence mechanisms, implementations that provide data from different information systems as ontologies can be developed (Cui et al. 2001). As a result, integration of legacy data in ontology-driven applications can be achieved (Yang et al. 1999).

7.3 Advanced Framework Features

In addition to the basic features, which may be implemented in different ways from rather naïve to very sophisticated, many frameworks also provide more functionality to improve the development of ontology-driven applications.

Some frameworks are rather focused on the data or object model, thus providing a basis for implementing ontology-driven applications on the level of an application's logic. Others already have specific user-interface components, such as textual or graphical ontology editors, or the means to develop those (Cardoso and Sheth 2006).

Ontology programming frameworks also differ in the way they support ontology description languages. While some frameworks are restricted, e.g., to specific dialects of OWL, others use only abstract models that can be expressed in arbitrary ontology languages. Thus, the latter are independent from a specific syntactic ontology representation.

There are different ways of accessing a model's parts when specific elements of an ontology are needed. The simple approach is to navigate the model graph until one has found those elements. Some frameworks also offer query languages to find elements in a model more efficiently. Such query languages are comparable to SQL, for querying relational databases, or to XPath (Clark and de Rose 1999), for querying XML documents.

Although almost all frameworks have interfaces to develop persistence adapters and reasoning tools, some come with ready-to-use implementations for different technologies and tools, while others provide only the outline for developers to use when developing their own implementations.

Frameworks also differ in the way in which they allow integration into developed applications. Some frameworks provide web-server-based APIs for remote access. A common example is the DL Implementation Group (DIG) interface (Bechhofer 2003), which allows remote access to a reasoner's functionality via a standardized HTTP-based interface.

When an ontology-based application is developed, that application may have to react to changes in an ontology. To this end, some frameworks provide event-listener or observer mechanisms (Gamma et al. 1995), which allow for easier implementation of applications reactive to ontology changes.

A crucial point, especially when working with large ontologies, is the question of whether an ontology always has to be loaded into memory as a whole, or whether there is the possibility of working directly with a persistent ontology. When an ontology's object model is built, an object is created in memory for each concept in the ontology. Thus, a large ontology containing many concepts requires a large amount of memory, and sufficiently large ontologies can cause a system to run out of memory (Kiryakov et al. 2005; Hepp 2006a). Therefore, some frameworks support a *lazy loading technique* where only those parts of a persistent ontology that are actually needed are loaded into memory (Fowler 2002).

7.4 Framework Examples

In the WonderWeb project, which involved partners from four European universities as well as an industrial advisory board with members from more than twenty-five international companies (WonderWeb Consortium 2003), the WonderWeb OWL API, often just called "OWL API," was developed. The focus of the OWL API is on representing OWL constructs in Java classes, allowing all dialects of OWL (i.e., Lite, DL and Full) to be used (Bechhofer et al. 2003).

A major design philosophy of the OWL API is the separation of interfaces and their implementations. Consequently, for each OWL construct, an interface and an implementation class, which defines a very basic implementation, exist. Developers can create their own, different implementations. Ontologies can only be manipulated indirectly via visitor classes (Gamma et al. 1995). With the standard implementation, ontologies are loaded into memory in full; lazy loading is not supported. Repository sources other than simple parsed files are also not included in the standard implementation (WonderWeb OWL API Consortium 2003). A reasoner, as described in Chapter 6, can be implemented and integrated into the framework, but is not included.

The Simple Ontology Framework API (SOFA) is another lightweight ontology programming framework. Like the WonderWeb API, its core is an ontology object model, but it is not restricted to OWL – although it contains all constructs defined in OWL and is therefore compatible with OWL ontologies (Alishevskikh 2005a).

SOFA includes parsers and serializers for OWL, RDF/S, DAML and N-Triples, a plain text format for encoding RDF graphs (W3C 2004f). Furthermore, an inference engine supporting simple reasoning on transitive, symmetric and inverse relations; a module for validating ontologies; and a persistence layer which is delivered with an adapter for relational databases is included. Ontologies are always loaded into memory as a whole. In contrast to the case with the OWL API, they can be manipulated directly. The framework also has a mechanism for turning an ontology into a directed graph for display purposes. One special feature of SOFA is that it provides some support for interoperability of ontologies, i.e., describing relations between ontologies, as a simple form of mappings (Alishevskikh 2005b). Figure 7.2 shows SOFA's architecture.

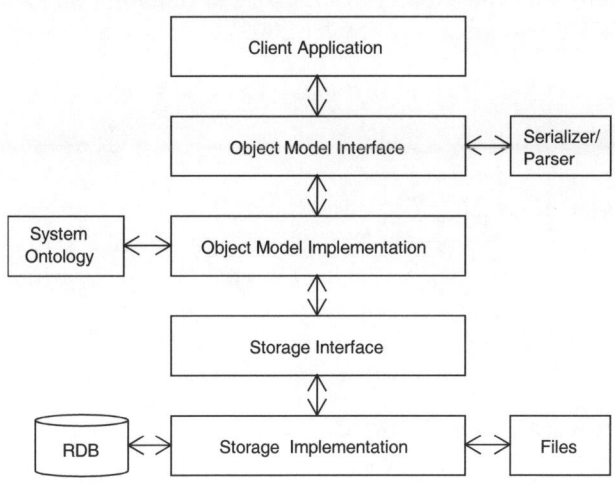

Fig. 7.2. SOFA architecture (based on Alishevskikh 2005b)

Another popular ontology programming framework is Jena2, which has been developed by HP Laboratories. The first version was released in 2000, and Jena2 has been available since 2003 (Carroll et al. 2003). Like SOFA, Jena2 uses an object model abstracted from OWL ontologies (using graphs instead) and it supports RDF/S, DAML and all dialects of OWL (Bechhofer and Carroll 2004).

Graphs can be loaded into memory completely as well as stored in external storage locations, such as relational databases, without having to load the ontology as whole when working with it; thus, lazy loading is supported. Operations on graphs can be performed with the SPARQL Protocol and RDF Query Language (SPARQL) (Prud'hommeaux and Seaborne 2007). SPARQL queries can also be used remotely using the Joseki SPARQL server (Joseki Consortium 2007).

Jena2 contains some built-in reasoners and allows for the connection of external ones and also supports the DIG interface (Carroll et al. 2003). The Jena architecture is shown in Figure 7.3.

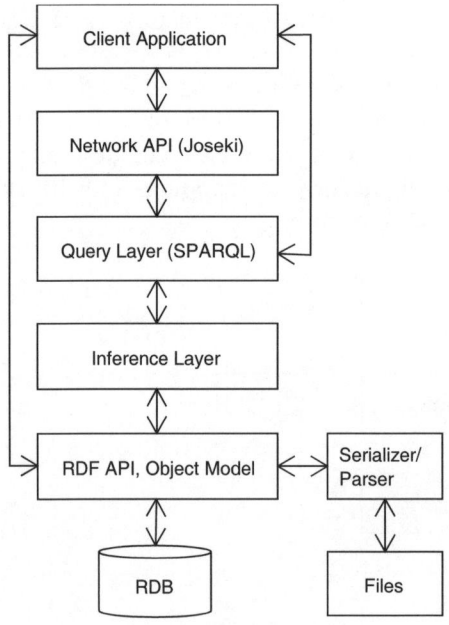

Fig. 7.3. Jena architecture (adapted from McBride 2002)

KAON2 is an ontology programming framework focussed mainly on reasoning. It was developed by the German FZI (Computer Science Research Center) in Karlsruhe, the University of Karlsruhe, and the University of Manchester (KAON2 Consortium 2007). Like Jena2, it allows SPARQL queries, and it has a Remote Method Invocation (RMI) interface for remote access. KAON2 supports OWL DL, Semantic Web Rule Language (SWRL) and F-Logic ontologies, stored as files or in databases. It offers its reasoning capabilities to other applications with a DIG interface (Motik and Sattler 2006). Figure 7.4 shows KAON2's architecture. There is a free version for non-commercial use as well as a commercial version called "OntoBroker," which also supports web-service access for service-oriented applications (Ontoprise 2007).

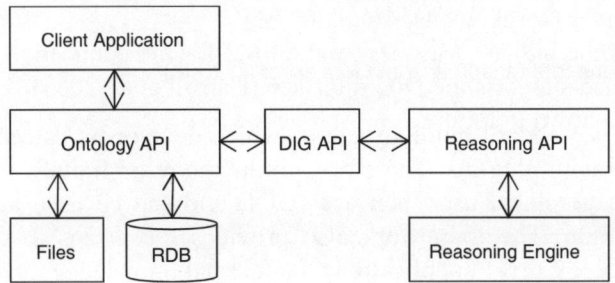

Fig. 7.4. KAON2 architecture (adapted from Motik and Sattler 2006)

Protégé, developed at the Stanford University School of Medicine, is a framework intended to develop ontology-driven applications with graphical editor components. Its original version, developed in 1987, was specialized to build tools for the field of medical planning only. Since then, it has evolved into a universal, domain-independent tool for arbitrary kinds of knowledge-based systems, going through several re-implementations. The current version, Protégé-2000, is Java based (a detailed description of the history of Protégé's development can be found in Gennari et al. 2003). Figure 7.5 shows the architecture.

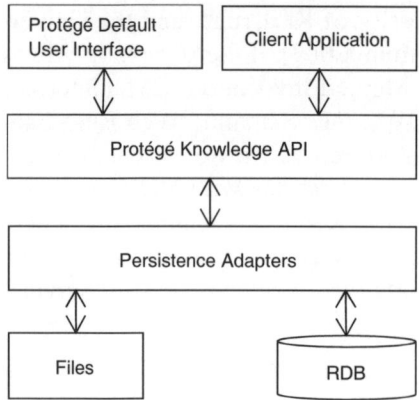

Fig. 7.5. Protégé architecture (adapted from Gennari et al. 2003)

Protégé contains a standard ontology editor which developers can manipulate and extend with plug-ins. Therefore, unlike the other frameworks mentioned, it has a graphical user interface (GUI) and can be used as a stand-alone application. The framework also provides the means to develop GUIs for ontology-driven applications. Its internal knowledge model abstracts from a specific ontology format, providing constructs such as metaclasses also. It has a back-end mechanism that allows for different data sources, such as files or databases. When working with ontologies persistent in databases, Protégé does not require them to be loaded into memory as a whole (Gennari et al. 2003).

Using a framework to develop ontologies-based software systems can increase the software's quality and earning potential (Fayad and Schmidt 1997). However, each of the frameworks presented has both advantages and drawbacks. The selection of an actual framework for conducting a software development project depends on several factors. From a business-oriented point of view, aspects such as licensing, support and documentation are important. Table 7.1 provides an overview of those aspects of the current versions.

Table 7.1. Comparison of ontology programming frameworks

	WonderWeb OWL API	SOFA	JENA2	KAON2	Protégé
Developers	WonderWeb Consortium	Alexey Alishev-skikh, Ganesh Subbiah	HP Labs	Consortium of FZI, University of Karls-ruhe, University of Manchester	Protégé Community
License	GNU Lesser General Public License, Open Source	GNU Lesser General Public License, Open Source	Proprietary Open License	Free for non-commercial use, commercial otherwise	Mozilla Public License
Documentation	Limited	Some	Good	None (just a few examples)	Good
Latest version	1.4.3 (for OWL 1.0), 2.1.1 (for OWL 1.1)	0.3	2.5.3	2007-08-01	3.3.1 (newer alpha and beta versions)

On the other hand, technical considerations also play an important role when choosing a framework. Table 7.2 summarizes the technical features of the frameworks introduced in this chapter.

If the software to be developed is intended to provide direct ontology-editing features, using a framework like Protégé is highly recommended, because it already has ready-to-use GUI components.

When using large ontologies, the framework should allow off-memory and lazy loading processing. In such cases, it also important to choose a framework that is flexible enough to exchange the persistence layer, so that highly performing persistence tools can be coupled with the framework.

Table 7.2. Feature matrix of ontology programming frameworks

	WonderWeb OWL API	SOFA	JENA2	KAON2	Protégé
Supported Formats	OWL Lite, OWL-DL, OWL Full, OWL 1.1	OWL, DAML+ OIL, RDF+ RDFS	OWL Lite, OWL-DL, OWL Full, DAML+ OIL, RDF/S	OWL-DL, F-Logic, SWRL	OWL Lite, OWL-DL, OWL Full, RDF/S, SWRL
Program-ming Lan-guage	Java	Java	Java	Java	Java
Event Mechanism	Yes	Yes	Yes	Yes	Yes
Ontology Validation	Yes	Yes	Via Plug-in	Yes	Yes
Reasoning	No (but can be plugged in)	Basic	Basic Reasoning built in; DIG reasoners can be plugged in	Yes	Can be plugged in
Query Lan-guage	None	None	SPARQL	SPARQL	SPARQL
Persistence	Files	Files, RDB (experimental)	Files, RDB	Files, RDB	Files, RDB
Proprietary Persistence Possible	Parsers and serializers can be added	Parsers and serializers can be added	Yes	Parsers and serializers can be added	integratable with Jena
Off-memory Processing	No	Yes	Yes	Yes	Yes
Remote Access	No	No	With Joseki Enhancement	Via RMI and DIG	No

If the ontologies that will be worked with already exist, the ontology languages supported can also become an important factor. In such a case, one has to choose a framework that supports the existing ontologies' languages, or one that supports developing and plugging in parsers for those languages.

If the system to be developed requires a specific architecture, it can make sense to use a framework that has corresponding interfaces; for example, KAON2 provides an RMI interface.

When reasoning capabilities are a crucial part of the system to be developed (for example, in expert's systems), a reasoner should be part of the framework, or it should at least be possible to plug one in. Likewise, when the system to be developed requires querying a knowledge base, especially if the actual queries are not known in advance, the framework should include a sufficiently powerful querying language.

Choosing a framework that fits the application to be developed is not a trivial task (Froehlich et al. 2000). Therefore, there can be no general recommendation for one specific framework. Instead, when developing ontology-driven software, a criteria catalogue has to be built, considering the specific needs and demands, and the potential frameworks have to be evaluated accordingly.

Part III

E-Business Integration with Semantic Technologies

8 A Methodology for Semantic E-Business Integration

The knowledge management technologies presented in the previous chapters can be combined into a consistent methodology for semantic e-business integration. Thus, superseding simple electronic document exchange performed today, the Semantic Web vision of machine-interpretable documents can become a reality. In the following chapters we present and discuss the methodology and application components developed.

8.1 Semantic Synchronization

As discussed above, the need for semantic synchronization in e-business arises out of the coexistence of multiple standards in information chains.

The term synchronization originates from the Greek *sýn* ("together") and *chrónos* ("time"). It denotes the provision of even speed for different activities. Literally, synchronization is the process of coordinating two different things to occur in unison. Carried over to the field of e-business communication, *semantic synchronization* can be understood as the process of reconciling differing structure or content elements between e-business standards, i.e., domain ontologies. If, for the reasons described above, the individual standards shall remain unchanged, then the purpose of reconciliation can be achieved by establishing references between their elements. Thus, determining references for elements can be seen as explicating their meaning. A statement such as "Term X in standard A is equal to term Y in standard B" is basically the explanation of the meaning, and a translation, of X. Matching their communication content on the semantic level reconciles business partners' languages and thus truly synchronizes their intentions.

8.1.1 Synchronization in E-Business Processes

For ease-of-use, it is desirable that a synchronization service is available generically and independently of actual processes or applications. As for a most straightforward and generic scenario, when the user finds a term with, to her, an ambiguous meaning, she can mark the term and request semantic referencing for it. A list of suitable references is returned. The user may either select a reference from the list, create a new reference, or proceed without using a reference. Figure 8.1 shows the basic process design.

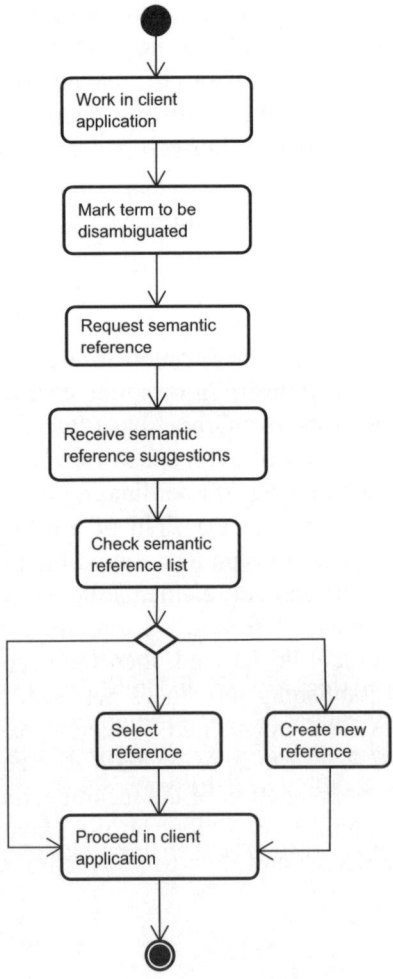

Fig. 8.1. Semantic synchronization

As stated in our research objectives, it is desirable that this functionality may be used with any type of application. Additionally, it should not require extensive software installation or training efforts. It should not be required to perform upfront work to set up the service or to create an initial collection of references.

8.1.2 Semantic References

As discussed above, e-business standards can be regarded as lightweight domain ontologies (Gómez-Pérez et al. 2004; Uschold and Gruninger 2004). Therefore, ontological engineering techniques as introduced in Part II can be applied, in particular mapping techniques. Relations, especially correspondences and similarities found between data elements of ontologies, may be represented and stored as mappings to be used as references. Because they describe semantic relations, we term them *semantic references*. They can be contemplated as multidimensional vectors. In extension of the work of Ehrig and Euzenat (2005), Shvaiko and Euzenat (2005) and Bouquet et al. (2005) we represent a reference as a 5-tuple as shown in Eq. 8.1.

$$<entity1,\ entity2,\ type,\ confidence,\ acceptance> \tag{8.1}$$

where
- *entity1* and *entity2* are the data elements of an ontology between which a relation is assumed
- *type* is the logical relation assumed between the entities
- *confidence* is a numerical value between 0 and 1 qualifying the relation
- *acceptance* is a numerical value between 0 and 1 describing the degree of reputation and trust in the assumed relation, which can be computed out of the users' feedback.

This form allows for encoding references in an arbitrary formal language, e.g., XML. Semantic identity thus can be expressed as well as any other kind of binary correspondence (Euzenat and Shvaiko 2007). As it is used here, the confidence represents the degree of truth of the statement. (Note that it does not stand for the degree of fuzziness of the statement, which would describe the degree of belief of the users (Russell and Norvig 2003) and is expressed by the acceptance.)

Applied to e-business standards in general, this facilitates statements about the relation of two terms from two different standards. The information of a statement such as `<Ontology1#X, Ontology2#Y, is equal to, 1.00, 0.95>` reads as "Concept X in Ontology1 and concept Y in Ontology2 are equal with a confidence of 100%, and 95% of all users agreed on that statement". For the relation type <is equal to>, a confidence value of 1 returns a "true" statement and denotes that two entities are alike. A value of 0 returns a "false" statement and denotes that two entities are not alike. Values between 0 and 1 describe the similarity of two entities and could also be expressed as <is similar to>. These relation types are similar to the thesauri relation types USE and UF as per ISO 5964. Further support for describing similarities can be provided with relation types such as <more general> or <most-specific superclass> and, vice versa, <more specific>, <most-general subclass> and <is overlapping>. These would correspond to BT, NT and, partly, RT in ISO 5964.

Each time an *acceptance value* based on user choice behavior is added, a relation is made more trustworthy and can become more precise and stable over time and change from the best possible to the most exact possible. With his selection decision, the user thus contributes to improving the quality of the respective reference.

8.2 Adaptive Semi-automated Semantic Referencing

An initial reference base, as a starting point for user-driven growth and quality improvement over time, can be established by means of automated tools. Users can also contribute to the reference collection by creating new references.

The process cycle includes an iteration, which is run each time new references are added to the reference repository or existing references are used and rated by the users. Thus, the system is self-learning and can adapt the reference collection over time. The process as a whole is the basis for realizing semantic synchronization in any kind of application. Figure 8.2 shows the process of adaptive semi-automated semantic referencing.

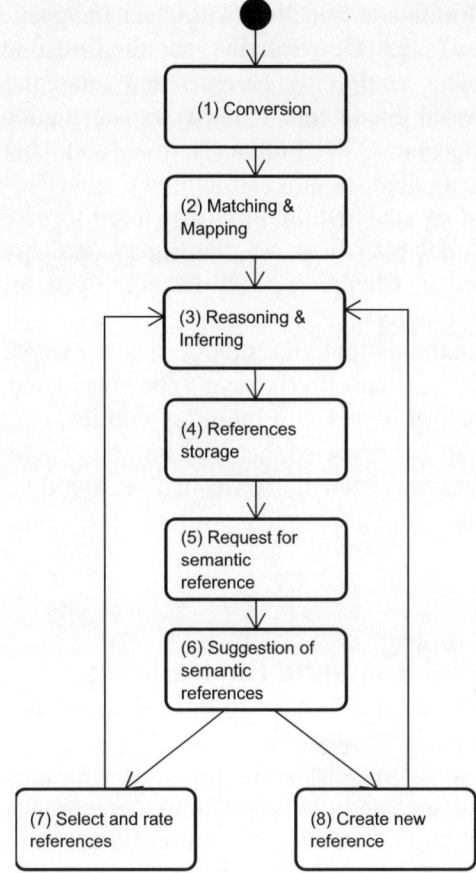

Fig. 8.2. Process of adaptive semi-automated semantic referencing

In the following section, the individual steps of the process are discussed.

8.2.1 Step 1: Conversion

Since knowledge bases can exist in different formats, they may be syntactically heterogeneous. For example, e-business standards are available in formats such as XLS, CSV, XML, XSD, as well as in plain text, formatted or in natural language. To make them processable, they have to be brought into a common syntactical format. In order to employ ontology engineering tools, they have to be converted to ontologies.

To transform XML into other formats, eXtensible Stylesheet Language Transformations (XSLT) may be utilized. This describes the modification from one XML dialect into another employing patterns and templates (Alexiev et al. 2005). For XML-based documents, an XSL transformation exists for turning them into ontologies in OWL format (Bohring and Auer 2005); similar mechanisms may be applied for other structured formats.

If knowledge, on the other hand, is available in an unstructured format, such as natural language in text documents or on webpages, ontology learning mechanisms, as described in Chapter 6, may be employed for converting those descriptions to ontologies.

The conversion of e-business standards into an ontology is not a trivial task due to the diversity of formats. Various criteria have to be considered, such as the approach used to transform terms into ontology entities, e.g., classes or properties. Research so far has revealed that no common generic approach can be applied. Therefore, converted standards can be stored together with their transformation rules and are readily available for further reuse.

8.2.2 Step 2: Matching and Mapping

Finding semantic references between the elements of structured knowledge bases is performed in step 2 of the referencing process.

In this step, the search for and measurement of the semantic similarity of the entities of two or more ontologies and the specification of semantic relations is performed, without merging the ontologies or modifying one of them. The relations are conceptualized in unidirectional form so that non-symmetric relating can be reflected.

Creating an initial set of mappings between the e-business standards to be related can be accomplished by means of automated processes. As discussed earlier, methods and techniques from ontology engineering and AI can be used in processing and combining existing knowledge (Shvaiko and Euzenat 2005). Due to the diversity of the methods, a combined approach can exploit all possibilities to enable mediation (de Bruijn et al. 2004).

In order to improve the quality of derived mappings and assist in resolving ambiguity, reference ontologies can be included into the matching operations. These may be top-level ontologies, supporting the linkage of various domain ontologies:

- OpenCyc, the open source version of the general knowledge base Cyc (OpenCyc 2006)
- Knowledge Representation Ontology (KR) (Sowa 1999)

- Suggested Upper Merged Ontology (SUMO) by IEEE (SUMO 2006)
- Descriptive Ontology for Linguistic and Cognitive Engineering (DOLCE) (WonderWeb 2006)
- the Common Warehouse Model (CWM) specifying metadata interchange among data warehousing, business intelligence, knowledge management and portal technologies (OMG 2007).

Linguistic ontologies can be selected to support monolingual as well as multilingual needs:

- WordNet is a thesaurus for the English language, developed at the Cognitive Science Laboratory at Princeton University. Nouns, verbs, adjectives and adverbs are grouped into cognitive synonyms. They are conceptually related in semantic and lexical relationships and form a net of meaningful related terms (WordNet 2006).
- EuroWordNet is a multilingual lexical-semantic database connecting various European monolingual word collections. The contained term definitions and concepts, respectively, are linked by relations such as synonymy or hyponymy and constitute a semantic net. Hence, the terms for expressing a concept in different languages are interlinked (EuroWordNet 2006).

Upper-level ontologies for specific application domains are concerned with many fields of knowledge collection, such as medical or gene ontologies. For economic purposes, those focused on business modeling and business execution include:

- Enterprise Ontology, a collection of terms and definitions relevant to business enterprises (Uschold et al. 1998)
- TOVE (TOronto Virtual Enterprise), a shared representation to allow for deducing answers for common sense questions (Fox 1992)
- Core Components of ebXML (ebXML 2007)
- OASIS standard UBL (Universal Business Language), a generic extendable XML interchange format for business documents (OASIS 2006a)
- Universal Data Element Framework (UDEF), a cross-industry initiative foreseen to provide naming conventions for indexing enterprise information (Open Group 2007)
- Business Data Ontology, a high level reference ontology for business data (Nagypál and Lemcke 2005)

Such ontologies may be used in the background for supporting the matching process, e.g., by measuring similarity of entity names through comparing character strings (Ehrig 2004b).

8.2.3 Step 3: Deducing New Knowledge

Since ontologies are formally expressed, the logic represented therein may be used for logical processing with reasoning and inference tools as described in Chapter 6. As shown in that chapter, new knowledge may be derived from existing knowledge.

Thus, after creating references through matching and mapping, these references may be used for inferring new references (Klein et al. 2003; Dameron et al. 2004). Formal semantics facilitate the possibility for deducing and thereby inferring statements. If the representation language of the ontology at hand is semantically sufficiently expressive, deduction of the allocation of objects to classes, the classification of subclasses and their equivalence can be made. Therefore, the complexity of the inference process and the efficiency of the algorithm implemented depend directly on the ontology language.

Additionally, with inference tools, the consistency of ontologies can be checked for (Antoniou et al. 2005).

8.2.4 Step 4: Storage

After their discovery, mappings are stored in a reference repository. Thus establishing a collection of references between ontologies creates persistent semantic interlinkages. The benefit of the reference collection increases with accumulation and further enhancement (Hepp 2006a). While references between them may be created, changed or deleted in the repository, the e-business standards themselves are kept in their original form.

Reference repositories may either be set up in-house or openly on a web server.

8.2.5 Steps 5 and 6: Reference Provision

The reference repository is used to answer user requests for semantic references. It may be accessed either by sending direct requests out of other applications or by using a web interface.

The system searches the knowledge base like a dictionary, out of which machine-generated suggestions are extracted and presented to the users for selection. For this, the synchronization system compiles a list of suitable references. From this list, the user can choose a reference, or, when none of the suggestions is considered appropriate, create a new reference. Alternatively, the user may proceed without selecting from the list.

8.2.6 Steps 7 and 8: Intelligence Collection

As discussed above, semantic heterogeneity often can not be resolved in a fully automated way. With a semi-automated approach, semantic references are subject to users' validation (Mitra et al. 2001). Through such manual intervention, ambiguousness can be resolved (Dameron et al. 2004; Hepp 2006a). Experiences with existing ontology engineering tools show that such domain expert knowledge is still needed to raise matching and mapping quality to an acceptable level (Zhdanova et al. 2004).

To avoid additional workload for the user, a very simple validation process is chosen. With its selection by a user, a suggested reference is accepted; all other suggestions are rejected. Each time a user decides for or against a particular reference or creates a new one, a positive rating is generated. Likewise, a negative rating is generated for each reference offered but not selected. With recurring selections or rejections by a greater number of users, references are strengthened or weakened over time. Figure 8.3 shows relations of different strength.

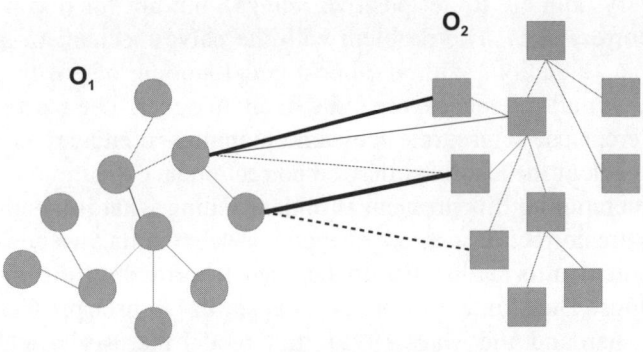

Fig. 8.3. Relations of different strength

The information thus learned is stored as the variable element, i.e., the acceptance parameter, of a reference. In its simplest form this may be the percentage of acceptances of a reference in relation to the number of times it has been suggested. In Chapter 8.3 we will discuss the rating mechanism in more detail.

If a reference for the same term is requested again, the reference suggestion list may be sorted by acceptance. In consequence, the probability that the correct reference is listed first increases. In contrast to other learning methods, e.g., neural nets (Huber 2005), the results thus become controllable and correctable by human intervention if necessary.

8.3 Context Sensitivity

To raise the quality of suggested references, the concept of context is used in our approach.

8.3.1 Ratings

As depicted above, users' selections lead to ratings for the references suggested by the application. These ratings are used to calculate the *acceptance value*, which in turn is input for the system's next suggestions.

To calculate the acceptance value, a naïve approach would be using the average value users' ratings, as shown in Eq. 8.2.

$$acc(Rf) = \sum_{R \in Ratings(Rf)} \frac{1}{\left|Ratings(Rf)\right|} \cdot acc(R). \qquad (8.2)$$

The naïve rating mechanism is feasible for filtering out erroneous mappings (which are very unlikely to get positive ratings), but not for disambiguating several correct ones. The problem with the naïve mechanism is that tie situations, i.e., situations with an almost equal amount of positive and negative ratings for all references, are quite likely to occur. The reason for this is that different users may rate the same mapping reference very differently – while each of these ratings may be correct on its own.

A core idea in overcoming this problem is understanding what it means that both mappings are correct: it means that each is correct in its own context. Therefore, context information has to be used to provide a disambiguation of mappings. That context information is similar to user profiles in social filtering (Shardand and Maes 1995): they model the user's field of work and interest. In order to implement an ontology-mapping disambiguation mechanism based on ratings and context, each rating is stored together with context information. This data can be used as a collection of cases for case-based reasoning (Allen 1994). Then, context-sensitive queries can be issued, such as context-sensitive queries in information retrieval (Baeza-Yates and Ribeiro-Neto 1999). Figure 8.4 illustrates the main principle of how these queries are processed.

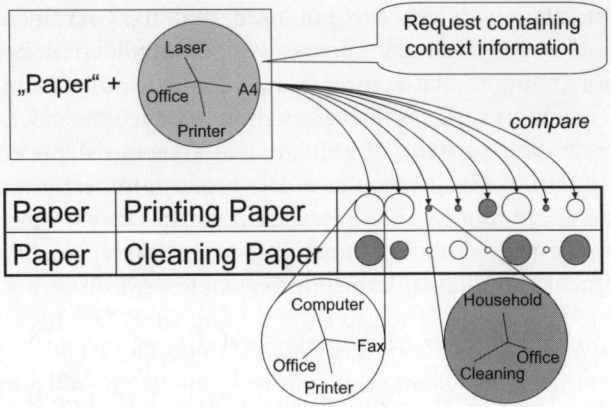

Fig. 8.4. Context-sensitive rating system

The query contains information on the querying user's context. Every mapping for the queried term has a series of positive (white in the figure) and negative (grey) ratings, each stored with information on the context in which the rating was issued. When processing the query, each rating's context is compared to the query's context, and the rating is weighted according to the similarity measure (in the figure, bigger circles represent a stronger weight). Thus, ties can be broken and mapping disambiguation can be achieved. Note that in the example given above, the naïve approach would result in a tie situation with four positive and four negative ratings each.

The result of the weighted ratings is an acceptance value that defines the mapping's appropriateness in the given context. Formally, the context-sensitive and ratings-based mapping service answers a query as follows:

Definition 1 (Context-sensitive referencing):
Given some context information $C(x)$, find those mappings for an element x from a set of ontologies O_1 to a set of ontologies O_2, with an acceptance value $acc_{C(x)}$ (which is the higher the more appropriate the reference is in this context), calculated dynamically for that context information and exceeding a minimum acceptance threshold acc_{min}.

By employing a minimum acceptance threshold, appropriate mappings can be separated from inappropriate ones.

8.3.2 Context Definition

A crucial task is determining which references are appropriate. Some vagueness or ambiguities can be resolved when the context is known. If the semantic synchronization services are not used within a confined, clearly distinct circle of users but rather across various application domains, disambiguation is required. Therefore, adding context information, and thus making the synchronization system sensitive to dynamic backgrounds, further enhances the process of semantic referencing depicted above. It enables the system, when it receives a user request, to perform a ranking of suitable references found in the repository and to present those which best fit the user's purpose in the top positions. Accordingly, a user's request for semantic synchronization is defined as shown in Eq. 8.3.

$$request := <term, standards_{from}, standards_{to}, context>. \tag{8.3}$$

It consists of the term for which semantic references are sought, a list of standards for each side, and context information. Both $standards_{from}$ and $standards_{to}$ are optional. If they are left out, references from and to all standards are returned. A typical request could be "What is the term that is called 'X' in UNSPSC called in eClass?" or "Are there any references in other standards for a term called 'Y' in xCBL?"

In order to make the system interface as simple to work with as possible, users should not have to explicitly determine the application domain they are working in. Instead, each query for references comes with information on the query term's context. The client application is responsible for gathering the term's context. Ideally, this can be done automatically, without the user having to explicitly point out which terms are context terms and which are not.

In order to provide the user with the best possible suggestions within his context, the context within which each user rating for a certain reference has been given is stored along with the actual rating. Therefore, a rating always consists of an acceptance value, between 0 for minimum and 1 for maximum agreement, together with the context. Eq. 8.4 depicts this.

$$rating := \{context, acceptance\}. \tag{8.4}$$

When observing the choices for or against a reference, the rating will be just 0 for a rejection or 1 or acceptance. Alternatively, floating values may be entered for more distinct expression. The ratings are used to dynamically calculate the value of the variable acceptance in the reference which is returned to the user.

The indistinctness and ambiguousness of terms' meanings can be resolved when the context of such a vague term is known. The more additional information regarding a term's context is identified, the more precisely the similarity of two contexts can be determined.

In order for a generic approach to make the semantic referencing services available to as many types of applications as possible, it is imperative to describe context as generally as possible. On the other hand, to reach maximum expressivity, context has to be described as specifically as possible. We deal with this dilemma by using pairs of context terms and distance values, as detailed below.

8.3.3 Context Description

The procedure used to determine the context of a term to be referenced depends on the kind of client application concerned. To achieve high-quality results, context information has to be as specific as possible. However, not all client applications out of which a user may request a semantic reference are capable of computing all forms of context possible. Different application types might use different methods to determine context. Systems for working with unstructured text may try to find out the syntactical function of a term in a sentence and take the words in front of and after the term in question. Systems working with structured documents may use context terms that are structurally close to the queried term, weighting different structural relations differently. One possible strategy might be using all ancestor elements, but only the closest siblings.

A dialogue system in which a term in an input filed should be referenced might use different context items, such as input fields, labels and contents of neighboring data fields. Furthermore, for applications belonging to a particular application domain, terms for describing the domain may also be part of the context. For example, in the case of a flight booking system, the terms "booking" and "travel" could be taken. Figure 8.5 illustrates these context determination options.

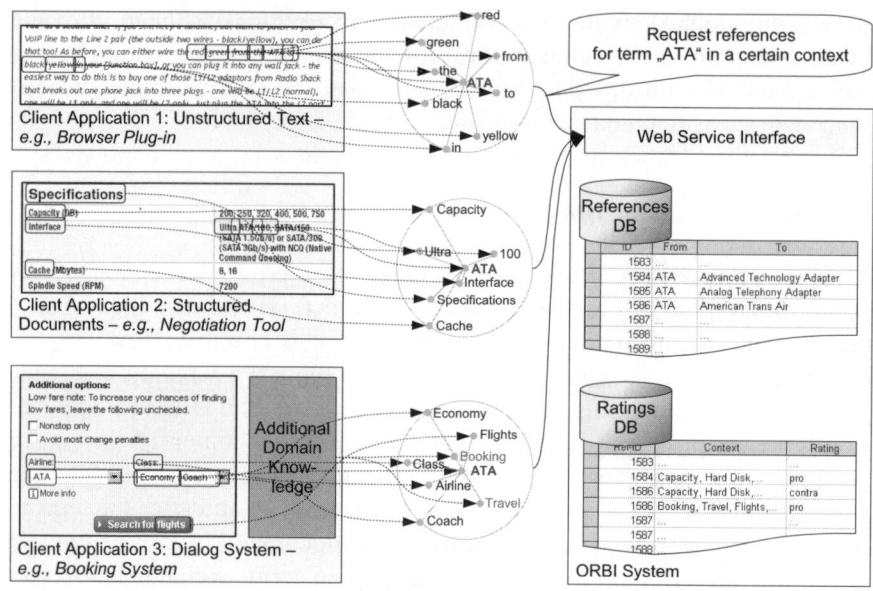

Fig. 8.5. Context description by different applications

When all client applications work according to the same context-description mechanisms, as described above, all ratings given by users of the semantic referencing services within one application can be used in another application as well. If, for example, a reference has been created for use in a structured business document, this may also be used in a totally different text document containing similar context elements. Therefore, all users of the semantic synchronization service can benefit from the knowledge collected from the different users of the various applications available in e-business.

8.3.4 Determination

As described in Chapter 6, context-sensitive referencing can be regarded as a case-based reasoning problem. For each term that could be queried to be disambiguated, an eager learning strategy, such as decision trees, would require learning one decision tree per term for which references could potentially be sought. Thus, only lazy learning strategies are feasible. Therefore, we use the distance-weighted k-nearest-neighbor approach (Dudani 1976). To this end, we have to determine context and define a similarity measure for context information.

To incorporate the context, a weighted sum is calculated instead of the naïve, unweighted arithmetic mean to obtain a more concise result, taking into account the query's and the rating's contexts. Thereby, each acceptance value is weighted by the similarity of the query's context and the rating's context as shown in Eq. 8.5. C designates the total of all contexts.

$$sim : C \times C \to [0,1].$$ (8.5)

When the similarity functions are determined for contexts, the acceptance can be calculated accordingly. Given a referenced term X and a query's context $C_Q(X)$, a reference's acceptance value is calculated as shown in Eq. 8.6.

$$acc_{C_Q(x)}(Rf) \begin{cases} \sum_{R \in Ratings(Rf)} \frac{sim(C_Q(x),C_R(x))}{sum_{sim}} \cdot acc(R) & if\ sum_{sim} > 0 \\ acc_{default} & if\ sum_{sim} = 0 \end{cases}.$$ (8.6)

Here, $C_R(x)$ designates the context of a rating and $C_Q(x)$ the context of the query. Each rating is weighted with the similarity of the rating's context $C_R(X)$ and the query's context. When there are no ratings whose context is comparable to the query's context, i.e., where the similarity of the query's context and each rating's context equals 0, a default acceptance value is used.

Thus, the distance-weighted k-nearest-neighbors technique from data mining is applied in a modified form. However, where the original algorithm predicts discrete classes, here a real-valued acceptance value is calculated instead. The context is the pattern, and the context similarity measure is the distance function. The system developed allows using either all ratings or filter the closest k before calculating the sum, where k is an adjustable parameter (Rebstock et al. 2007).

In the reference suggestion list, the user may receive all those results or the number of results may be filtered according to a preset acceptance limit or a predefined number of results.

For semantic synchronization as presented here, the task of determining the context of the rating of a reference request is conceptualized as a task of the e-business application in use, which acts as a client system to the semantic synchronization system. That way, each system can use its own individual technique for gathering context. This implies that the definition of context must be as general as possible in order to allow a wide variety of client systems. For this reason, a shallow approach seems more attractive. In order to avoid overloading the client with the need to determine semantic information, the most straightforward approach is a relational one, where a distance value is stored for each context word. Mathematically, the context of a term can be understood as a set of terms C(x), expressed in a normalized distance function for this context, as shown in Eq. 8.7.

$$dist_{C(x)} : C(x) \rightarrow [0,1] \text{ with } \max_{y \in C(x)} dist_{C(x)}(y) = 1.$$ (8.7)

The terms contained in C(x) can be arbitrary strings. Term x is the context's core, i.e., the term to be referenced, and is not contained in C(x). The closer a term y is to the core, and the smaller $dist_{C(x)}(y)$ is, respectively, the more important it is for determining the meaning of x. The distances are normalized with the maximum of 1, so that later the similarity of two contexts can be calculated more easily.

Since every client application can use its own method to determine context, and references are shared between different client applications, the ratings' contexts are produced by different mechanisms. This yields the problem that two applications could decide to use different radiuses, since they may have different mechanisms for determining context. For example, one application might consider only the next four neighboring terms within a document, while another one might consider up to twenty or more. The problem is that if both clients determine the context of a term in the same document, the contexts produced will look different although they are the same in the original document. A different radius upon determining the context around a term to be referenced would lead to incorrect results when comparing the context of a reference rating and a context delivered by a client application at the time of receiving the user request.

Through normalizing, two contexts can be checked to determine if they are identical. To do so, the intersection of terms contained in both contexts is constructed. For each context, the distance of the term contained in the intersection with maximum distance is set to 1 and the other distances are scaled accordingly. Terms whose distance is scaled to a value bigger than 1 are discarded. Figure 8.6 illustrates the normalization process for two example contexts.

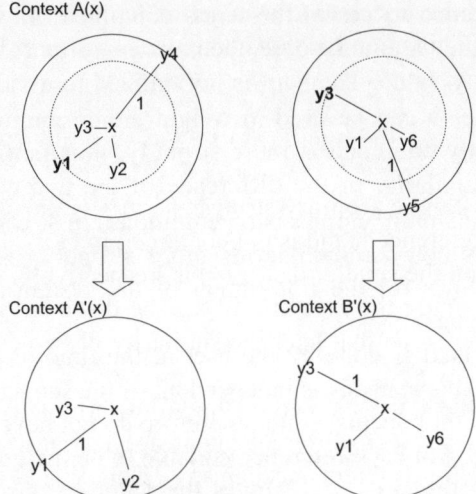

Fig. 8.6. Context normalization

In this example, the most distant terms in the two contexts' intersection are y1 and y3. Their distance is set to 1, and the more distant terms y4 and y6 are discarded. The remaining terms allow for a meaningful comparison and performance of the actual measurement. For two such contexts, A(x) and B(x), the normalized context A'(x) is defined as seen in Eq. 8.8.

$$A'(x) := \left\{ y \in A(x) \mid dist_{A'(x)}(y) \le 1 \right\}$$

$$\text{with } dist_{A'(x)}(y) := \frac{dist_{A(x)}(y)}{\max\limits_{z \in A \cap B} dist_{A(x)}(z)} \qquad (8.8)$$

B'(x) is defined analogously. Then, context measurement is carried out on the two contexts A'(x) and B'(x). A'(x) and B'(x) are empty sets if and only if there are no common terms in A(x) and B(x); therefore, the similarity of A(x) and B(x) is set to 0. Furthermore, A'(x) and B'(x) can only be both empty or both non-empty sets. Therefore, in the following, it is assumed that A'(x) and B'(x) are non-empty sets. The similarity of A(x) and B(x) is then defined as seen in Eq. 8.9.

$$sim(A(x), B(x)) := \frac{\sum\limits_{y \in A'(x) \cap B'(x)} \lambda \cdot \left(1 - \left| dist_{A'(x)}(y) - dist_{B'(x)}(y) \right| \right) + \sum\limits_{y \in A'(x) \Delta B'(x)} (1-\lambda) \cdot dist_{A'(x) \Delta B'(x)}(y)}{\lambda \cdot \left| A'(x) \cap B'(x) \right| + (1-\lambda) \left| A'(x) \Delta B'(x) \right|} \qquad (8.9)$$

The first summand in the numerator sums up the distance differences of the terms that both contexts have in common, subtracted from one, thus making the similarity value bigger the closer the common terms are. The second summand adds the distance values of the terms contained only in one context. Hence, the closer they are to the core, the more important they are, thus the lesser the similarity value. The sum is normalized to a value between 0 and 1. The parameter λ can be used to weight either common terms or terms contained in only one context more strongly, thus putting more emphasis either on the similarity or the difference of the two contexts. A value of λ close to 1 puts more emphasis on common terms, while a value close to 0 emphasizes non-common terms more strongly. This parameterization possibility allows for the fine-tuning of the system according to individual requirements.

The interpretation of the context is done by the user at the time of requesting a semantic reference. This analysis is independent of the semantic synchronization system and its components, which therefore do not have to support context sensitivity at all. For each reference suitable to be included into a suggested reference list, the system computes the value of acceptance. These calculated acceptance values are used to rank the semantic references. A rating is expressed as a floating point value between 0 and 1. Since the acceptance value is calculated as a number between 0 and 1, it can also be read as a percentage value, allowing statements such as "In this context, the reference is appropriate to a degree of 87%".

Basically, to extend a client application with a context-description functionality, different similarity measurements as suggested in Chapter 6 can be chosen. In the above example, the formulas used to determine a reference's acceptance value in a given context provide some parametrical degree of freedom, as different values for λ in measuring context similarity, and different values for k in the weighted k-nearest-neighbor algorithm can be chosen.

The best set of values strongly depends on the domain and on the type of client application used. Typical influencing factors in choosing settings can be as follows:

- The variance of context information, as this depends on the e-business application in use. For example, a flight booking system is used in a very narrow domain and will produce context with less variance than a general e-procurement system that is used for sourcing MRO commodities. If the context has little variance, it may be useful to look at the differences; on the other hand, if there are a lot of variances, it is more appropriate to try to focus on common terms. Therefore, the higher the variance of context information, the lower the value for λ should be.
- The client application system users' degree of expertise. A lower degree of expertise could result in more faulty ratings, which the system has to

cope with. If faulty ratings are likely to occur, care must be taken that their influence on the result is not too high.

The insight that different parameter sets are needed in different application domains leads to these individual possibilities of deployment. The semantic referencing system allows the configuration of different parameter sets for each client system, and differently deployed versions may share one common repository of references and ratings. Using this approach, we can share knowledge between domains, but still produce optimal results for individual application domains.

8.4 Comprehensive Semantic Support

The approach presented allows for the creation of semantic references for context-sensitive semantic synchronization services. Context-sensitive ontology-mapping disambiguation, as described above, is a mechanism that is almost universally applicable due to the various types of context information available.

Gathering context information in a generic way, as described above, allows to narrow down disambiguation in accordance with the application domain or background of users. Extracting context through the collection of neighboring terms can lead to the transmission of a different meaning (Karabatis 2006). Therefore, client applications can be individually optimized to describe context as expressively as possible by providing extensions for context gathering that are as suitable as possible for the particular application domain or community. In fact, a community-based approach can be seen as a special case of context-sensitive, ratings-based mapping disambiguation. This leads to semantic synchronization services either being used openly for the general public or being fine-tuned for the confined surroundings of a particular community. Formally, the community-driven ontology-matching service answers the user's query as follows:

Definition 2 (Community-based referencing):
Given a user being member in a non-empty set of communities S_U, find those mappings for an element x from a set of ontologies O_1 to a set of ontologies O_2 that have been created by a user being member in a non-empty set of communities S_C under the condition that $S_U \cap S_C$ is not empty.

If we understand community identifiers as context terms, we can use a context-sensitive mechanism to implement a community-based one.

An application requiring semantic references has information about a user's communities. When references are needed, the user's community identifiers are used to form context information and handed over to the context-sensitive, rating-based service. In this scenario, the community identifiers serve as context terms. Thus, the context consists of those identifiers, each having the distance value 1.

Suppose that for each mapping, a positive rating exists, with the community identifiers of the mapping's creator providing the rating's context. The most straightforward way to ensure that precondition is to automatically create the rating when a user creates the mapping itself. This is another example of how implicit ratings can be generated.

We have to choose a similarity measure that yields 0 if the query's context and the rating's context have no common terms, i.e., the querying user and the creator share no communities. Otherwise, the similarity has a value bigger than zero. Thus, all mappings created by users who share no community with the querying user will have a calculated acceptance value of 0; mappings whose creator shares at least one community with the querying user will have an acceptance value bigger than zero. Therefore, filtering the results with a lower threshold of 0 will disambiguate mappings so that only mappings relevant in the querying user's domain are returned.

This shows that context-sensitive mapping disambiguation is a universal mechanism. The algorithm can be extended in such a way that it processes several dimensions of context, e.g., using a community dimension and a context-terms dimension. The referencing methodology presented here has been implemented in the ORBI Ontology Mediator. After an access control methodology has been described in Chapter 9, the Mediator itself is described in Chapter 10.

9 Access Control for E-Business Integration

by Patrick Röder and Omid Tafreschi

9.1 Rationale

Many standards today are commonly used and open to public use. International organizations like UN/CEFACT intentionally publish their standards and standards elements freely on the Web to foster their use. Many industry consortiums do the same. Still, many other standards are used without being open to the public or without the public even knowing about them.

Thus, access to standards, in part or as a whole, may be restricted. We can distinguish three major reasons, detailed further in the next paragraphs, for this:

- Business models can be based on the commercial use of intellectual property rights for standards, standards elements or references.
- Some standards are not open to the public, e.g., company-wide internal standards or standards within consortiums.
- Some references are not open to the public, e.g., because those references would unveil ongoing research and development activities.

The commercial use of intellectual property rights for electronic media has been on the research agenda for some time now (e.g., Thurow 1997; Shapiro and Varian 1999) and has been intensely discussed for topics like public domain software (Nycum 1993; Siponen 2006), wikis or peer-to-peer (P2P) music downloads and is already applied in business domains today. Examples include the software, entertainment or news industries. Stable business models for commercial use of property rights for electronic media emerge even in the more challenging industries, such as the music industry.

The development of a standard and its elements is an intellectual endeavor that deeply deserves protection of use. If political or strategic considerations do not imply that a standard should be available to the public without restrictions, a company or consortium that has developed a standard may want the option of benefiting commercially from this property.

Instead of using a standard commercially, a company or consortium may want to restrict access to this domain knowledge to users within the company or consortium, e.g., because this knowledge is considered to be a competitive advantage. The same holds true for references between standards. Reasons for not unveiling this information may be similar.

Besides being a competitive advantage or very company specific, a new standard element or reference may also unveil, if made public, information about ongoing research and development or marketing activities to competitors. For example, if a new element is added to a product in a bill of material, this may alert the competitor that the company plans to add this new feature to the given product. Or, if in a procurement catalog a new ingredient or part is added, this may reveal that the company is changing recipes or bills of materials and is preparing to come to market with a new or modified product.

For these reasons, access to standards and references between standards may need to be restricted. Therefore, appropriate access-control mechanisms have to be applied. In the next section, we present a scenario to illustrate the challenges involved in controlling access to standards.

We begin by explaining the reasons why access control is required for standards. Then, we provide a scenario where we illustrate the challenges involved in controlling access to standards. After this, we explain our history-based model for defining access control, which can be used with standards. We present a security architecture with an efficient workflow for editing standards and show how our model can be used to enforce the policies of the presented scenario. Next, we discuss related work. Finally, we draw conclusions.

9.2 Scenario

Here, we describe a scenario to illustrate the challenges of controlling access to standards. Companies share a common IT system to maintain their confidential standards and to share these standards with their business partners. In addition, some companies collaborate to maintain a common standard. In our scenario, we consider three companies. The first company is SmartChips, which is a supplier of car computers. The other two companies are EcoCars and FastCars, both of which are car manufacturers and, also, competitors. Each company has its own standard. There are also public standards that can be accessed by all companies without restrictions.

Competitors should not be able to access the standards of their adversary. SmartChips and EcoCars have a strong collaboration. Therefore, Smart-Chips is allowed to edit the standard of EcoCars and can copy parts of its own standard to EcoCars' standard. Since SmartChips is also a supplier to FastCars, SmartChips has read access to the FastCars standard and can copy parts of this to its own standard. Figure 9.1 shows the permitted data flows in our scenario.

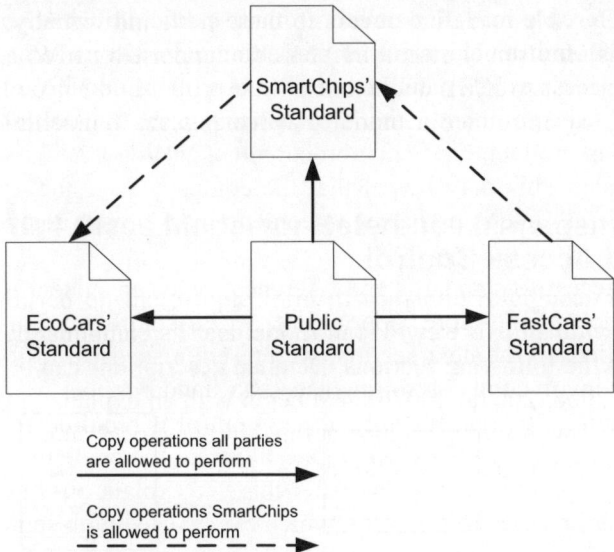

Fig. 9.1. Permitted data flows

In our example, we consider a negotiation between SmartChips and FastCars, during which SmartChips views the standard of FastCars and copies some parts of this to its own standard. From FastCars' point of view, SmartChips should not be able to copy parts of FastCars' standard to EcoCars' standard. Therefore, after it accesses FastCars' standard, Smart-Chips' access to EcoCars' standard must be restricted. Depending on the requirements of the scenario, we can define three alternatives for limiting the access of SmartChips. In the first instance, SmartChips is not permitted to access the standard of EcoCars. In the second, SmartChips is not al-lowed to edit the standard of EcoCars. In the third, SmartChips is allowed to edit the standard of EcoCars, as long as no data is transferred from FastCars' standard. This case occurs when SmartChips transfers data from a public standard to EcoCars' standard.

This simple scenario illustrates several challenges with regard to access control. First, we need a mechanism for recording accesses to standards, which are stored in documents. This recorded information must contain information about each operation performed and its context. The context must include relevant data for access decisions, e.g., the subject that performed the operation and the time at which the operation was performed. Second, we must be able to define access to documents depending on former accesses. As a consequence, we need a model where access is defined based on the history of previous operations. Third, since standards contain descriptive texts which can be partly reused in other standards, the access-control system has to be able to define access to these parts individually. Fourth, since standards are usually stored in XML documents, we need a model that can define access to XML documents.

In the next section, we introduce a model that handles the four challenges mentioned above.

9.3 History-Based Access Control

In this section, we provide an overview of our model and its components, which are explained in the following sections. Detailed descriptions can be found in Röder et al. (2006; 2007a; 2007b). We begin with an explanation of the histories, continue with the operations defined in our model and, finally, present the syntax for access-control rules.

9.3.1 Histories

We use histories to keep track of changes caused by the operations `create`, `copy`, `delete`, and `change attribute`, which we describe in detail in the next section. We keep one history for the corresponding XML element itself, including its attributes, and one history for its text content. The latter history uses dedicated markup elements to divide the text into text blocks with block IDs. This mechanism enables us to keep track of subelements of arbitrary size. In other words, we can split the text content of an element into smaller units, which can be distinguished by our access-control rules.

A new text block is created in two cases. First, we create a new text block as a result of a copy operation, at both the source and the destination element. Second, we create a new text block whenever text is added to an existing element. This mechanism is required, since part of the text of a standard can be copied to other standards.

In addition to the histories, we maintain a unique element ID for each element in order to reference it independently of its current position within the document. Each document also has a unique document ID.

We use these IDs to keep track of copy operations by maintaining an *is-copy-of* relation among the elements and text blocks. Two objects are in is-copy-of relation to one another if one object is a copy of the other.

Figure 9.2 shows a graphical illustration of the is-copy-of relation of the objects mentioned in the scenario. We refer to this kind of illustration as a copy-graph. In this example, all objects are text blocks. In the general case, objects can be XML elements as well.

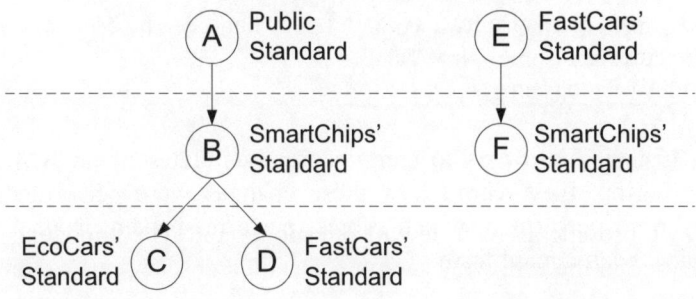

Fig. 9.2. Examples of copy-graphs

The data structure for adding histories to each element is listed in Table 9.1, where cardinality denotes the minimum and maximum number (* for no maximum) of occurrences of a specific element.

Table 9.1. Data structure for histories

Cardinality	Element	Type
1, 1	Element ID	Integer
0, *	Element History Entry	(Action, Context)
0, *	Text History Entry	(Action, Context)

A history entry consists of an action element, which contains details on the operation and a context description. A context is a tuple of Date, Subject and Role, where Date refers to a date, including time, and Role is the role of the Subject that performs the corresponding operation. In addition to the operation, an action element can have up to two arguments that describe the action more precisely. The actions and their arguments are listed in Table 9.2. For the actions related to attributes, we store the name of the corresponding attribute. The `change attribute` and `create attribute` operations also store the new value of the attribute. The `create text` and `delete text` operations store the block ID of the corresponding text block.

Table 9.2. Actions and their arguments

Operation	Argument 1	Argument 2
Create Element	-	-
Delete Element	-	-
Create Text	Block ID	-
Delete Text	Block ID	-
Create Attribute	Attribute Name	New Value
Change Attribute	Attribute Name	New Value
Delete Attribute	Attribute Name	-

To sum up, histories allow us to capture previous states of an XML document. In addition, they record how these changes were performed; e.g., when they were performed, which subject performed them or where specific parts have been copied from.

9.3.2 Operations

In this section, we describe the details of the operations supported in our model. These are `view`, `create`, `delete`, `change attribute` and `copy`. Most of the operations can be applied to elements, text and attributes. Each operation has an effect on the document itself as well as on the histories. In the case of the view operation, the viewing of an element is logged in the histories at the time the corresponding view is created. The `create` operation is divided into creating elements, creating attributes and creating text.

The `create element` operation creates an element without any attributes or text. In addition to the element itself, the history of the element is created. The first entry of the history for the element describes its creation. The attributes of an element are created with the `create attribute` operation, which is also logged with an entry in the history of the enclosing element. Standards can require that elements have mandatory attributes. This requirement should be checked on the application level and not within the access-control system. This also applies to the deletion of mandatory attributes.

The `create text` operation is used to add new text to an element. This operation has an argument that specifies the position of the new text.

This position can be in an existing text block, before an existing text block or after an existing block. In the first case, where the position is within an existing text block, we must split the existing block at the position where the new content should be placed. The new content is placed in-between the split blocks. The split blocks keep their original histories, whereas the new content gets a new history with one entry describing its creation.

The `delete` operation is used to delete elements, attributes, text or parts of the text. Since elements and their attributes are checked in rules, we need to keep them after deletion. For that purpose, the context (role, subject, date) of a delete operation is captured in the element history with a delete action entry.

The `copy` operation is used to copy elements, text or parts of the text. In all cases, we apply the corresponding `create` operation to create a new instance at the destination, as a copy from the source, which is registered in the destination element. Additionally, the is-copy-of relation of the elements among each other is updated.

The `view` operation displays elements which have not been deleted. When a user wants to view a standard, the `view` operation is invoked for every element of the corresponding document, and also for its attributes and text. In contrast to the read operation of some other systems (e.g., Brewer and Nash 1989; Bell and LaPadula 1973), the view operation does not imply a data transfer. The view operation is logged in the history at the time the view is created and presented to the user.

The `change attribute` operation allows users to change the value of a specific attribute. Since former values of an attribute can be checked by rules, we record the change with an entry in the element history.

9.3.3 Rules

In this section, we define the syntax for access-control rules, which can express policies that depend on the content of the current document, the recorded history information and the content of dependent documents. These are documents with parts that have been copied to or from the current document. Generally speaking, a rule has the typical structure of subject, operation, object and mode. The `mode` field of a rule defines whether it is positive (allow) or negative (deny). We use roles to model the subjects. For this purpose, we use the concept of Role-Based Access Control (RBAC), which was introduced in Sandhu et al. (1996). Instead of being assigned directly to subjects, access rights, called permissions in RBAC terminology, are assigned to roles. Such a role is used to model a specific task. Therefore, all permissions that are required to perform a specific task are assigned to a role, e.g., a role `cashier` can be used to collect all permissions that are required for performing the job of a cashier. In addition to assigning permissions to roles, RBAC assigns subjects to roles. Furthermore, RBAC introduces role hierarchies, which define a partial order among the roles of the system. This partial order defines a specialization relationship among the roles, where the more special role inherits all permission from the less special role. As a consequence, more special rules have more permission than less special rules.

If the access to an object is neither allowed nor denied by a rule, then the object is not accessible. If conflicts occur, we take the rule with the superior role and, finally, apply "deny takes precedence over allow". In addition, a subject needs the view permission to perform an operation on an object.

Instead of listing individual objects in rules (Graham and Denning 1972), we describe objects by their properties, e.g., location within a document or attribute values. For this purpose, we use the XML Path Language (XPath) (Berglund et al. 2007) to describe the objects for which a rule is applicable. XPath is a language used to select parts of an XML document. We use XPath because its clearly defined semantics makes the interpretation of the resulting rules unambiguous. Moreover, XPath has a predefined set of mechanisms that can be used for our purpose, which simplifies the implementation of our model.

XPath patterns are designed to select elements, attributes and text based on their position in the document and on their properties, e.g., `/Standard[@class='public']` matches all public standards. A condition on a set of elements is placed in square brackets. The most common syntax elements and their descriptions are given in Table 9.3. XPath also defines a large set of functions which can be used for more advanced conditions; e.g., the pattern `/Standard[count(.//categories) > 5]` uses the function `count()` to match all standards which contain more than five categories.

Table 9.3. Excerpt of the syntax elements of XPath

Syntax element	Description
@	Selects an attribute
.	Selects the current element
//*	Selects all elements in the document
/	Selects from the root element
[n]	Selects the n-th element of a set

We define two types of rules. The first type of rule defines permissions for the unary operations `create`, `view`, `delete` and `change attribute`. The objects of an access-control rule are defined by an XPath pattern. The second type of rule defines permissions for the binary `copy` operation, which requires the specification of a source and a destination object. We use two XPath patterns for this. The syntax of both types of rules is listed in Table 9.4.

Table 9.4. Syntax of access-control rules

Unary Rule		Copy Rule	
Element	Description	Element	Description
Role	Role	Role	Role
Operation	Operation	Operation	Copy
Object	XPath	Object	XPath
		Destination	XPath
Mode	allow | deny	Mode	allow | deny

We use XPath patterns in rules to define access depending on histories. As a consequence, we need a mechanism for accessing the histories within an XPath pattern. Therefore, we have extended the function library of XPath by a set of functions. In Röder et al. (2007b) we present further details about our XPath extension functions.

9.4 Security Architecture

In this section, we present a security architecture for applying history-based access control in an environment where multiple users can edit standards concurrently. Its components are explained in the following sections.

9.4.1 Architecture Overview

Our security architecture and its components are depicted in Figure 9.3. The system uses four databases. The document database (Doc DB) contains all the documents of the system. The rule database (Rule DB) contains the access-control rules, which specify allowed or denied accesses to the documents and their parts. The copy database (Copy DB) stores the is-copy-of relation of the objects. Finally, the user database (User DB) stores the credentials of the users of the system as well as the corresponding roles, including their hierarchy.

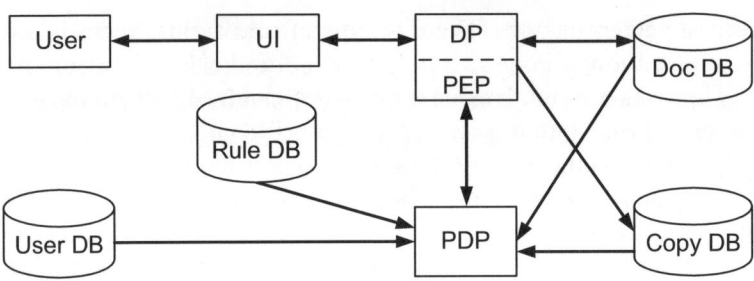

Fig. 9.3. Security architecture

The user interface (UI) presents documents to the user and offers operations that can be performed on the documents. If the user invokes such an operation, the corresponding request is sent to the document processor (DP), which performs the requested operation, if it is permitted. Inside the DP, the policy enforcement point (PEP) intercepts each operation and asks the policy decision point (PDP) whether the requested operation is allowed. The PDP uses the four databases to decide whether to allow or deny the requested operation. This architecture allows us to access distributed documents when a rule is evaluated. In the following section, we explain the workflow for editing a document in order to illustrate the processes within our architecture.

9.4.2 Workflow

A document containing a standard must be opened before it can be viewed or edited. Therefore, the UI offers a command for opening a document. This command is sent to the DP, which loads a copy of the corresponding document from the document database. We refer to this process as *check-out*, since it has semantics similar to the check-out command of a version control system (Tichy 1985). After the check-out, the user can edit the document by applying the operations of our model. We evaluate the access-control rules before executing the operation to determine whether it is allowed. The changed content of an opened document, including the corresponding histories, becomes relevant for access decisions of other documents after it is checked in. Until then, the content of the opened document is only relevant for access decisions concerning that document itself. The document and the corresponding histories are kept as a local copy in the DP. To *check-in* a document, the user must invoke the corresponding command of the UI. The DP then stores the copy of the document back to the document database.

The check-in and check-out concept is more efficient and offers a higher usability compared to working directly on the policy-relevant version of a document. The former is more efficient because changed content must be propagated less often. More precisely, the changed content must be propagated only when a document is checked-in. This also reduces the overhead of recalculating permissions. The usability is also higher, because of the transaction semantics of the approach. With this concept a user can decide when the changing of a document is done, instead of having potentially unwanted intermediate states before receiving relevant access decisions.

In the next section, we show how to model access to standards as described in our scenario.

9.5 Modeling Access to Standards

In this section, we model our scenario using the mechanisms that we have presented in the previous sections. We assume that the role hierarchy depicted in Figure 9.4 is used and that all subjects act in one of these roles. We use the generic role `employee` to describe an employee of any of the three companies of our example. We use special roles for the employees of each company and derive these roles from the generic role `employee`. For example, we use the role `employee-smartchips` as a role for employees of the company SmartChips.

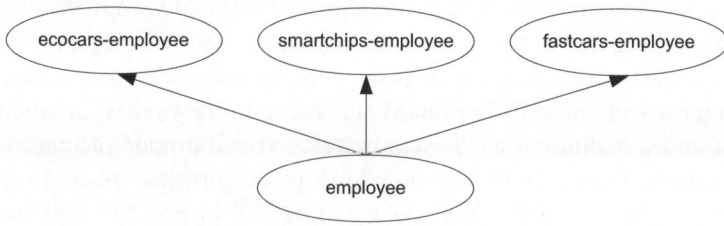

Fig. 9.4. Role hierarchy of the scenario

Moreover, we assume that every XML document defining a standard has a `class` attribute at its root element. This attribute defines which company the standard belongs to or that the standard is public. In the first case, the attribute is set to the name of the corresponding company, whereas in the second case, the attribute is set to `public`. We assume that a security administrator maintains the attribute `class` and that other subjects are not allowed to change this attribute.

For each statement of the scenario, which defines an allowed or forbidden action, we need to specify one or more access-control rules. Because of the default semantics of our model, all unspecified operations are denied. As a consequence, we only need to define allow rules and, in addition, exceptions from these rules.

First of all, we need a set of rules to define the fact that each company is allowed to view and edit their own standard. We refrain from listing all those rules. Instead, we present Rule 1 as an example of such a rule. This rule states that employees of the company SmartChips are allowed to view documents that have a root element with the attribute `class` set to `SmartChips`. In other words, employees of SmartChips are allowed to view their own standard. Similar rules must be defined for the remaining operations (`create`, `delete`, `copy` and `change-attribute`) and for the other two companies (EcoCars and FastCars).

Rule 1. Allow employees of SmartChips to view their own standard

Role	`employee-smartchips`
Operation	`view`
Object	`/*/@class == 'SmartChips'//*`
Mode	`allow`

Next, we define a rule that states that every employee is allowed to view parts that were copied from a public standard. In this rule, we use the functions `ac:copies` to determine where the part was originally copied from, where the namespace of our functions is indicated by the prefix `'ac:'`. This function returns all nodes that are in is-copy-of relation with the current node. The returned list of nodes is sorted according to the time of creation of the nodes, in ascending order. We can retrieve the first node of this list with the expression `ac:copies()[1]`. This is the original node from which all other nodes on the list have been copied. We inspect the attribute `class` of the corresponding document containing the first node and check whether the attribute is set to `public`. In this case, the viewing is allowed.

Rule 2. Allow viewing if the object is copied from a public standard

Role	`employee`
Operation	`view`
Object	`fn:root(ac:copies(.)[1])/@class == 'public'`
Mode	`allow`

In addition to the previous rule, we define Rule 3, which allows the copying of parts of public standards. In this rule, we also use the function `ac:copies`. Using this function offers the advantage that public parts within a company's standard can also be copied. For example, this rule allows the copying of parts of a public standard that reside in the standard of SmartChips. Moreover, this rule defines no restriction for the destination. In other words, it allows copying parts of a public standard to anywhere. Since our model requires a view permission on an object to perform another operation, a subject can only copy parts to locations for which it also has the view permission. This restriction avoids the possibility that Eco-Cars could copy parts of a public standard to FastCars' standard, since employees of EcoCars have no permission to view the standard of FastCars.

Rule 3. Allow copy if source is public

Role	`employee`
Operation	`copy`
Object	`fn:root(ac:copies(.)[1])/@class == 'public'`
Destination	`//*`
Mode	`allow`

We stated in the scenario that employees of SmartChips are allowed to view both the standard of EcoCars and the standard of FastCars. Rule 4 expresses this statement by inspecting the attribute class of the corresponding root element of the element in question.

Rule 4. SmartChips' employees can view other standards

Role	`employee-smartchips`
Operation	`view`
Object	`//*[(/*/@class == 'EcoCars') or (/*/@class == 'FastCars')]`
Mode	`allow`

Recall that we did not restrict the destination of `copy` operations in Rule 3. In addition, Rule 4 adds view permissions on FastCars' standard for employees of SmartChips. These added view permissions enable employees of SmartChips to copy parts of public standards to the standard of FastCars, since view permissions are required to perform any other operation. However, employees of SmartChips should not be allowed to modify FastCars' standard. As a consequence, we need a rule that prevents unwanted copy operations. For this purpose, Rule 5 explicitly denies all transfers to FastCars' standard for employees of SmartChips. Rule 5 takes precedence over Rule 3, since deny rules take precedence over allow rules.

Rule 5. Deny copying to FastCars' standard by SmartChips

Role	`employee-smartchips`
Operation	`copy`
Object	`//*`
Destination	`//*[/*/@class == 'FastCars']`
Mode	`deny`

As stated in the scenario, SmartChips' employees are allowed to copy parts of their own standard to the standard of EcoCars. Rule 6 fulfills this condition. In this case, we inspect the original location of the parts instead of their current location. We retrieve the standard where the part was created by using the `ac:copies` function. With this access-control rule, we also allow the employees of SmartChips to copy parts of their standard that are located in the standard of EcoCars to another location within EcoCars' standard.

Rule 6. Allow SmartChips' employees to copy to EcoCars standard

Role	`employee-smartchips`
Operation	`copy`
Object	`fn:root(ac:copies(.)[1])/@class == 'SmartChips'`
Destination	`//*[/*/@class == 'EcoCars']`
Mode	`allow`

As described in the scenario, employees of SmartChips are allowed to copy parts from FastCars' standard to their own standard. Rule 7 implements this condition and uses similar mechanisms to Rule 6. In this case, we also inspect the original location of these parts, which also allows copying them from other locations, e.g., from SmartChips' standard.

Rule 7. Allow SmartChips' employees to copy from FastCars

Role	`employee-smartchips`
Operation	`copy`
Object	`fn:root(ac:copies(.)[1])/@class == 'FastCars'`

Rule 7. continued

Destination	`//*[/*/@class == 'SmartChips']`
Mode	`allow`

Under their agreement with EcoCars, employees of SmartChips need to edit the standard of EcoCars. As a consequence, we must define the corresponding permissions by a set of rules. We need a rule for create, delete and change attribute. Rule 8 is the corresponding rule for the create operation. Since the other two rules differ only in their operation field, we refrain from listing these rules.

Rule 8. Allow SmartChips' employees to edit the standard of EcoCars

Role	`employee-smartchips`
Operation	`create`
Object	`//*[/*/@class == 'EcoCars']`
Mode	`allow`

When editing EcoCars' standard, employees of SmartChips should not delete objects or modify attributes that have not been created by them. Rule 9 implements this restriction by checking the creation context of an object before granting a delete or change-attribute operation. The corresponding context is retrieved with the function `ac:getCreationContext()`. Then, we inspect the `role` attribute of the retrieved context. An employee is not allowed to delete or change an object if he did not create this object.

Rule 9. Deny deleting elements and changing attributes by SmartChips

Role	`employee-smartchips`
Operation	`delete, change-attribute`
Object	`//*[ac:getCreationContext()/@role != employee-smartchips]`
Mode	`deny`

Since employees of SmartChips can both read the standard of FastCars and edit the standard of EcoCars, they could transfer knowledge from EcoCars to FastCars. There are several possibilities for defining restrictions to prevent this. We can model this condition in three alternative ways, for which we present access-control rules in the following paragraphs:

1. After an employee of SmartChips has accessed the standard of Fast-Cars, we deny him the viewing of EcoCars' standard. Since view permissions are required for any other operation, employees of SmartChips cannot perform any operation on EcoCars' standard in this case.
2. After an employee of SmartChips has accessed the standard of Fast-Cars, he is still allowed to view the standard of EcoCars. However, we deny editing of the standard.
3. After an employee of SmartChips has accessed the standard of Fast-Cars, he is still allowed to edit the standard of EcoCars. However, we deny the copying of parts of FastCars' standard to EcoCars' standard.

Within each of these three alternatives, we have two options regarding which subjects we define the restrictions for:

1. We can restrict access for all employees of SmartChips after any of them has accessed the standard of FastCars.
2. We can restrict access only for the specific subject that has accessed the standard of FastCars.

We start by modeling the first alternative. As stated above, we have two options for how to model this alternative. The most restrictive option is to deny any access to the standard of EcoCars after any employee of Smart-Chips has accessed the standard of FastCars. Rule 10a implements this version of the scenario.

Rule 10a. Deny access to EcoCars' standard for SmartChips

Role	employee-smartchips
Operation	view
Object	`//*[((/*/@class == 'EcoCars') and (fn:count(ac:accessed(any, cur-rent)[/*/@company == 'FastCars']) > 0)]`
Mode	deny

This rule revokes the view permissions, which are needed as a basis for any other operation. The rule checks two conditions. First, the corresponding object must reside in the standard of EcoCars. The second condition uses our `ac:accessed` function to check whether any employee of SmartChips has previously accessed FastCars' standard. This function has the parameters `user` and `role` that define conditions on the returned nodes. The first parameter `user` specifies that only nodes that have been accessed by the specified user should be returned. Analogously, we define the parameter `role`. Both parameters can be set to `any` to indicate that nodes accessed by any user or in any role should be returned. In Rule 10a, we use `any, current` as parameters for the `ac:accessed` function, which indicates that all objects accessed by any subject who was active in the same role as the current subject should be returned. As a result, all objects that were accessed by an employee of SmartChips are returned. If we use `current, current` as parameters for the `ac:accessed` function, we get different semantics. In this case, all objects that were accessed by the current subject are returned. As a result, access is blocked only for an individual employee, while the access of other employees is not blocked. The requirements of the scenario determine which of the two options is chosen. If access is restricted at the level of employees, we retain more flexibility since other employees of SmartChips can continue to work on EcoCars' standard while only employees that have accessed FastCars' standard are not permitted to edit it. On the other hand, if the information in the FastCars' standard is very confidential, this flexible version might not be sufficiently restrictive; employees of SmartChips could pass their knowledge on outside the IT system, and a different employee could transfer the confidential information. In such cases, the more restrictive version should be applied.

Next, we explain how to express the second alternative with our access-control rules. Instead of denying any access, we can deny edit access only. To do this, we need to define rules similar to Rule 10a, where we need one rule for each of the editing operations `create`, `delete`, `change-attribute` and `copy`. In a similar fashion to the case where we denied the viewing, we can deny the editing both at the level of employees as well as at the level of the entire company. Rule 10b_1 and Rule 10b_2 deny editing access for all employees of SmartChips if any employee of Smart-Chips has accessed FastCars' standard. Alternatively, editing can be denied for only the specific employee if the parameters of the `ac:accessed` function are set to `current, current`.

Rule 10b_1. Deny editing by SmartChips after access to FastCars' standard

Role	employee-smartchips
Operation	create, delete, change-attribute
Object	//*[((/*/@class == 'EcoCars') and (fn:count(ac:accessed(any, current)[/*/@company == 'FastCars']) > 0)]
Mode	deny

Rule 10b_2. Deny copying by SmartChips after access to FastCars' standard

Role	`employee-smartchips`
Operation	`copy`
Object	`//*[fn:count(ac:accessed(any, cur-` `rent)[/*/@company == 'FastCars']) > 0]`
Destination	`//*[/*/@class == 'EcoCars']`
Mode	`deny`

The third alternative is the least restrictive one. In this case, we only deny explicit transfers of parts of FastCars' standard to EcoCars' standard. Rule 10c is the access-control rule for this alternative. It is the least restrictive version of the three sketched alternatives since both viewing and editing are still allowed.

Rule 10c. Deny copying after access to FastCars' standard.

Role	`employee-smartchips`
Operation	`copy`
Object	`//*[fn:root(ac:copies(.)[1])/@class` `== 'FastCars']`
Destination	`//*[/*/@class == 'EcoCars']`
Mode	`deny`

The three alternatives show that our history-based approach is sufficiently expressive to offer different ways to define access to standards.

9.6 Related Work

The model proposed in Bertino and Ferrari (2002) supports selective authorizations to parts of documents based on the semantic structure of XML documents. Authorizations can be defined for different nodes together with propagation options. Regarding these aspects, the model is very similar to our work. However, the supported operations and their semantics are different, since our approach is able to differentiate between objects with different histories. The support of copying data differs from our work, since the model proposed in Bertino and Ferrari (2002) supports only a push of different views of a document to different sets of users whereas our model allows us to define which elements of one document may be reused in other documents. Similar approaches can be found in Damiani et al. (2000, 2002), Gabillon and Bruno (2002), and Murata et al. (2003), where Gabillon and Bruno and Murata et al. consider access-control rules for the read operation only. All these approaches consider the XML element as the smallest unit of protection. In contrast, our approach is capable of handling parts of the text content.

Iwaihara et al. (2005) allow for defining access based on the version relationship of documents and elements among each other. They define six operations including *copy*, which is similar to our copy operation but can only be applied to elements or subtrees and not to text content or parts of text content. In contrast to our model, the modification of the text content of an element is modeled by the operation *update* only, which states that the entire content of a node is replaced with new content. Concerning access control, Iwaihara et al. only consider read and write operations and do not define a copy operation as part of their privileges. Consequently, they cannot express which transfers among documents are permitted or denied. Moreover, they do not consider the concept of splitting copied elements in order to have different history information for parts from different sources.

9.7 Conclusion

In this chapter, we have shown how to model access to standards. To illustrate the challenges of this task we presented a scenario. Then, we described our history-based model for defining access control for XML documents. We have defined five operations which can be invoked by human subjects to view and manipulate standards which are stored in XML documents. The effects of the operations are recorded in histories. This history information includes the source of the parts of a document that were transferred from different documents as well as the former states of each document. We have presented access-control rules that use history information, and we have proposed a security architecture with an efficient workflow for editing standards.

Additionally, we have demonstrated how our model can be used to enforce the policies of the presented scenario. The resulting rules allow several alternative methods for enforcing policies, with different levels of flexibility and security.

10 Case Study: An Application for Dynamic Semantic E-Business Integration – The ORBI Ontology Mediator

The ORBI Ontology Mediator is a system designed to support users of arbitrary applications with semantic synchronization services. Its purpose is to reconcile, and thus mediate, the differences between ontologies. As a framework, it connects ontology engineering and artificial intelligence tools and combines them with application components based on the methodology developed above.

In the following, we first describe the integration scenarios for the system's services. We then discuss the system's functionality in more detail.

10.1 E-Business Integration Scenarios

As stated in Chapter 1, the main objective of the research reported here is to allow the integration of e-business processes and information flows – especially in open, dynamic and interactive environments, where classical, static approaches will not work satisfactorily. The way the mediator system is designed, it addresses the requirements stemming from such application scenarios.

The ORBI Ontology Mediator is realized using web-based technologies, thus exploiting the generally high acceptance and universal availability of the Internet and its underlying technologies. All relevant system functionality is available as web services. Designing the application as a configurable framework allows for its use as an openly available service as well as its deployment for specific purposes within organizations.

To be able to support dynamic integration settings, the mediating service provides semantic synchronization at run-time. Due to its flexible framework design, there are several configuration alternatives for using the ORBI synchronization functionality.

First, the system can be accessed via the Internet using its browser-based *user interface*. Alternatively, using the ORBI *browser plug-in* allows requests from within any webpage or web-based application by means of a pop-up context menu. Third, the ORBI *web services* can be called directly from any application that is web-service-enabled. This option is used if the referencing services are to be integrated into a specific business application.

Concerning the user community addressed, the systems usage may be open or restricted. The systems' services may be freely available via the Internet. Alternatively, an in-house setup may be envisioned for exclusive use within a single enterprise only. Within extranets or comparable networks, specific enterprise reference collections may serve as a continuous comprehensive communication support tool among network partners.

10.1.1 User Interface

The ORBI Ontology Mediator provides a web-based user interface, which is implemented with Java Server Faces (JSF) (JSR-127 Expert Group 2004), including some interactive components implemented in Flash, a format for interactive webpage elements displayed by a browser plug-in (Adobe 2007). Figures 10.1 and 10.2 show screenshots of the interface.

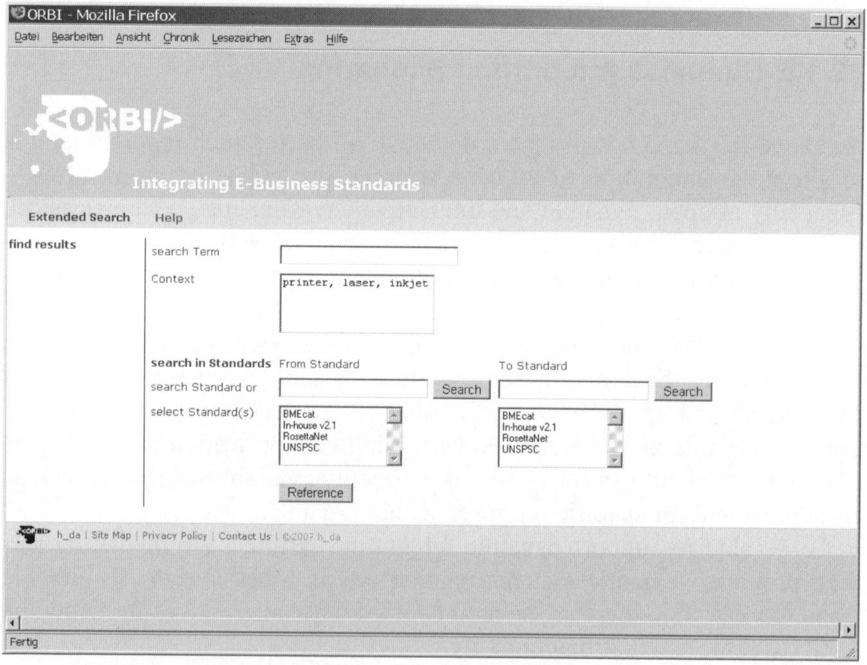

Fig. 10.1. ORBI user interface: extended search mask

From the core system's point of view, the web-based user interface is yet another client application, using the same web services as other client applications.

The interface is designed to allow easy, intuitive use of the ORBI Ontology Mediator's functionality without advance training. It can be used if an application cannot be connected to the ORBI Ontology Mediator via web services, if the user only wants to inquire about e-business standards and their relations, or for administrative purposes.

To allow access with minimum installation effort, the interface is web-based and runs on an application server (not necessarily the same one as the ORBI Ontology Mediator). Further design principals include:

- Simple and self-explanatory use
- Fault tolerance (e.g., using intelligent search mechanisms)
- Easy customizability

Users can search for references, using either a simple or an extended search mask, as can be seen in Figure 10.1. The result list returned is shown in Figure 10.2.

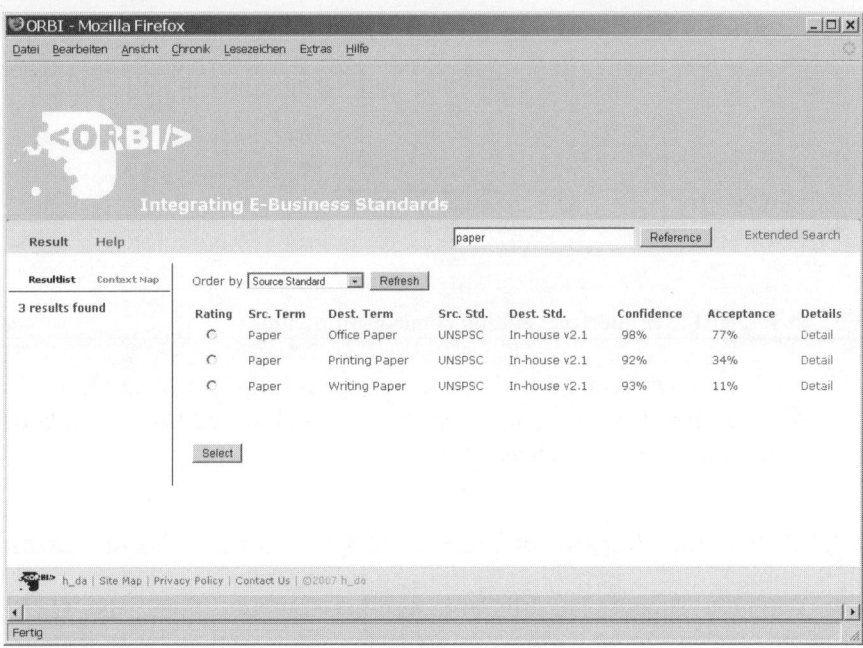

Fig. 10.2. ORBI user interface: result list

Results can be selected and are copied to the clipboard for further use. When a reference is selected, a rating is automatically generated. The result list can be ordered according to the user's preferences, e.g., by term, by standard, or other criteria.

Interactive graphics support the user in manipulating their context information, as can be seen in Figure 10.3, creating new references and browsing standards for understanding a reference.

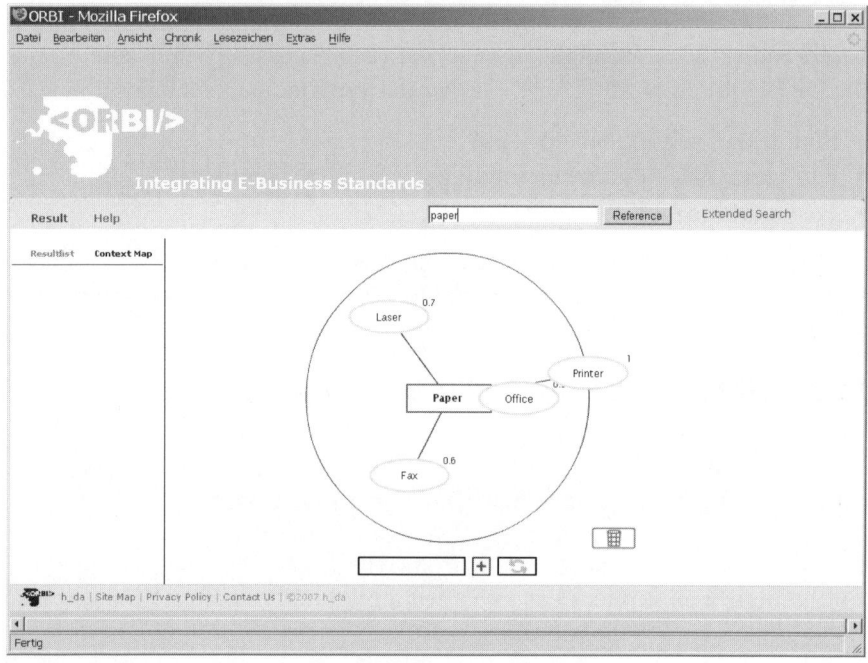

Fig. 10.3. ORBI user interface: editing context information

For access to advanced functions, a user needs to log in. After login, users are thus provided with options such as to import additional standards and to edit and delete references.

10.1.2 Browser Plug-In for Web-Based E-Business Applications

For semantic support in arbitrary web-based applications, the ORBI browser plug-in can be used. Thus, extensive additional software installation can be avoided. Users can mark terms in the webpages displayed by the application and retrieve semantic references with the help of the plug-in. The user can flag suggested references as either appropriate or inappro-

priate and thus create feedback. In this case, context information for disambiguating different references is extracted from the actual webpage. The
plug-in is capable of determining the context by including the neighboring
terms of the marked term to be referenced, up to a certain distance. Figure
10.4 shows an example.

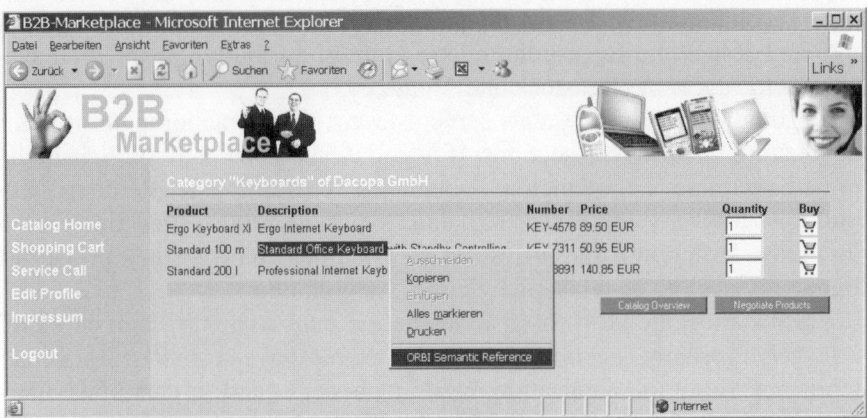

Fig. 10.4. ORBI browser plug-in context menu

10.1.3 Web-Service-Based Application Integration

For using the ORBI functionality from within arbitrary business applications, ORBI web services can be called directly. As examples for the wide
range of integration possibilities, we discuss two configurations in more
detail.

Multiple Data-Source Querying

The first scenario is multiple data-source querying. For example, this can
support the task of retrieving offers from different electronic marketplaces.
In this case, a common query interface is presented to the user, where
query information can be entered. The common interface transforms the
entered information into the individual metadata formats in order to gather
and aggregate the search results. Those results are retransformed into the
metadata format used by the common query interface and presented to the
user.

As metadata formats can be described as ontologies, the common query
interface can use the semantic synchronization service to retrieve references from the interface's internal metadata format to the individual data

sources' metadata formats. For the resolution of ambiguous results returned by different queries, the systems' disambiguation methods can be used.

Electronic Negotiation Platform

As a second example for the integration of semantic referencing services into an application, we use the bilateral, multi-attributive negotiation system *MultiNeg/M2N* (Rebstock and Thun 2003).

Negotiation support systems serve as a virtual interaction platforms for negotiating business transactions. If negotiations do contain more than just price bargaining, i.e., if they are conducted regarding multiple items with multiple, arbitrary attributes, semantic synchronization often becomes a necessity. Different names or values for positions, items or their properties frequently need to be reconciled during a negotiation.

For instance, the need for disambiguation may come up when checking an offer. Presently, negotiation partners would have to reconcile unclear terms outside of the application, e.g., by phone, e-mail or chat, thus interrupting the electronic process. Using the ORBI web service allows requesting a semantic reference at any point during a negotiation. Figure 10.5 shows an activity diagram depicting the respective process.

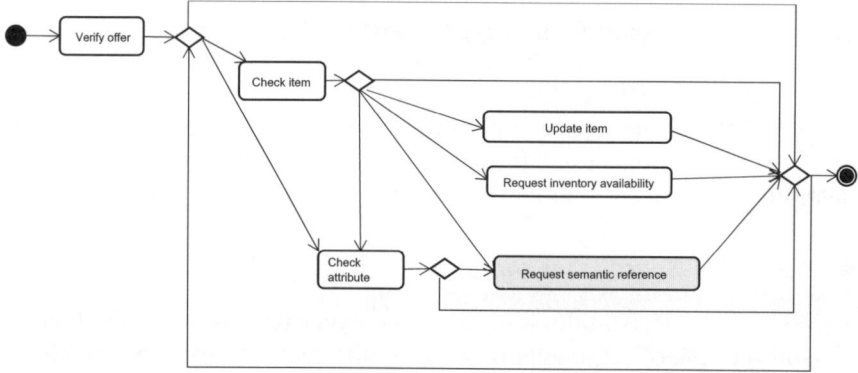

Fig. 10.5. Activity diagram: check offer

To clarify the content negotiated, when changing the offer a reference for a term in the partner's version of the offer to one's own term in the new version of the offer may be added. Thus, in the course of the negotiation, semantic reference attributes can be negotiated like any other item or attribute. Upon the conclusion of a negotiation, the semantic reference attributes become part of the contract. Figure 10.6 shows the activity diagram for such an offer modification process.

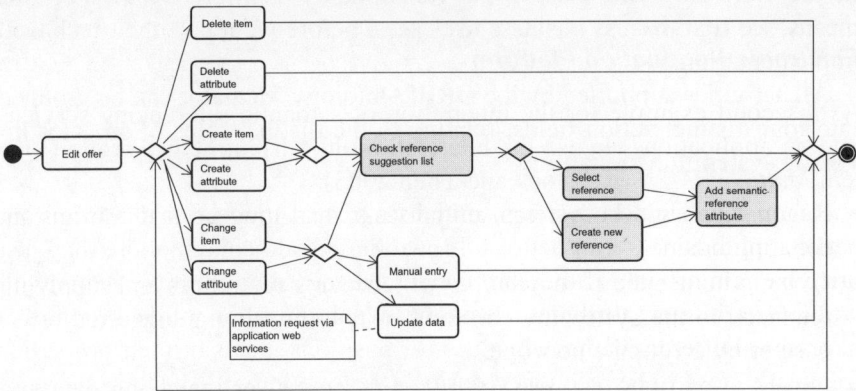

Fig. 10.6. Activity diagram: modify offer

Figure 10.7 shows an example of an ORBI web service call from within the MultiNeg/M2N electronic negotiation support system and the successive storing of reference attributes (Simon et al. 2007).

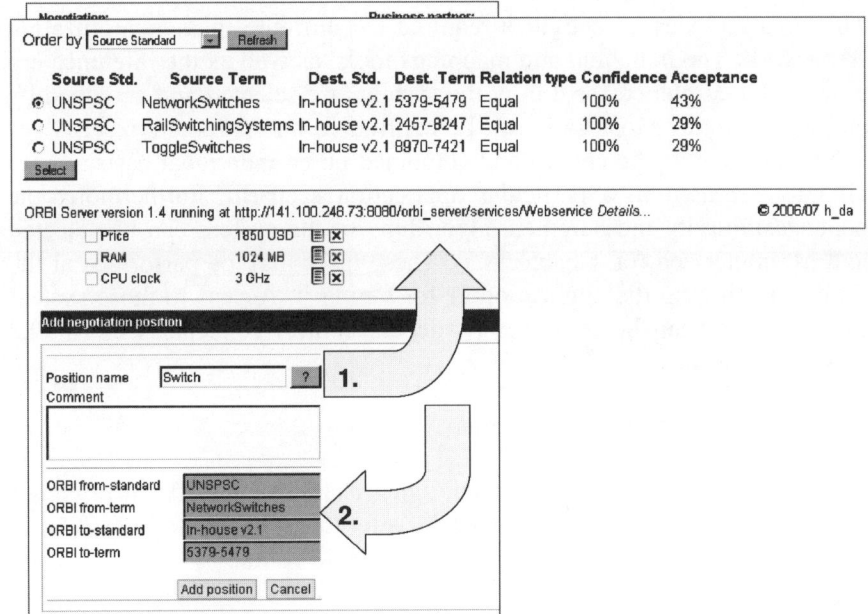

Fig. 10.7. Integration of semantic referencing into MultiNeg/M2N

10.2 Use Cases

In the following, we discuss the functionality in more detail. For this means, we first discuss business use cases, before we report their technical implementation.

All activities supported by the ORBI Ontology Mediator can be grouped into four distinct action fields, relating to the distinct roles of an actor invoking system functionality:

- *Administrators*, who perform initial tasks of setting up and configuring the application.
- *Users,* who use the *core functions* of retrieving references and supplying feedback to the system by choosing or not choosing a suggested reference or by creating a new one.
- *Expert users*, who can use *advanced functions* for managing data and have more options of extending and enhancing the reference collection.
- The *system* itself, when working autonomously for creating and assessing references.

10.2.1 Administrator Activities

This area includes all activities required to configure the synchronization framework. The matching and mappings tools, as well as the inference engines to be combined for use by the system, are selected and activated by an administrator. Most tools can be configured and parameterized. Algorithms can thereby be chosen and combined on an individual basis as specifically required in a particular application scenario. Furthermore, the context similarity measurement algorithms of the system can be selected and parameterized (cf. Chapter 8.3). These tasks may be performed at the time of setting up the application or for tuning it. Access to those system functionalities can be restricted by access control concepts. Figure 10.8 shows the use cases.

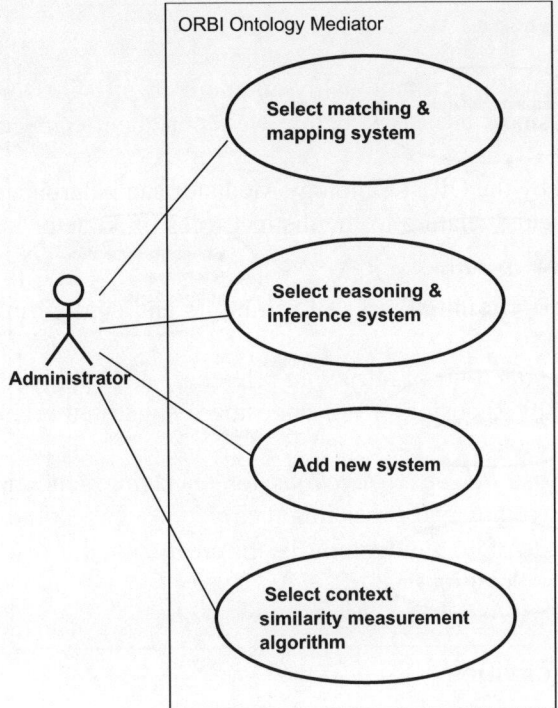

Fig. 10.8. Use case diagram: administrator activities

10.2.2 User Activities

This area is the core area for realizing ontologies-based reconciliation. Users retrieve semantic references and choose from the suggested reference list. In general, arbitrary client applications may be invoked. The referencing services can be used by one user or by several users at once, depending on the type of application supported and the kind of integration implementation chosen. Figure 10.9 shows the use cases.

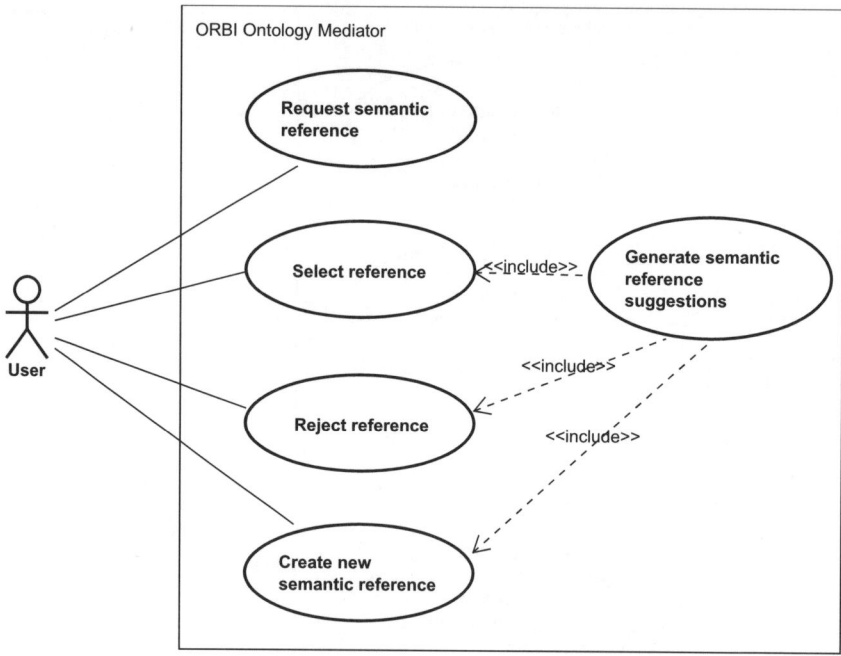

Fig. 10.9. Use case diagram: user activities

10.2.3 Expert User Activities

This area comprises the activities required for the creation and maintenance of the reference collection and initiates the actions constituting the
adaptive semi-automated referencing process as introduced above. New
standards can be converted into ontologies and imported into the system.
New references can be entered manually, and existing ones can be edited
or deleted. Figure 10.10 depicts the respective use cases.

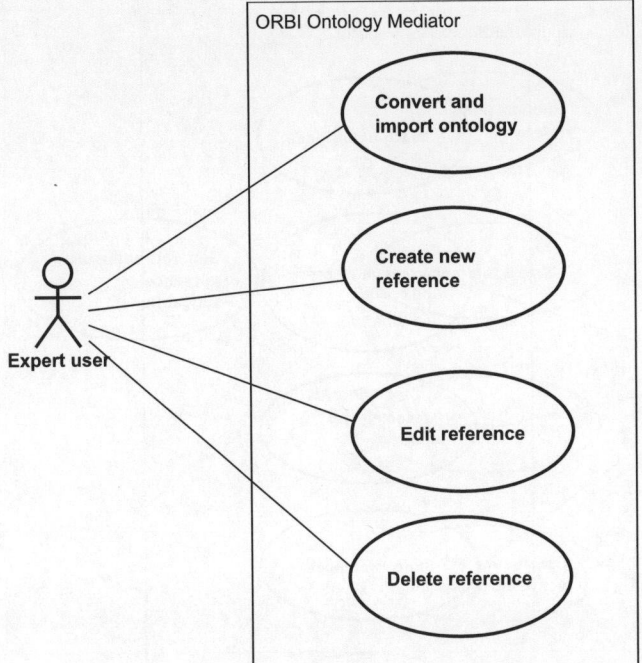

Fig. 10.10. Use case diagram: expert user activities

10.2.4 System Activities

The system will automatically match and establish mappings between the ontology entities. The discovered correspondences are specified and stored for further use. Also, the reference collection is used for deriving new knowledge. These activities are performed autonomously by the system; they may be started automatically by the system or triggered manually by a user. Figure 10.11 shows the use cases.

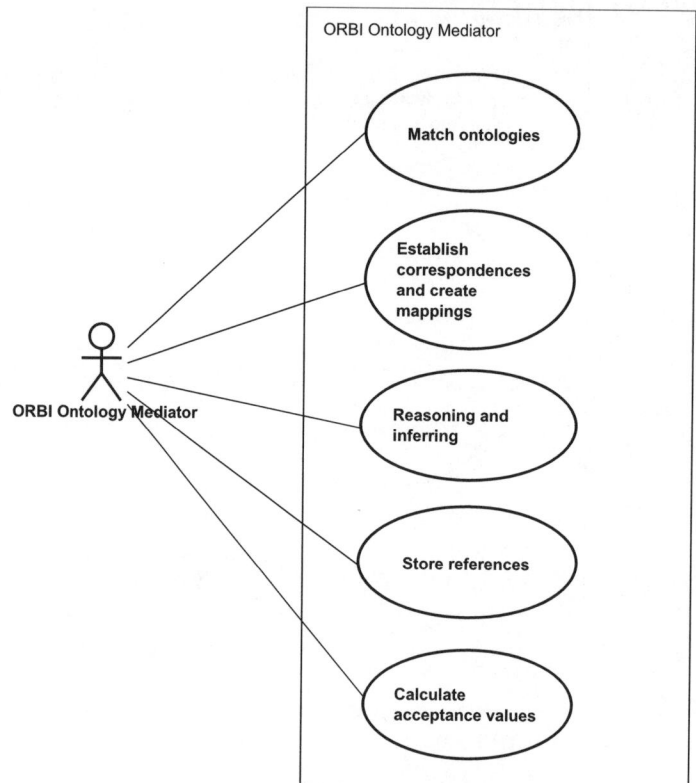

Fig. 10.11. Use case diagram: system activities

10.3 Web Service Functionality

The following functionality implements the use cases. It can be divided into *core functions*, *advanced functions* and *support functions*. Administrative activities for system configuration as well as internal, autonomous system activities are not offered as web services. Support functions are not directly called by users and have therefore not been specified by use cases.

As administrators perform configuration activities that are not available as a web service, two user types access web service functionality: (standard) users and expert users. As mentioned before, the web services available can either be called by the ORBI Ontology Mediator's own web interface, by its browser plug-in or by external client applications.

10.3.1 Core Functions

The ORBI Ontology Mediator's core functions assist users in their work with semantic references. Therefore, those functions are designed according to basic use cases. Those basic use cases are as follows:

- Request semantic reference (for a term in a given context)
- Rate semantic reference in a given context by selecting or rejecting
- Create new semantic reference

These functions are straightforward implementations of basic users' needs: the user requests a list of possible references. When the result list does not contain the reference needed, the user can create a new reference, which is possible using the applicable function.

If the result list contains the reference needed, which is of course the most desirable case, the user can select that reference in order to work with it. Selecting a reference means giving, implicitly, that reference a positive rating; on the other hand, not selecting the other references presented in the result list means giving those references a negative rating. Thus, all of the references presented in the result list receive either a positive or a negative rating as a result of just one user action: selecting a reference.

10.3.2 Advanced Functions

Expert users have access to additional functionality, including the following:

- Convert and import ontology (i.e., standard)
- Edit reference
- Delete reference

When importing an additional standard, the expert user inserts (or uploads) a new file representing the standard into the system. That file is internally converted to the framework's object model by a conversion plug-in. Every file format for which a conversion plug-in is present can be processed (see below). Note that a format is not only a technical file format, such as CSV or XML, but can also include further information on the files' structure. Such information can include the definition of columns and their meanings in CSV files, e.g., for importing the Excel versions of UNSPSC, or the structure and meaning of elements of XML files, e.g., for importing the XML files of the RosettaNet Business Dictionary.

After the file has been converted to the framework's object model, it is converted again, for storage, into the storage model, e.g., a relational database model, by the persistence layer, as depicted in Figure 10.12. The conversion steps are taken in the opposite direction when retrieving a stored standard and presenting it to the user.

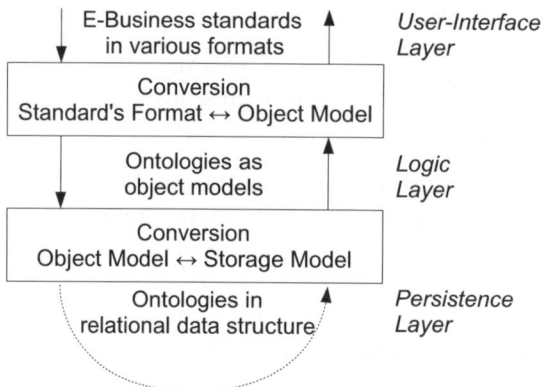

Fig. 10.12. Data conversion in different steps

While standard users can only use the collection of semantic references by creating and rating them, expert users can also alter references directly, i.e., changing the relation type, the referenced terms or the confidence value. They can also delete a reference when it has proven to be inappropriate.

10.3.3 Support Functions

Both core and administrative functions require additional support functions that are not directly called by user actions. These include the following:

- Retrieve a list of all standards
- Retrieve a list of all supported formats for standards
- Find terms in a standard
- Retrieve a subset from a standard

The system can display a list of standards to the user for information purposes. This list can be used to restrict a query's search result to certain standards.

The list of supported formats is needed when a new standard is to be added; it shows which formats for the standard can be processed by the system. The expert user can provide a standard file in one of those formats, which then is stored as described above.

When a new reference is created, the user first has to identify the terms to be referenced in the standards. This can be done in two different ways:

- Directly searching for the term in the standard by its name, for which a support function is provided.
- Browsing the standard visually. Since standards can be large, it is more convenient to look at just parts of them. For visualizing parts of standards, a support function for retrieving a subset of a standard is provided.

When the terms to be referenced are identified using either one of those two methods, they can be linked by a semantic reference, using the core function of creating a new reference.

10.4 Class Model for Reference Management

Based on the 5-tuple form of semantic references introduced earlier, the class model has been developed. Figure 10.13 shows the class diagram.

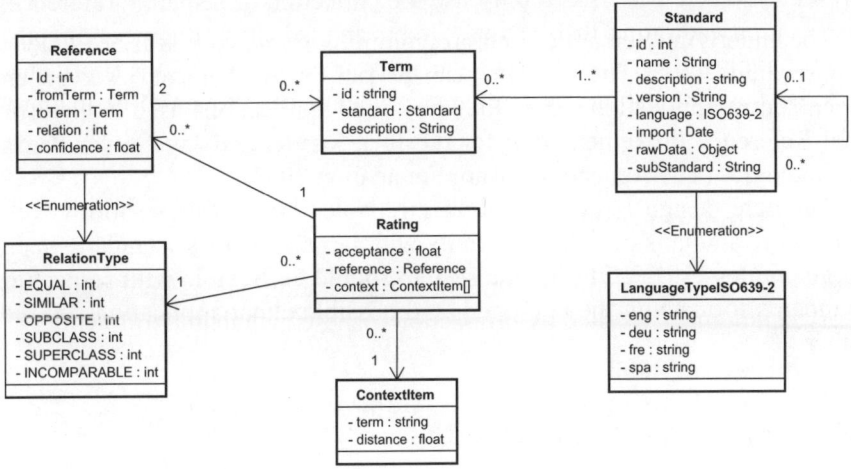

Fig. 10.13. Class diagram: reference management

Modeling the relation between the classes Term and Standard with the cardinality 0..* allows for the usage of terms that do not belong to an ontology or standard, respectively. For the class RelationType, an enumeration is foreseen. Upon the coupling of mapping tools, this can be extended or amended according to the results of the particular tool. Accep-

`tance` is not modeled as an individual class as its dynamically changing value is computed individually for each reference request at run-time.

10.5 Implementation

The ORBI Ontology Mediator is implemented on top of open-source Java and Semantic Web technologies. Its modular design uses adapters, plug-ins and a run-time configuration mechanism to maximize flexibility and extensibility.

10.5.1 Technology

In order to allow the use of the system's functionality in as many different integration scenarios as possible, its functions can be accessed as web services, using SOAP via HTTP requests or using the Apache AXIS (Apache Web Services Project 2007), which is an open-source implementation of the W3C recommendation for the SOAP web services standard (W3C 2007).

The underlying Semantic Web programming framework is JENA2 (Jena Consortium 2007). The mediator can be run on the Tomcat 5 server, an open-source application server for Java-based applications used in the official Reference Implementation for the Java Servlet and JavaServer Pages technologies (The Apache Software Foundation 2007).

The core design issue is creating a reliable service that performs well with large amounts of data, especially with large e-business standards, i.e., large ontologies. In addition, the system should be flexible with respect to standards formats on the one hand, and possible client applications on the other.

10.5.2 System Architecture

The ORBI Ontology Mediator's core system is divided into two main parts: the references subsystem and the ratings subsystem, as shown in Figure 10.11. The references subsystem is responsible for storing semantic references as well as the referenced standards. If adapters to mapping and inference systems are configured, it also calls those systems to find semantic references automatically. Mapping and inference systems are called asynchronously with a scheduling mechanism; they may need more time to compute, so in this way the system is not blocked and can still answer users' queries. Examples of the detailed interaction of the subsystems and connected components are shown in Figure 10.14.

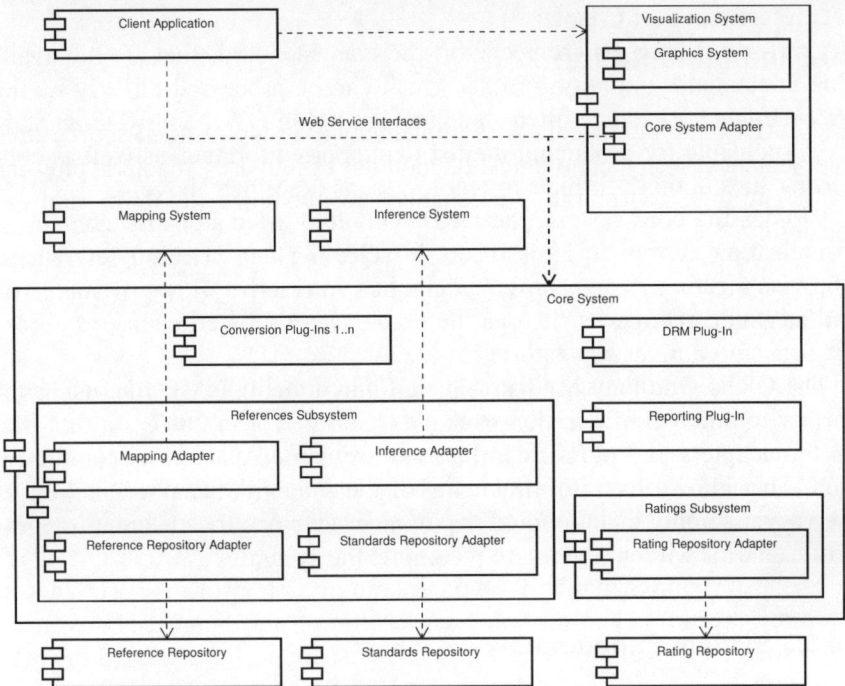

Fig. 10.14. ORBI Ontology Mediator architecture

The ratings subsystem is responsible for storing and evaluating the users' ratings of semantic references, including the ratings' context information. It calculates the references' acceptance values, depending on the querying user's context, and presents references ordered by that acceptance value, as described in Chapter 6.

Standards, references and ratings are stored in repositories, which are connected to the core system via adapters. The storage format is defined by those adapters that are actually used and can range from text or XML files to relational databases. The adapters are capable of rendering standards and references in arbitrary representations, such as RDF/S or OWL. In this way, for the purpose of visualizing and employing reasoning tools, the applicable format is selectable.

The core system's functionality can be further enhanced by several plug-ins. A reporting plug-in can monitor the system's performance (qualitative as well as quantitative) and generate reports showing the system's behavior over time.

An access control and digital rights management (DRM) plug-in can be used if there is information in the system that should be restricted to certain users. Such information can include private standards as well as private references (see Chapter 9).

Conversion plug-ins are needed if there are standards that are not available in standard ontology formats which can be processed directly by the JENA framework, since often standards are not in OWL and RDF/S. They are responsible for producing the list of supported formats, as well as converting files in those formats to ontologies, as described above.

Besides the core system, the ORBI Ontology Mediator also contains a visualization system to assist users in selecting and creating references. The visualization system provides graphic, interactive views of standards and semantic references. It uses the core system's functionality to access the data stored in the repositories.

The ORBI Ontology Mediator is configured via an XML file, using Jakarta's common configuration package (Jakarta Project 2007). In that file, all the adapters and plug-ins to be used are named as well as parameterized. That allows for the influencing of the system's behavior as well as the easy assembly of individual deployment versions for different integration scenarios without having to recompile the system.

10.5.3 System Functionality

Each time a request is directed to the core system or its web service interface – i.e., a core, administrative or support function is called – the core system calls functions on the subsystems to answer the requests. The most commonly used function, a query for semantic references, uses both the references and the ratings subsystem, as shown in Figure 10.15.

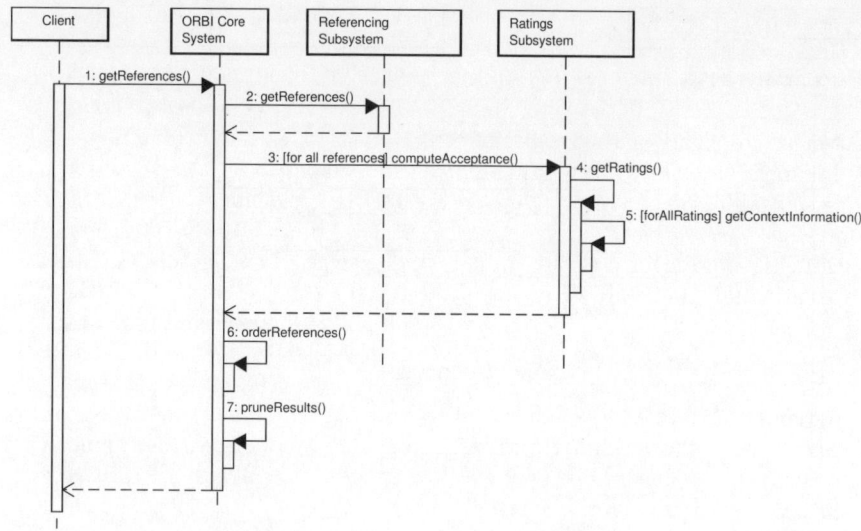

Fig. 10.15. Sequence diagram: request semantic reference

First, all references that could potentially fit the query are retrieved by the referencing subsystem. That means that a wildcard search is done on the search term entered by the user; the search might be restricted to certain standards if the user decided only to look for references within some, not all, standards. These references are called reference candidates. Then, the acceptance value for each reference candidate is calculated by the ratings subsystem, taking into account all ratings for the reference candidate and weighting each rating according to its context information. After calculating the acceptance values, the list of results is ordered according to these values and pruned according to certain criteria. These criteria can include employing a minimum acceptance threshold, thus presenting only semantic references that are suitable to at least a certain degree, or only presenting the uppermost references. The pruning step thereby turns a reference candidate into a reference. The list of references is then returned to the user.

The function of creating a reference is processed as shown in Figure 10.16.

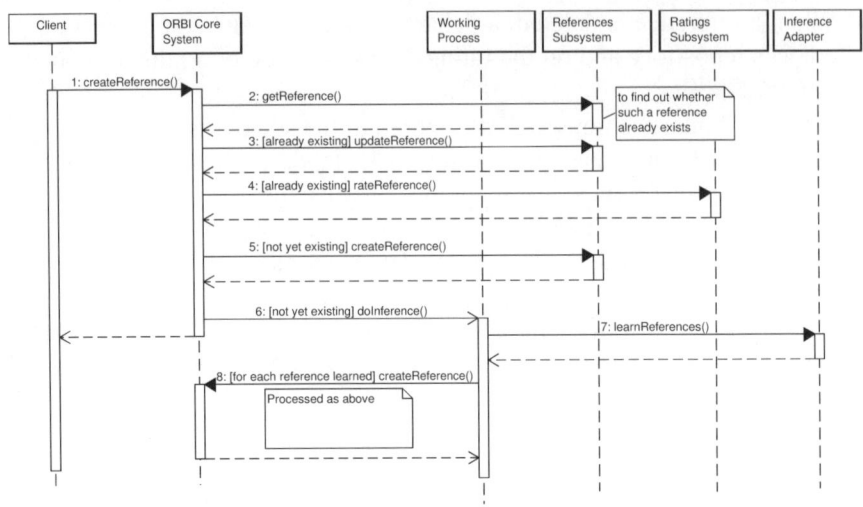

Fig. 10.16. Sequence diagram: create new semantic reference

First, the system checks if a reference like the one to be created already exists. If a reference which has the same relation type and the same terms is found in the reference repository, its confidence value is updated and set to the value of the reference the user wanted to create. Then, a rating in the user's context is stored by the ratings subsystem (which is the action also triggered when a user rates a reference).

If, on the other hand, such a reference does not yet exist, it is created and stored in the repository. If an inference system is connected to the core system with an adapter, it is called to derive new references from the newly created one. The call to the inference adapter is processed by an asynchronous working process, so that the client's query can be closed. For each reference found by the inference system, the process of creating a new reference is started again. This implies that the inference system can be called many times, until no more new references are found. A scheduling mechanism guards the calls to the inference adapter to make sure that they are executed in a reasonable order, avoiding unnecessary calls.

The other functions are implemented similarly. Altering a reference works in the same way as creating a reference, omitting steps 2 and 3. Most of the other functions require a call of just one or two single adapters:

- When a reference is rated, the rating is stored directly in the ratings repository.

- When a reference is deleted, a delete operation is carried out on the references repository and on the ratings repository, deleting the reference's ratings as well.
- When a standard is imported, it is stored in the standards repository. The mapping adapter is called once for each standard already contained in the system; thus it runs dual mappings on all standards and thereby finds references from the new standard to all standards in the system. For each reference found, the inference adapter is called, as shown in steps 7 and 8 in Figure 10.16.
- The functions for retrieving a list of standards, finding a term in a standard and retrieving a subset of a standard are processed directly by the standards repository.

10.5.4 External Systems Adapters

The framework provides adapters for coupling additional mapping and reasoning systems. A variety of tools for ontology matching and mapping is presently available, and these are often concentrated on implementing a specific method, as introduced in Chapter 5. Many of the open-source or freely available tools have the status of an academic prototype and may not scale according to real-world business requirements. Some experiments regarding the processing of realistic data loads have been conducted already. The object of investigation has been eClass. For example, due to the data file size of 25 MB in OWL, performance problems occurred when using Protégé (Hepp 2006a). However, the amount of enterprise data stored in relational databases and processed in daily business operations with the assistance of standard COTS software is usually considerably higher (Hepp 2006a; Bouquet et al. 2005). This presents a challenge for many ontology engineering tools (Hu et al. 2006).

There exist state-of-the-art open-source tools for determining ontology mappings without merging the source ontologies. These are not matching or mapping systems concentrating on the procedure alone, but rather tools with a framework character, since the mappings generated can be manipulated or composed within the given infrastructure (Euzenat and Shvaiko 2007). Readily available are COMA++ (COMA 2006), from the field of schema matching, and FOAM (FOAM 2007) and the Alignment API (Euzenat 2006), from the field of ontology matching. COMA++ (Combination of Match Algorithms) focuses on combining different match operators for finding semantic correspondences into an infrastructure for processing large amounts of data. FOAM (Framework for Ontology Alignment and Mapping) uses QOM (Quick Ontology Mapping) as the tool for mapping creation and concentrates on the trade-off necessary between quality and efficiency. In this framework several methods are combined, and through adapting the results, performance enhancements are achieved with only minor quality reductions (Ehrig and Staab 2004). The Alignment API offers functionality for editing the mappings discovered. Table 10.1 provides an overview.

Table 10.1. Overview of open state-of-the-art mapping tools

	COMA++	FOAM/QOM	Alignment API
Developer	University Leipzig (D)	University Karlsruhe (D)	INRIA Alpes (Fr)
Focus	Schema Matching	Ontology Mapping	Ontology Mapping
Input	XSD / OWL	RDF/S / OWL	RDF/S / OWL
Output	1:1-mapping pairs	unspecified mapping pairs	mapping pairs with all cardinalities
Syntactical match on element level	string-, language-based, data types	string-, language-based, data types	string-, language-based
external information	Thesauri, mapping reuse	WordNet	yes
Syntactical match on structure level	yes	yes	yes
Java based	yes	yes	yes
Prerequisite	MySQL	KAON2	OWL API

In order to exploit the different approaches of these mapping tools, an automated parallel iterative mapping process can be developed, with each cycle using another of the tools. Combining these tools provides results of higher quality (Ehrig 2007). The CROSI mapping tool is a framework enabling the coupling of several mapping tools into a hybrid system. It does not perform several cycles, but conducts searches based on different algorithms in parallel. In addition to internal match operators, FOAM and the Alignment API can be added as external matchers. Since the findings of these tools are very different, they can complement each other. The aggregation of their computing outcomes provides meaningful results (Kalfoglou 2005b).

Similarly, in the field of inference engines, there are several tools available. Among the major Semantic Web reasoners there are some commercially available and two openly available implementations (Liebig 2006). They are well defined by being based on model theoretic semantics. Both Pellet (Sirin et al. 2007) and FaCT++ (Tsarkov and Horrocks 2006) are fully implemented and under active development. Table 10.2 provides an overview.

Table 10.2. Overview of open state-of-the-art reasoners

	Pellet	FaCT++
Developer	University of Maryland (US)	University of Manchester (UK)
Input	OWL-DL	OWL-DL
Multiple ontologies	E-Connections	merge with owl:imports
ABox Query	yes	yes
TBox Query	yes	standard
Java based	yes	no (C++)
Interface	various	DIG
Combination	OWL API	OWL API

Still, recent tests show bugs in these systems and scalability issues (Liebig 2006). Furthermore, in the literature so far, no attempts seem to have been made regarding a possible combination of these approaches. Further developments have to be awaited.

10.6 System Evaluation

Experiments have been carried out with large numbers of simulation queries in order to examine the ranking mechanism's qualitative performance. To this end, artificial context data with certain statistic features, created using heuristics, was used. As intuitively assumed, the smaller the number of references to disambiguate is, the better the ranking mechanism works.

Figure 10.17 shows the most relevant simulation results. Different curves in the diagram show results for different numbers of references (r) to be disambiguated. The number of ratings (N) is noted on the x-axis. It can thus be interpreted as a time axis, because the number of ratings increases over time, as the system is used. On the y-axis, a normalized value of the correctness of the result (C) is noted; 1 meaning that the desired reference is presented in the first position of the result list and 0 that it is presented in the last position.

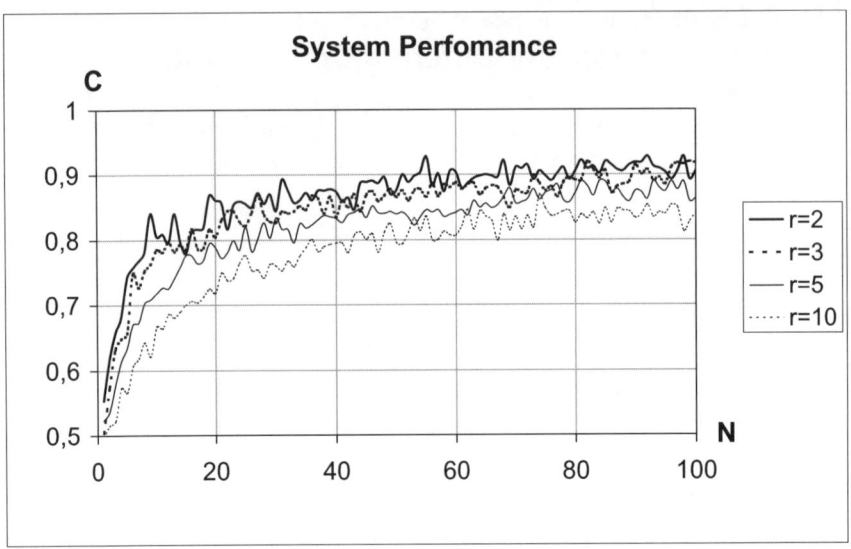

Fig. 10.17. Performance for different numbers of references

It can be observed that the maximum value for result correctness lies between 0.8 and 0.95, depending on the average number of references that
have to be disambiguated for answering a query. It can be assumed that for
$r > 10$, the results will lie below the lowest curve. But despite the actual
number of references, it can be seen that the system's performance im-
proves with an increasing number of ratings, arriving at a fair quality with
approximately 40 ratings. This means that the more ratings there are per
reference, the more accurately the system can tell appropriate references
from inappropriate ones, given a certain context.

The experiments have also shown that the system's performance depends heavily on the nature of context information used, as demonstrated
in Figure 10.18. The three graphs represent different simulation scenarios,
which differ in terms of two parameters: a) the average similarity of sets of
context data for the same reference, called sim_{same}, and b) the average similarity of sets of context data for different references, called sim_{diff}.

The experiments have shown that the crucial factor is the difference of
these two parameters, $d = sim_{same} - sim_{diff}$. The best results are achieved for
a high value of that difference, i.e., for a high value of sim_{same} and a low
value of sim_{diff}. In Figure 10.18, the performance measures for difference
values $d = 5$, 20, and 70 are shown.

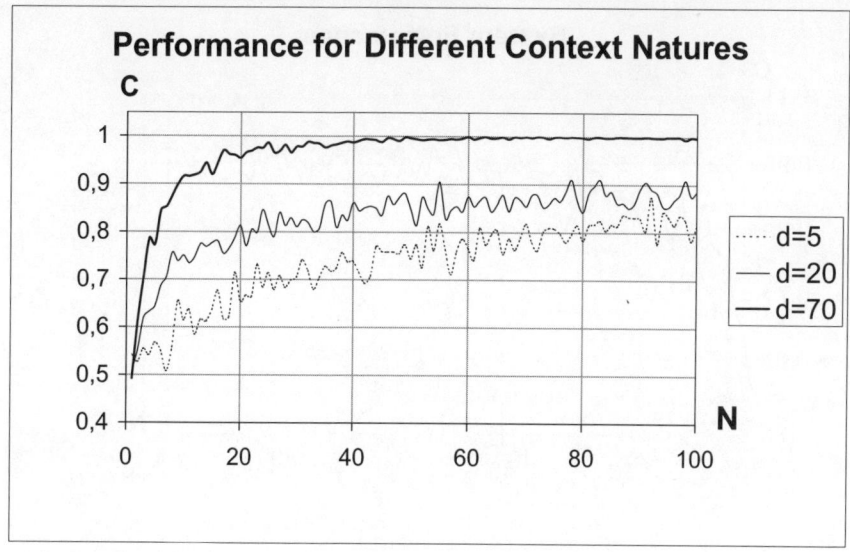

Fig. 10.18. Performance for different kinds of context natures

The first observation is that for a high difference value, the system's qualitative performance has a limit of 1, which means that it almost always presents the desired information in the top position. The second observation is that even for the poor case, in which the difference is only 5, the limit of C is still about 0.8.

A high value of sim_{same} and a low value of sim_{diff} result in a high acceptance value for references that fit the query's context, since positive ratings are assigned high weights and negative ratings are assigned a low weight. Likewise, with a low value of sim_{diff} and a high value of sim_{same}, even appropriate references erroneously receive a low acceptance value. If sim_{same} and sim_{diff} are equal, the system is not able to separate appropriate references from inappropriate ones, because their acceptance values will be the same on average.

It might be expected that the size of context information (s) given is a crucial factor for the system's quality. However, as Figure 10.19 shows, context size does not influence the system's quality to a large extent. Based on the findings shown above, it can be concluded that the difference of context similarities is the crucial factor; context size itself is not.

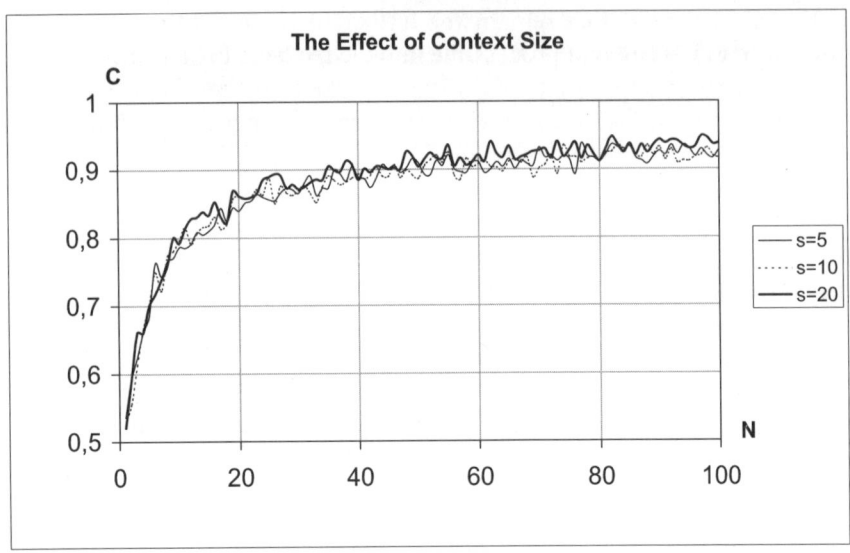

Fig. 10.19. Effect of context size on the quality of results

As an extreme example, a situation can be constructed where the system produces optimal results even with context information consisting of only one element. Consider this context element as the primary key of the reference looked for. In this case, the similarity with the context of positive ratings will always be 1 (for the contexts are identical), and the similarity with contexts of negative ratings will always be 0 (for the contexts have no elements in common). Thus, the acceptance value is 1 for the reference in question, 0 for all other references. Of course, this example is purely artificial, since if the reference's primary key was known, the reference would be as well, which would mean that it would not be necessary to query the system at all. Nevertheless, the example demonstrates that context size as such is not a crucial factor.

10.7 Discussion

The prototypical implementation of the ORBI Ontology Mediator available today and its practical application have shown and proven not only the conceptual strength but also the practical relevance of our approach. Still, a number of aspects remain subject to future research, which we will highlight in the following discussion. Based on further results, the platform will be continuously improved.

Technical aspects that remain for further research deal with the questions of how to store and process the knowledge base for business integration in the most appropriate and efficient way. For very large databases, performance issues are critical. Criteria of special interest for performance evaluation in our context are ontology size, number of references and ratings, and the number of context terms attributed to individual ratings.

The experiments described above have only dealt with qualitative performance, i.e., whether the results the system produces have a satisfactory degree of correctness. The other major issue is quantitative performance, i.e., the time (and memory) consumed to compute the results, so that the user gets a result for his query within a reasonable time.

When working with real-world e-business standards and their representation as ontologies, one has to take into account that the amount of data can be very large. This means that scalability is one of the main technical focus points. Presently, scalability issues could be partly resolved by means of automated partitioning.

Research regarding the comparison and combination of mapping tools has been conducted. However, research on interoperability and coordination of different reasoning tools is still necessary and will be conducted in future steps. Such further research can potentially help in finding individual solutions for different application domains.

The experiments examining the quality of the mechanism for ranking semantic references described above have shown that the system's qualitative performance is better when more ratings are stored. On the other hand, that means that all ratings for one reference have to be processed each time the reference is to be displayed to the user. Thus, efficient storage and processing of ratings and their context information is also a key issue when it comes to quantitative performance.

On the lowest level, performance issues are addressed when selecting repositories that are optimized for larger amounts of data. The ORBI Ontology Mediator's framework architecture allows arbitrary repository solutions, from simple flat files to storage solutions that have been designed to work with large amounts of data, such as OWLIM (Kiryakov et al. 2005). The same holds true for the storage of references, ratings, and context information, where scalable and high-performance storage solutions have to be found.

On the higher levels, when working with large ontologies, it is often impossible to load an entire ontology into memory. Therefore, the framework was implemented in such a way that all operations necessary to the ontologies themselves (mainly the retrieval of parts of ontologies to display or process) can be mapped to queries on the repository, e.g., as a SPARQL query (W3C 2006b), which is processed directly on the persisted data.

Adapters to other existing systems are also implemented in such a fashion that the systems are supplied with partial ontology data on demand, rather than whole ontologies.

Another important factor concerning performance is the number of ratings and the size of context information. As shown, the quality of the acceptance values calculated for a reference increases with the number of ratings available. The downside is, of course, that the time consumed to calculate that value also increases. Given N ratings, each with an average context size s, that time is at least $O(Ns)$, given an efficient implementation of a context similarity measure that touches each element only a constant number of times.

The two possible ways of optimizing the system's response time would therefore be reducing the number of ratings to be processed, and reducing the average context size.

Reducing the number of ratings and using as many ratings as possible to get a result of high quality are clearly conflicting objectives. Hence, it is more promising to try to reduce the average context size, especially since the findings shown above demonstrate that context size does not directly influence the results' quality. At any rate, context size must be reduced in a way that still leads to a high value of $sim_{same} - sim_{diff}$. Producing small context information that fulfills this postulation is a non-trivial task that has to be performed by the client applications, which requires further research activities.

11 Business Integration – Past, Present and Beyond

Business integration has been a manual task for centuries. In Greek and Roman times, document exchange relied on courier runners. The horse-carriage-based postal system developed in medieval Europe, with regular lines and connections, added more regularity and reduced exchange times and costs. Electric and electronic media such as telegraphs, the telephone, telex, fax machines and early computer networks contributed to the same objectives. But even with these advances, the final document and process integration remained a manual, i.e., human task.

The advent of advanced electronic means for business automation established the promise of automated business processes and integration. Standardized business processes can already be executed automatically by using WfMS internally and EDI externally, thus decreasing costs and increasing efficiency, speed and quality. But the vision is that potentially all documents, i.e., information, traveling electronically through business processes can be handed over from process step to process step and from application to application automatically. As we have seen, such a scenario brings with it a great deal of prerequisites. Information has to be *machine-readable* and *-processable,* but not just on a technical and a syntactical level. For documents to be interpreted and integrated into different applications automatically, their content has to be *machine-interpretable*. Solutions have to be flexible enough to cope with dynamic application situations, in which business partners, processes, document types and structures are continuously in flux. Making the semantics of documents machine interpretable was the starting point of the Semantic Web initiative and the many projects that have been and are contributing to this overall objective. This goal is still a long way off; the *"not-yet-semantic Web"* (Allsopp 2007, 5) remains today's reality.

We believe that the results presented in this book are a substantial step towards dynamic e-business integration. We have presented and discussed methods for the dynamic integration of e-business information flows on the semantic level. We have analyzed, designed and built ontologies-based application components supporting such dynamic business integration.

In addition to its results, our work has also produced an outline of the work that lies ahead. With respect to this work, we can distinguish technical, business and conceptual challenges, which we will discuss briefly in the following paragraphs.

11.1 Technical Challenges

Within our actual implementation, storing the knowledge base on a central server brings with it the advantages of a central database: manageability, consistency, security in general and access control specifically. On the other hand, decentralized storage of the knowledge base in a P2P architecture could contribute to the application's dissemination and enhance its availability. In order to be able to deploy and evaluate the application on a P2P platform, questions concerning replication of the database, management of users, and user access require further research.

The actual system architecture is based on the internal storage of references plus the standards themselves. This means easier data retrieval and data management. But, as most standards will be managed by external bodies, updates have to be made for the internal ontologies whenever a new version of a standard is available. Although standards versions can be managed by the application, this means additional system-administration overhead. An architectural alternative is to store only references in the knowledge base of the application itself and to refer to externally stored standards only. So the knowledge base would be free of standards management, if standards are handled by an external body. The retrieval and performance issues of this architectural option remain to be evaluated.

Another aspect is how to deal with evolution of e-business standards. As new versions of standards become available, they are often used in parallel to older ones. References have to be versioned as well in order to be able to reconstruct semantic references between any versions of standards. Thus, transaction documents using older references can be kept readable. On the other hand, when new versions of a standard are available, they should inherit as much of the existing references as possible in order to preserve knowledge. Intelligent versioning mechanisms for standards, references and their ratings that meet these challenges have to be deployed.

As mentioned above, there is no comprehensive domain-specific evaluation of mapping and inference tools available at present. Since the developed system allows the coupling of different subsystems, results regarding the efficiency of existing tools solutions in different domain areas and with differing sizes of data are of special interest in judging system's overall performance. As the architecture allows the parallel use of multiple tools – for example, different inference tools – their specific strengths and weaknesses depending on a specific application situation remain to be examined. An interesting question in this respect is to what extent the results of these tools may be combined in an advantageous manner. Therefore, both the possibility of measuring the result quality at run-time and the possibility of calculating an adaptively formed, weighted combination from the measurement results must be evaluated.

Future research also has to address the topic of if and how much bias arises when the acceptance of a rating is computed with a small number of ratings only. It needs to be determined whether a minimum threshold of candidate ratings needs to be defined and if acceptances with less than this threshold should be ignored. Alternatively, it is possible to extend the existing calculation methods with a variable showing the user the absolute number of ratings the acceptance is based on, so that each user may decide individually for or against using a suggested semantic reference.

11.2 Business Challenges

The success of our results in everyday business use will be greatly influenced by the benefits generated and the costs induced for the average user. To reduce these costs as much as possible, the application functionality is delivered as web services that, to the largest extent possible, are transparent for standard users. Still, more research is needed to prove user acceptance and deal with user evaluation. For expert users, the usability of the graphical interface for ontology navigation and management has to be researched further. In general, the objective is to limit the amount of technical knowledge required of business users and to supply them with the most easy-to-use interface possible.

At the company level, only extensive longitudinal or case-based research can prove the overall cost reduction, as well as time and quality improvements, propagated. Unfortunately, such research has to cope with the well-known problem of assessing IT effects on business processes and company performance. The determination of whether IT increases the productivity of businesses raises some severe methodological problems. Those problems have been reared within the *productivity paradox* discussion for some time now (Brynjolfsson 1993; Brynjolfsson and Hitt 2003), with no final answer given to date. Still, case-based research may be able to isolate some productivity effects by controlling as many of the side conditions as possible.

The ORBI Ontology Mediator service, like other groupware or social software systems, needs a critical mass of users to function in an optimal way. As the reference collection is envisioned to evolve and improve over time through the user feedback, users actively adopting and engaging in sharing their knowledge are crucial to achieving this growth. A critical number of users is considered the key factor to successful groupware acceptance, even before perceived ease of use and usefulness (Lou et al. 2000). Technology characteristics and the quality of the services delivered contribute to the intention to use software and user satisfaction, which lead to, but again also influence, the critical mass of users (Seen et al. 2007). By providing an open system that can be accessed via a web browser, a browser plug-in, or by arbitrary applications that are able to call web services, the platform is well prepared to reach a critical mass quickly. As experiences from other Web-2.0 communities show, critical mass can be reached easily and quickly if the platform delivers sufficient benefits for the community and is easy and open to use. Still, additional longitudinal research should unveil more about the success conditions for the services developed.

11.3 Conceptual Challenges

Developing the methods and components for ontologies-based business integration has enhanced the options for semantic interoperability. Proceeding to the level of pragmatics, in addition to the information exchanged and the documents in which it is contained, *processes* have to be considered. *Pragmatic integration*, i.e., the integration of business processes, is currently being attempted by only a few initiatives. Exceptions are RosettaNet or ebXML. In any case, process integration is impossible without communicating process-flow layouts to business partners in a structured way. This structured, in some cases even standardized, way of communicating process layouts is achieved by exchanging *process models*. Pragmatic e-business integration thus means integration of process models. Methods and tools for *dynamic model integration* require additional aspects to be considered. Such methods and tools are still missing.

The methods and tools discussed in this book were developed for dynamic e-business integration. Still, as we are using a very generic conceptual as well as technical approach, we are convinced that our results can be transferred to other application domains. Indeed, when looking at our results, we see strong potential for using some of our generic methods and tools as an input for research and development for this next step: pragmatic e-business integration driven by dynamic process-model integration. In the MODI project (MODI 2007), we pursue further research in this area.

As we have elaborated, our results represent an important step towards real e-business integration. Still, with the research questions formulated above, the field of e-business integration promises to remain challenging and rewarding for the coming years.

List of Abbreviations

AI	Artificial Intelligence
ANSI ASC X12	American National Standards Institute Accredited Standards Committee X12
API	Application Programming Interface
APS	Advanced Planning and Scheduling
ASCII	American Standard Code for Information Interchange
B2B	Business-to-Business
BBS	Bulletin Board System
BEC	Classification by Broad Economic Categories
BI	Business Intelligence
BIC	Bank Identifier Code
BPEL	Business Process Execution Language
BPIM	Business Process and Information Modeling
CAD	Computer Aided Design
CAE	Computer Aided Engineering
CBO	Common Business Objects
CC	Core Component
CCTS	Core Component Technical Specification
CEN	Comité Européen de Normalisation (European Committee for Standardization)
CIF	Cost, Insurance and Freight
COTS	Commercial Off-the-Shelf Software
CPC	Central Product Classification
CPP/CPA	Collaboration Protocol Profile / Agreement
CPV	Common Procurement Vocabulary
CRM	Customer Relationship Management
CSV	Comma Separated Values
CWM	Common Warehouse Model
cXML	Commerce eXtensible Markup Language
DAML	DARPA Agent Markup Language
DIG	D(escription) L(ogics) Implementation Group
DOLCE	Descriptive Ontology for Linguistic and Cognitive Engineering
DP	Document Processor

DRM	Digital Rights Management
DW	Data Warehouse
EAI	Enterprise Application Integration
EAN	European Article Number
EANCOM	EAN + Communication
ebBPSS	ebXML Business Process Specification Schema
ebMS	Electronic Business Messaging Service
ebXML	Electronic Business eXtensible Markup Language
EDI	Electronic Data Exchange
EDIINT	EDI for Internet
EDM	Engineering Data Management
eOTD	ECCMA Open Technical Dictionary
EPC	Electronic Product Codes
ERM	Entity Relationship Model
ERP	Enterprise Resource Planning
FOB	Free on Board
FTAM	File Transfer Access and Management
FTP	File Transfer Protocol
GPC	Global Product Classification
GUI	Graphical User Interface
HL7	Health Level Seven
HS	Harmonized Commodity Description and Coding System
HTTP	Hypertext Transport Protocol
ICT	Information and Communication Technologies
IDoc	Intermediate Document
IMAP	Internet Message Access Protocol
INCOTERMS	International Commercial Terms
IRC	Internet Relay Chat
ISBN	International Standard Book Number
ISIC	International Standard Industrial Classification of All Economic Activities
IT	Information Technology
JIT	Just-in-Time
KIF	Knowledge Interchange Format
KR	Knowledge Representation Ontology
LAN	Local Area Network
LES	Logistics Execution Systems
LISP	List Processing
MES	Manufacturing Execution Systems
MIME	Multipurpose Internet Mail Extensions
MIS	Management Information Systems

MRO	Maintenance, Repair and Operation
NACE	Nomenclature générale des activités économiques dans les Communautés Européennes
NAICS	North American Industry Classification System
NLP	Natural Language Processing
OCL	Object Constraint Language
OCML	Operational Conceptual Modelling Language
ODBC	Open Database Connectivity
OEM	Original Equipment Manufacturer
OIL	Ontology Inference Layer
OKBC	Open Knowledge Base Connectivity
ORBI	Ontologies-based Reconciliation for Business Integration
OWL	Web Ontology Language
P2P	Peer-to-Peer
PDP	Policy Decision Point
PEP	Policy Enforcement Point
PIDX	Petroleum Industry Data Exchange
PIP	RosettaNet Partner Interface Process
PLM	Product Lifecycle Management
POP3	Post Office Protocol Version 3
PPS	Production Planning and Scheduling
R&D	Research and Development
RDF	Resource Description Framework
RDF/S	RDF-Schema
Reg/Rep	ebXML's Registry/Repository
RFID	Radio Frequency Identification
RMI	Remote Method Invocation
RNTD	RosettaNet Technical Directory
RTF	Rich Text Format
SAT	Satisfiability
SBO	Semantic Bridge Ontologies
SCM	Supply Chain Management
SFA	Sales Force Automation
SME	Small and Medium-sized Enterprises
SNITEM	Syndicat National de l'Industrie des Technologies Médicales
SOA	Service Oriented Architecture
SOAP	Simple Object Access Protocol
SOFA	Simple Ontology Framework API
SQL	Structured Query Language
SSL	Secure Socket Layer

SSML	Security Services Markup Language
STEP	Standard for the Exchange of Product Model Data
SUMO	Suggested Upper Merged Ontology
SWIFT	Society for Worldwide Interbank Financial Telecommunication
SWRL	Semantic Web Rule Language
TCP/IP	Transmission Control Protocol/Internet Protocol
TPA	Trading Partner Agreement
UBL	Universal Business Language
UCC	Uniform Code Council
UDDI	Universal Description, Discovery and Integration
UDEF	Universal Data Element Framework
UI	User Interface
UML	Unified Modeling Language
UMM	United Nations Modeling Methodology
UN/CEFACT	United Nations Centre for Trade Facilitation and Electronic Business
UN/EDIFACT	United Nations/Electronic Data Interchange For Administration, Commerce, and Transport
UNDP	United Nations Development Programme
UNeDocs	United Nations electronic Trade Documents
UNSPSC	United Nations Standard Products and Services Code
UNTDED	United Nations Trade Data Element Directory
UPC	Uniform Product Code
URI	Unique Resource Identifier
VAN	Value Added Network
VMI	Vendor Managed Inventory
W3C	World Wide Web Consortium
WAN	Wide Area Network
WfMS	Workflow Management System
WM	Warehouse Management
WWW	World Wide Web
xCBL	XML Common Business Library
XLINK	XML Linking Language
XML	eXtensible Markup Language
XMLDsig	XML Signature Syntax and Processing
XOL	XML-based Ontology Language
XPath	XML Path Language
XSD	XML Schema Definition
XSLT	eXtensible Stylesheet Language Transformations

List of Figures

List of Tables

References

Abecker A, Stojanovic L (2005) Ontology Evolution: MEDLINE Case Study. In: Ferstl Otto K, Sinz Elmar J, Eckert S, Isselhorst T (eds) Wirtschaftsinformatik 2005 eEconomy, eGovernment, eSociety 7. Internationale Tagung Wirtschaftsinformatik 2005. Physica, Heidelberg, pp 1291-1308

Adobe (2007) Flash CS3 Professional. http://www.adobe.com/products/flash/, 2007-06-20

Alexiev V, Breu M, de Bruijn J, Fensel D, Lara R, Lausen H (2005) Information Integration with Ontologies Experiences from an Industrial Showcase. Wiley & Sons, Chichester

Alishevskikh A (2005a) SOFA Design Whitepaper. http://sofa.projects.semweb central.org/doc/design/index.html, 2007-06-27

Alishevskikh A (2005b) Getting Started with the SOFA API. http://sofa. projects.semwebcentral.org/doc/getstarted/index.html, 2007-06-27

Allen BP (1994) Case-Based Reasoning: Business Applications. Communications of the ACM 37(3):40-42

Almeida R, Mozafari B, Cho J (2007) On the Evolution of Wikipedia. In: Proceedings of ICWSM International Conference on Weblogs and Social Media. http://www.icwsm.org/papers/paper2.html, 2007-08-15

Allsopp J (2007) Microformats: Empowering Your Markup for Web 2.0. Springer, New York

Antoniou G, Franconi E, van Harmelen F (2005) Introduction to Semantic Web Ontology Languages. In: Eisinger N, Maluszynski J (eds) Reasoning Web, Proceedings of the Summer School, LNCS 3564. Springer, Berlin Heidelberg New York

Apache Web Services Project (2007) WebServices – Axis. http://ws.apache. org/axis/, 2007-06-13

API (2007) American Petroleum Institute Petroleum Industry Data Exchange (PIDX) Committee Standards. http://committees.api.org/business/pidx/ standards/index.html, 2007-06-30

Aristotle (1984) The complete works of Aristotle: the revised Oxford translation edited by Jonathan Barnes. Princeton University Press, Princeton, N.J.

ASC X12 (2006) About ASC X12 Vision and Mission. http://www.x12. org/x12org/about/VisionMission.cfm, 2006-12-10

Baeza-Yates R, Ribeiro-Neto B (1999) Modern Information Retrieval. ACM Press, New York

Bao J, Cao Y, Tavanapong W, Honavar V (2004) Integration of Domain-Specific and Domain-Independent Ontologies for Colonoscopy Video Database Annotation. http://www.cs.iastate.edu/~honavar/Papers/baojieike04. pdf, 2005-10-18

Barry & Associates, Inc. (2006) XML standards and vocabularies. http://www.service-architecture.com/xml/articles/index.html, 2006-12-10

Bechhofer S (2003) The DIG Description Logic Interface: DIG/1.1. In: Proceedings of the 2003 International Workshop on Description Logics (DL-2003). CEUR-WS.org, Aachen, http://CEUR-WS.org/Vol-81/, 2007-09-14

Bechhofer S, Lord P, Volz R (2003) Cooking the Semantic Web with the OWL API. In: Fensel D, Sycara K, Mylopoulos J (eds) Proceedings of 2nd International Semantic Web Conference ISWC 2003, LNCS 2870. Springer, Berlin Heidelberg New York, pp 659-675

Bechhofer SK, Carroll JJ (2004) Parsing OWL DL: Trees or Triples?. In: Proceedings of the 13th international conference on World Wide Web. ACM Press, New York, pp 266-275

Beckmann H, van der Eijk P, Hjulstad H, Madsen BN, Ondracek N, Schmitz V (2004) CEN Workshop Agreement 15045:2004 E Multilingual catalogue strategies for eCommerce and eBusiness. CEN Brussels, ftp://ftp.cen orm.be/PUBLIC/CWAs/e-Europe/eCat/CWA15045-00-2004-Jul.pdf, 2006-12-10

Bell DE, LaPadula LJ (1973) Secure Computer Systems: Mathematical Foundations and Model. Technical Report M74-244, MITRE Corp., Bedfort, MA

Bergamaschi S, Guerra F, Vincini M (2002) A Data Integration Framework for E-commerce Product Classification. In: 1st International Semantic Web Conference (ISWC2002). http://www.dbgroup.unimo.it/prototipo/paper/iswc2002.pdf, 2005-01-01

Berge J (1994) The EDIFACT Standards. Blackwell Publishing, Oxford

Berglund A, Boag S, Chamberlin D, Fernández MF, Kay M, Robie J, Siméon J (2007) XML Path Language (XPath) Version 2.0. W3C Recommendation. http://www.w3.org/TR/xpath20/, 2007-05-06

Berners-Lee T, Hendler J, Lassila O (2001) The Semantic Web. Scientific American.com, http://www.sciam.com/article.cfm?articleID=0004814410 D2-1C70-84A9809EC588EF21, 2007-07-30

Bertino E, Ferrari E (2002) Secure and Selective Dissemination of XML Documents. ACM Transactions on Information and System Security 5(3):290-331

Bichler M (2001) The Future of eMarkets. Cambridge University Press, Cambridge

Bieber M, Hiltz S, Stohr E, Engelbart D, Noll J, Turoff M, Furuta R, Preece J, Van de Walle B (2001) Virtual Community Knowledge Evolution. In: Proceedings of the 34th Annual Hawaii International Conference on System Sciences (HICSS-34). IEEE Computer Society, Washington DC, (8):8003

BITKOM (2004) Daten zur Informationsgesellschaft, Status quo und Perspektiven Deutschlands im internationalen Vergleich. BITKOM, Berlin

BITKOM (2005) Daten zur Informationsgesellschaft, Status quo und Perspektiven Deutschlands im internationalen Vergleich. BITKOM, Berlin.

http://www.bitkom.org/files/documents/BITKOM_Daten_zur_Information sgesellschaft_2005.pdf, 2005-03-04

BITKOM (2007) Daten zur Informationsgesellschaft, Status quo und Perspektiven Deutschlands im internationalen Vergleich. BITKOM, Berlin. http://www.bitkom.org/files/documents/Datenbroschuere_ 2007.pdf, 2007-07-10

BME e.V. (2006) BMEcat – der richtige Katalogstandard für ihr E-Business. Flyer.   http://www.bmecat.org/download/BMEcat_Flyer_2006_DE.pdf, 2007-07-03

Bohring H, Auer S (2005) Mapping XML to OWL Ontologies. In: Jantke KP, Fähnrich KP, Wittig WS (eds) Marktplatz Internet: Von e-Learning bis e-Payment. 13. Leipziger Informatik-Tage, LIT 2005. GI-Edition – Lecture Notes in Informatics (LNI), Leipzig, 72:147-156

Booch G, Rumbaugh J, Jacobson I (2005) Unified Modeling Language User Guide. Addison-Wesley Professional, Boston, USA

Bouquet P, Ehrig M, Euzenat J, Franconi E, Hitzler P, Krötzsch M, Serafini L, Stamou G, Sure Y, Tessaris S (2005) D2.2.1 Specification of a common framework for characterizing alignment. http://www.inrialpes.fr/exmo/ co-operation/kweb/heterogeneity/deli/kweb-221.pdf, 2007-08-03

Bray T, Paoli J, Sperberg-McQueen CM, Maler E, Yergeau F (eds) (2006) Extensible Markup Language (XML) 1.0 (Fourth Edition) W3C Recommendation 16 August 2006, edited in place 29 September 2006. http://www.w3.org/TR/REC-xml/, 2007-07-28

Brewer FD, Nash JM (1989) The Chinese Wall Security Policy. IEEE Symposium on Security and Privacy. IEEE Computer Society Press, http://www.gammassl.co.uk/topics/chwall.pdf, 2007-07-26

Brynjolfsson E (1993) The Productivity Paradox of Information Technology. Communications of the ACM 36(12):66-77

Brynjolfsson E, Hitt LM (2003) Costly Bidding in Online Markets for IT Services. Management Science 49(11):1504-1520

Buono P, Costabile MF, Guida S, Piccinno A, Tesoro G (2001) Integrating User Data and Collaborative Filtering in a Web Recommendation System. In: Revised Papers from the International Workshops OHS-7, SC-3, and AH-3 on Hypermedia: Openness, Structural Awareness and Adaptivity, LNCS 2266. Springer, Berlin Heidelberg New York, pp 315-321

Bussler C (2001) B2B Protocol Standards and their Role in Semantic B2B Integration Engines. Bulletin of the IEEE Computer Society Technical Committee on Data Engineering 24(3):1-11

Calì A, Calvanesel D, Cuenca Grau B, De Giacomo G, Lembo D, Lenzerini M, Lutz C, Milano D, Möller R, Poggi A, Sattler U (2005) State of the Art Survey – Deliverable D01. http://www.sts.tu-harburg.de/tech-reports/2006 /tonesdeliv01.pdf, 2007-07-25

Canny J (2002) Collaborative Filtering with Privacy. In: Proceedings of the IEEE Symposium on Security and Privacy. IEEE Computer Society, Washington DC, pp 45- 57

Cardoso J, Sheth AP (eds) (2006) Semantic Web Services, Processes and Applications. Springer Science + Business Media, LLC, New York

Carroll JJ, Dickinson I, Dollin C, Reynolds D, Seaborn A, Wilkinson K (2003) Jena: Implementing the Semantic Web Recommendations. Technical Report HPL-2003-146, Digital Media Systems Laboratory, HP Laboratories Bristol. http://www.hpl.hp.com/techreports/2003/HPL-2003-146.pdf?jum pid=reg_R1002_USEN, 2007-06-27

CEN (ed) (2006) CEN Workshop Agreement CWA 15556-3:2006 E Product Description and Classification - Part 3: Results of development in harmonization of product classifications and in multilingual electronic catalogues and their respective data modelling. CEN Brussels, http://www.c en.eu/cenorm/businessdomains/businessdomains/isss/cwa/cwa155563.pdf, 2007-04-04

Chang SK (ed) (2002) Handbook of Software Engineering & Knowledge Engineering, Vol. 2 Emerging Technologies. World Scientific, New Jersey London Singapore Hong Kong, p 297

Chari K, Seshadri S (2004) Demystifying Integration. Communications of the ACM 47(7):58-63

Chopra S, Meindl P (2001) Supply Chain Management. Prentice Hall, Upper Saddle River

Chowdhury GG (2004) Introduction to modern information retrieval, 2nd ed. Facet, London

Clark J, De Rose S (eds) (1999) XML Path Language (XPath) Version 1.0. W3C Recommendation 16 November 1999. http://www.w3.org/TR/xpath, 2007-07-18

Claypool M, Brown D, Le P, Waseda M (2001) Inferring user interest. IEEE Internet Computing 5(6):32-299

COMA++ (2007) COMA++ Schema and Ontology Matching with COMA++. Universität Leipzig, http://dbs.uni-leipzig.de/Research/coma .html, 2007-01-03

Conen W, Klapsing R (2001) Utilizing Host Formalisms to Extend RDF Semantics. In: Proceedings of the Semantic Web Working Symposium (SWWS). http://www.semanticweb.org/SWWS/program/full/ paper24.pdf, 2007-09-14

Coverpages (2006) Core Standards Extensible Markup Language (XML) XML: Proposed Applications and Industry Initiatives. http://xml.coverpag es.org/xml.html, 2006-08-03

Crysmann B, Frank A, Kiefer B, Müller S, Neumann G, Piskorski J, Schäfer U, Siegel M, Uszkoreit H, Xu F, Becker M, Krieger HU (2002) An integrated architecture for shallow and deep processing. In: Proceedings of the 40th Annual Meeting on Association for Computational Linguistics. Association for Computational Linguistics (ACL). http://www.aclweb.org/anthol ogy/P02-1056.pdf, 2007-09-14

Cui Z, Jones DM, O'Brien P (2002) Semantic B2B Integration: Issues in Ontology-based Approaches. ACM SIGMOD Record 31(1):43-48

cXML (2006) cXML FAQ. http://www.cxml.org/prnews/faq.cfm, 2006-12-06

Cyc (2002) OpenCyc Selected Vocabulary and Upper Ontology. http://www.

cyc.com/cycdoc/vocab/upperont-diagram.html, 2007-08-06

Dameron O, Noy NF, Knublauch H, Musen MA (2004) Accessing and Ma-nipulating Ontologies Using Web Services. In: Proceedings of the ISWC 2004 Workshop on Semantic Web Services: Preparing to Meet the World of Business Applications. CEUR-WS.org vol 119, http://sunsite.informa tik.rwth-aachen.de/Publications/CEUR-WS/Vol-119/paper7.pdf, 2007-12-04

Damiani E, De Capitani S, Paraboschi S, Samarati P (2000) Securing XML Documents. In: Zaniolo C, Lockemann PC, Scholl MH, Grust T (eds) Pro-ceedings of the 7th International Conference on Extending Database Tech-nology, LNCS 1777. Springer, Berlin Heidelberg New York, pp 121-135

Damiani E, di Vimercati S, De Capitani S, Paraboschi S, Samarati P (2002) A Fine-Grained Access Control System for XML Documents. ACM Transac-tions on Information and System Security (TIS-SEC) 5(2):169-202

Dan A, Dias DM, Kearney R, Lau TC, Nguyen TN, Parr FN, Sachs MW, Shaikh HH (2001) Business-to-business integration with tpaML and a business-to-business protocol framework. IBM Systems Journal 40(1):68-90

Daum B, Merten U (2002) System Architecture with XML. Morgan Kaufmann Publishers Inc, San Francisco, USA

David PA, Foray D (2003) Economic Fundamentals of the Knowledge Society. Policy Futures in Education 1(1):20-49

Davies J, Fensel D, van Harmelen F (2003) Towards the Semantic Web Ontol-ogy-driven Knowledge Management. Wiley & Sons, Chichester

DCMI Dublin Core Metadata Initiative (2006) Dublin Core Metadata Element Set, Version 1.1. http://dublincore.org/documents/dces/, 2007-08-09

de Bruijn J (2003) Using Ontologies, Enabling Knowledge Sharing and Reuse on the Semantic Web. DERI Technical Report DERI-2003-10-29, http://w ww.inf.unibz.it/~jdebruijn/publications-type/debr-2003a.html, 2005-06-04

de Bruijn J (2004) Semantic Information Integration Inside and Across Organ-izational Boundaries. DERI Technical Report DERI-2004-05-04A, http://deri-korea.org/publication/technical/DERI-TR-2004-05-04a1.pdf, 2006-12-27

de Bruijn J, Ehrig M, Feier C, Martin-Recuerda F, Scharffe F, Weiten M (2006) Ontology Mediation, Merging and Aligning. In: Davies J, Studer R, Warren P (eds) Semantic Web Technologies trends and research in ontol-ogy-based systems. Wiley & Sons, Chichester

Decker S, Melnik S, van Harmelen F, Fensel D, Klein M, Broekstra J, Erd-mann M, Horrocks I (2000) The Semantic Web: The roles of XML and RDF. IEEE Internet Computing 4(5):63-73

DEDIG (2004) DEDIG Deutsche EC/EDI-Gesellschaft e.V. EDI-Classico. http://www.e-gateway.de/dedig/classico.cfm, 2004-10-06

Devedzic V (2002) Understanding Ontological Engineering. Communications of the ACM 45(4):136-144

DINsml.net (2007) NA 128 Product Property Standards Committee. DIN Deut-sches Institut für Normung e. V. http://www.nsm.din.de/ cmd?workflowna me=InitCommittee&search_committee=nsm&contextid=nsm, 2007-06-20

DNB (2007) D&B D-U-N-S Number. http://www.dnb.com/US/duns_update/, 2007-06-01

Doan A, Madhavan J, Domingos P, Halevy A (2003) Learning to Map between Ontologies on the Semantic Web. The VLDB Journal The International Journal on Very Large Data Bases 12(4):303–319

Doan AH, Madhavan J, Domingos P, Halevy A (2004) Ontology Matching: A Machine Learning Approach. In: Staab S, Studer R (eds) Handbook on Ontologies. Springer, Berlin Heidelberg New York, pp 385-403

Domingue J (1998) Tadzebao and Webonto: Discussing, Browsing, and Editing Ontologies on the Web. http://kmi.open.ac.uk/people/domingue/ban ff98-paper/domingue.html, 2007-08-01

Dou D, McDermott D, Qi P (2004) Ontology Translation on the Semantic Web. In: Spaccapietra S (ed) Journal on Data Semantics II. Springer, Berlin Heidelberg, pp 35-57

Drucker H, Wu D, Vapnik VN (1999) Support Vector Machines for Spam Categorization. IEEE Transactions on Neural Networks 10(5):1048-1054

Dudani SA (1976) The distance-weighted k-nearest-neighbor rule. IEEE Transactions on Systems, Man and Cybernetics 6:325–327

eBSC (2005) eBusines Standardization Commitee BMEcat - Leading companies agree on a standard for electronic trade. http://www.bmecat.org/ English/index.asp?main=Ueber&pid=, 2007-08-14

ebXML (2007) About ebXML. http://www.ebxml.org/geninfo.htm, 2007-08-06

EC (2004) The European e-Business Report 2004 edition A portrait of e-business in 10 sectors of the EU economy 3rd Synthesis Report of the e-Business W@tch. European Communities, Luxembourg

EC (2005a) Special Report (July 2005) Overview of International e-Business Developments Monitoring activities, key results and policy implications. European Commission Enterprise & Industry Directorate, Brussels

EC (2005b) Special Report (September 2005) e-Business Interoperability and Standards A Cross-Sector Perspective and Outlook. European Commission Enterprise & Industry Directorate, Brussels

EC (2005c) Special Report (September 2005) ICT Security, e-Invoicing and e-Payment Activities in European Enterprises. European Commission Enterprise & Industry Directorate, Brussels

EC (2006) The European e-Business Report 2005 edition A portrait of e-business in 10 sectors of the EU economy 4th Synthesis Report of the e-Business W@tch. European Communities, Luxembourg

EC (2007) European Commission (ed) The European e-Business Report 2006/07 edition A portrait of e-business in 10 sectors of the EU economy 5th Synthesis Report of the e-Business W@tch. European Communities, Luxembourg

ECCMA (2007) About us. http://www.eccma.org/AboutUs.php, 2007-07-04

eClass (2005) The leading classification system. White Paper. http://www.e class.de/user/documents/eng_white_paper_v1_1_%5Bjune_2005%5D.pdf,

2007-08-14

eClass (2007a) General conditions of use. http://www.eclass.de/index. html/
JTI2bmF2aWQlM0QzNzExJTI2bm8lM0RpbnRbyUyNnNpZCUzRG40Nj
kyMTI5NGJhMDY4JTI2YiUzRA==.html, 2007-07-30

eClass (2007b) What is eclass?. FAQs on the current status of eClass.
http://www.eclass.de/index.html/JTI2bmF2aWQlM0QzODQxJTI2bm8lM
0RpbnRybyUyNnNpZCUzRG40NmIxYTk4OTEyMTA5JTI2YiUzRA==.
html, 2007-08-01

EDIFICE (2007) The European B2B Forum for the Electronics Industry
EDIFICE REPOSITORY 2007-1 Endorsed on 30 May 2007. http://reposi
tory.edifice.org/default.aspx, 2007-07-30

EDIFrance (2007) EDITEX. http://www.edifrance.org/asso_gdeep_desc.php
?id=27, 2007-08-20

Ehrig M (2004a) Ontology Mapping. In: Proceedings of Information Interpretation and Integration Conference (I3CON) Workshop, at: Performance
Metrics for Intelligent Systems PerMIS '04. NIST National Institute of
Standards and Technology. http://www.isd.mel.nist.gov/research_areas/re-
search_engineering/Performance_Metrics/PerMIS_2004/Proceedings/Ehri
g.pps, 2006-12-28

Ehrig M (2004b) Ontology Mapping - An Integrated Approach. In: Bussler C,
Davis J, Fensel D, Studer R (eds) Proceedings of the First European Se-
mantic Web Symposium, LNCS 3053. Springer, Berlin Heidelberg New
York, pp 76-91

Ehrig M, Staab S (2004) QOM - Quick Ontology Mapping. Technical Report,
Institut AIFB, Universität Karlsruhe, http://www.aifb.uni-karlsruhe.de/
Publikationen/showPublikation?publ_id=776, 2007-01-03

Ehrig M, Euzenat J (2005) Relaxed Precision and Recall for Ontology Matching. In: Ashpole B, Ehrig M, Euzenat J, Stuckenschmidt H (eds) Proceedings of the Workshop on Integrating Ontologies. *CEU*R-WS.org vol 156,
http://sunsite.informatik.rwth-aachen.de/Publications/CEUR-WS/Vol-
156/paper5.pdf, 2006-08-04

Ehrig M (2007) Ontology Alignment Bridging the Semantic Gap. Springer Science + Business Media, New York

EITO (2005) European Information Technology Observation 2005. http://ww
w.eito.com/download/EITO_2005_ICT_markets%20press%20kit.pdf,
2005-03-04

EITO (2006) European Information Technology Observatory, ICT markets
2006.   http://www.eito.com/download/EITO%202006%20-%20ICT%20-
market%20March%202006.pdf, 2006-12-13

Emery P, Hart L (2004) Artic, an Ontology Mapping Engine. In: Proceedings
of Information Interpretation and Integration Conference (I3CON) Workshop, at Performance Metrics for Intelligent Systems PerMIS '04. http://w
ww.atl.lmco.com/projects/ontology/i3con/present ations.html, 2006-12-29

Eurostat (2007a) Metadata Statistical Classification of Economic Activities in
the European Community, Rev. 1.1 (2002). http://ec.europa.eu/eurostat/
ramon/nomenclatures/index.cfm?TargetUrl=LST_NOM_DTL&StrNom=N

ACE_1_1&StrLanguageCode=EN&IntPcKey=&StrLayoutCode=HIERAR CHIC&IntCurrentPage=1, 2007-08-20

Eurostat (2007b) Metadata classifications. http://ec.europa.eu/eurostat/ramon/ nomenclatures/index.cfm?TargetUrl=LST_NOM&StrGroupCode=CLASS IFIC&StrLanguageCode=EN, 2007-07-10

EuroWordNet (2006) EuroWordNet Objectives. http://www.illc.uva.nl/Euro WordNet/objectives-ewn.html, 2006-12-28

Euzenat J (2005) Evaluating ontology alignment methods (extended abstract). In: Kalfoglou Y, Schorlemmer M,. Sheth A , Staab S, Uschold M (eds) Dagstuhl Seminar Proceedings 04391, Semantic Interoperability and Integration. http://drops.dagstuhl.de/opus/volltexte/2005/36, 2005-06-06

Euzenat J (2006) An API for ontology alignment (version 2.1). http://ww w.gforge.inria.fr/docman/view.php/117/251/align.pdf, 2007-08-06

Euzenat J, Shvaiko P (2007) Ontology Matching. Springer, Berlin Heidelberg New York

Fayad ME, Schmidt DC (1997) Object-Oriented Application Frameworks. Communications of the ACM 40(10):32-38

Fensel D (2001) Ontologies and Electronic Commerce. IEEE Intelligent Systems 16(1):8-14, http://ieeeexplore.ieee.org/iel5/9670/19693/01183337.pd f?tp=&arnumber=1183337&isnumber=1969, 2006-11-10

Fensel D, Ding Y, Omelayenko B, Schulten E, Botquin G, Brown M, Flett A (2001) Product Data Integration in B2B E-Commerce. IEEE Intelligent Systems 16(4):54-59

Fensel D (2004) Ontologies: A Silver Bullet for Knowledge Management and Electronic Commerce, 2nd edn. Springer, Berlin Heidelberg New York

Ferris C, Farrell J (2003) What are Web Services?. Communications of the ACM 46(6):31

Fischer G (1996) Seeding, Evolutionary Growth, and Reseeding: Constructing, Capturing and Evolving Knowledge in Domain-Oriented Design Environments. In: Sutcliffe A, Benyon D, van Asche F (eds) Domain Knowledge for Interactive System Design. Chapman & Hall, pp 1-16

Fluit C, Sabou M, van Harmelen F (2003) Supporting User Tasks through Visualisation of Light-weight Ontologies. In: Staab S, Studer R (eds) Handbook on Ontologies in Information Systems. Springer, Berlin Heidelberg New York, pp 415-434

FOAM (2007) FOAM Framework for Ontology Alignment and Mapping. Universität Karlsruhe, http://www.aifb.uni-karlsruhe.de/WBS/meh/foam/, 2007-01-03

Fowler M (2002) Patterns of Enterprise Application Architecture. Addison-Wesley Professional, Boston, USA

Fox, MS (1992) The TOVE Project: Towards A Common-sense Model of the Enterprise. Enterprise Integration Laboratory Technical Report, University of Toronto, http://www.eil.utoronto.ca/enterprise-modelling/papers/fox-tove-uofttr92.pdf, 2007-04-05

Fricke M, Götze K, Renner T, Pols A (2006) eBusiness-Barometer 2006/ 2007.Wegweiser GmbH, Berlin

Froehlich G, Hoover HJ, Sorenson PG (2000) Choosing an Object-Oriented Domain Framework. ACM Computing Surveys (CSUR) 32(1):1-6

Gabillon A, Bruno E (2002) Regulating Access to XML Documents. In: Proceedings of the Working Conference on Database and Application Security. Kluwer Academic Publishers, pp 299 - 314

Gamma E, Helm R, Johnson R, Vlissides J (1995) Design Patterns. Elements of Reusable Object-Oriented Software. Addison-Wesley Longman, Amsterdam

Gennari JH, Musen MA, Fergerson RW, Grosso WE, Crubézy M, Eriksson H, Noy NF, Tu SW (2003) The evolution of Protégé: an environment for knowledge-based systems development. International Journal of Human-Computer Studies archive 58(1):89–123

Gómez-Pérez A, Fernández-López F, Corcho O (2004) Ontology Engineering. Springer, London Berlin Heidelberg

Graham GS, Denning PJ (1972) Protection - Principles and Practice. In: Proceedings Spring Joint Computer Reference 40:417-429

Granada Research (2001) Using the UNSPSC United Nations Standard Products and Services Code. White Paper, HTTP://WWW.UNSPSC.ORG/DOCUMENTATION.ASP, 2006-12-06

Gruber, TR (1993a) Toward Principles for the Design of Ontologies Used for Knowledge Sharing. International Journal Human-Computer Studies 43:907-928, http://tomgruber.org/writing/onto-design.pdf, 2007-08-01

Gruber TR (1993b) A Translation Approach to Portable Ontology Specifications. http://ksl-web.stanford.edu/KSL_Abstracts/KSL-92-71.html, 2005-06-06

GS1 (2006a) An Introduction to the Global Trade Item Number (GTIN). http://barcodes.gs1us.org/dnn_bcec/Documents/tabid/136/DMXModule/731/Command/Core_Download/Default.aspx?EntryId=59, 2007-08-10

GS1 (2006b) GS1 Identification Keys (ID Keys). http://www.gs1.org/productssolutions/barcodes/technical/id_keys.html, 2007-08-01

GS1 (2006c) Global Product Classification (GPC). http://www.gs1.org/productssolutions/gdsn/gpc/, 2006-12-09

GS1 (2007a) EANCOM Overview. http://www.gs1.org/productssolutions/ecom/eancom/overview/, 2007-07-30

GS1 (2007b) eCom Standards in the GS1 Community 2006. Brochure, http://www.gs1.org/docs/ecom/eCom_Standards_in_the_GS1_Community_2006.pdf, 2007-08-20

GS1 Germany (2007) SEDAS. http://www.gs1-germany.de/inter net/content/produkte/ean/ecommerce_edi/sedas/index_ ger.html, 2007-08-05

Hameed A, Preece A, Sleemann D (2004) Ontology Reconciliation. In: Staab S, Studer R (eds) Handbook on Ontologies. Springer, Berlin, pp 231-250

Hammer H (2001) The Superefficient Company. Harvard Business Review, pp 82-91. http://harvardbusinessonline.hbsp.harvard.edu/hbsp/hbr/articles/article.jsp?ml_action=getarticle&articleID=R0108E&ml_page=1&ml_subscriber=true, 2007-08-09

Hammer M, Champy J (1993) Reengineering the Corporation A Manifesto for

Business Revolution. HarperBusiness, New York

Han J, Kamber M (2000) Data Mining: Concepts and Techniques. Morgan Kaufmann, San Francisco

Hearst MA (1992) Automatic acquisition of hyponyms from large text corpora. In: Proceedings of the 14th conference on computational linguistics. Association for Computational Linguistics (ACL) 2:539-545

Henrich A, Morgenroth K (2003) Supporting Collaborative Software Development by Context-Aware Information Retrieval Facilities. In: Proceedings of the 14th International Workshop on Database and Expert Systems Applications (DEXA'03). IEEE Computer Society, Washington DC, pp 249-253

Hepp M (2003) Güterklassifikation als semantisches Standardisierungsproblem. Dissertation, University Würzburg. Universitätsverlag, Wiesbaden.

Hepp M, Leukel J, Schmitz V (2005) Content Metrics for Products and Services Categorization Standards. In: Proceedings of the IEEE International Conference on e-Technology, e-Commerce and e-Service (EEE-05). http://www.heppnetz.de/files/mhepp-jleukel-vschmitz-quantitative-analysis-eClass.pdf, 2006-12-10

Hepp M (2006a) Products and Services Ontologies: A Methodology for Derivin OWL Ontologies from Industrial Categorization Standards. International Journal on Semantic Web & Information Systems (IJSWIS) 2(1):72-99

Hepp M (2006b) The True Complexity of Product Representation in the Semantic Web. In: Proceedings of the 14th European Conference on Information System (ECIS 2006). http://www.heppnetz.de/files/hepptruecomplexity-ECIS2006.pdf, 2007-01-02

Hepp M (2006c) eClassOWL 5.1 – Products and Services Ontology for e-Business. User's Guide, Version 1.0 June 16, 2006. http://www.heppnetz.de/eclassowl/eclassOWL-Primer-final.pdf, 2007-08-02

Hepp M, Siorpaes K, Bachlechner D (2006) Towards the Semantic Web in E-Tourism: Can Annotation do the Trick?. In: Proceedings of the 14th European Conference on Information System (ECIS 2006). http://www.heppnetz.de/files/hepp-siorpaes-bachlechner-annotation-ECIS2006.pdf, 2006-03-27

Herman I (2007) Semantic Web. http://www.w3.org/2001/sw/, 2007-08-01

Hesse W (2005) Ontologies in the Software Engineering process. In: Lenz R, Hasenkamp U, Hasselbring W, Reichert M (eds) EAI 2005 - Proceedings Workshop on Enterprise Application Integration. GITO-Verlag, Berlin

Hill NC, Ferguson DM (1989) Electronic Data Interchange: A Definition and Perspective. EDI Forum: The Journal of Electronic Data Interchange 1(1):1-12

Hill W, Stead L, Rosenstein M, Furnas G (1995) Recommending and Evaluating Choices in a Virtual Community of Use. In: Proceedings of the SIGCHI conference on Human Factors in Computing Systems, pp 194-201

HL7 (2007) What is HL7?. http://www.hl7.org/, 2007-07-03

Hofreiter B, Huemer C (2002) B2B Integration – Aligning ebXML and Ontology Approaches. In: Shafaz H, Tjoa AM (eds) Proceedings of EURASIA-ICT'02 Information and Communication Technology, LNCS 2510. Springer, Berlin Heidelberg New York

Hofreiter B, Huemer C, Klas W (2002) ebXML: Status, Research Issues and Obstacles. In Proceedings of the 12th International Workshop on Research Issues on Data Engineering (RIDE 02). IEEE Computer Society, San Jose, CA

Hofreiter B, Huemer C, Naujok KD (2004) UN/CEFACT's Business Collaboration Framework - Motivation and Basic Concepts. In: Bichler M, Holtmann C, Kirn S, Müller JP, Weinhardt C (eds) Coordination and Agent Technology in Value Networks. Gito, Berlin, pp 93-108

Hofreiter B, Huemer C, Liegl P, Schuster R, Zapletal M (2006) UN/CEFACT's Modeling Methodology (UMM) A UML Profile for B2B e-Commerce. In: Proceedings of the 2nd International Workshop on Best Practices of UML at International Conference on Conceptual Modeling (ER 2006), LNCS 4231. Springer, Berlin Heidelberg New York

Hori K, Nakakoji K, Yamamoto Y, Ostwald J (2004) Organic Perspective of Knowledge Management: Knowledge Evolution through a Cycle of Knowledge Liquidization and Crystallization. Journal of Universal Computer Science 10(3):252-261

Hu W, Zhao Y, Qu Y (2006) Partition-Based Block Matching of Large Class Hierarchies. In: Mizoguchi R, Shi Z, Giunchiglia F (eds) Asian Semantic Web Conference ASWC 2006, LNCS 4185. Springer, Berlin Heidelberg New York, pp 72–83

Huber H (2005) Selbstlernende Suche Ein Praxisprojekt. Informatik-Spektrum, Heidelberg 28(3):189-192

Huemer C (2001) <<DIR>>-XML2 - Unambiguous Access to XML-based Business Documents in B2B E-Commerce. In: Proceedings of the 3rd ACM Conference on Electronic Commerce EC'01. ACM. DOI 501158.501181

ICC (2007) Preambles to Incoterms 2000. http://www.iccwbo.org/incoterms/id3040/index.html, 2007-08-01

Ide N, Véronis, J (1998) Introduction to the Special Issue on Word Sense Disambiguation: The State of the Art. Computational Linguistics 24(1):1-40

IFLA (2005) IFLA (The International Federation of Library Associations and Institutions) Guidelines for Multilingual Thesauri. Working Group on Guidelines for Multilingual Thesauri Classification and Indexing Section, IFLA, http://www.ifla.org/VII/s29/pubs/Draft-multilingualthesauri.pdf, 2006-12-27

ISBN (2007) Frequently Asked Questions about the ISBN. http://www.isbn.org/standards/home/isbn/us/isbnqa.asp, 2007-06-01

ISO (2004) ISO/IEC Guide 2:2004 Standardization and related activities - General vocabulary, 8th edn. ISO, Geneva, Switzerland

Iwaihara M, Chatvichienchai S, Anutariya C, Wuwongse V (2005) Relevancy Based Access Control of Versioned XML Documents. In: Proceedings of the 10th ACM Symposium on Access Control Models and Technologies.

ACM Press, New York, pp 85-94

Jena Consortium (2007) Jena Semantic Web Framework. http://jena.source
forge.net/, 2007-06-13

Joseki Consortium (2007) Joseki - A SPARQL Server for Jena. http://www.jos
eki.org/, 2007-06-27

JSR-127 Expert Group (2004) JSR 127: JavaServer Faces. http://www.jc
p.org/en/jsr/detail?id=127, 2007-06-13

Kalakota R, Robinson M (2000) E-Business 2.0: Roadmap for Success. 2nd ed,
Addison-Wesley Professional, Boston

Kalfoglou Y, Schorlemmer M (2003) IF-Map: An Ontology-Mapping Method
based on Information-Flow Theory. In: Spaccapietra S, March S, Aberer K
(eds) Journal on Data Semantics I, LNCS 2800. Springer, Berlin, Heidelberg, New York, pp 98-127

Kalfoglou Y, Schorlemmer M (2005) Ontology Mapping: The State of the Art.
In: Kalfoglou Y, Schorlemmer M, Sheth A, Staab S, Uschold M Semantic
Interoperability and Integration. Dagstuhl Seminar Proceedings No 04391,
Internationales Begegnungs- und Forschungszentrum fuer Informatik
(IBFI) Schloss Dagstuhl. http://drops.dagstuhl.de/opus/volltexte/2005/40,
2007-02-04

Kalfoglou Y, Hu B, Reynolds D, Shadbolt N (2005a) Semantic Integration
Technologies Survey. CROSI project, 6th month deliverable. University of
Southampton, Technical Report E-Print No #10842. http://www.akt
ors.org/crosi/deliverables/, 2006-12-06

Kalfoglou Y, Hu B, Reynolds D, Shadbolt N (2005b) CROSI project final report. University of Southampton, Technical Report E-Print No#11717.
http://www.aktors.org/crosi/deliverables/, 2006-12-06

KAON2 (2007) KAON2. http://kaon2.semanticweb.org/, 2007-06-27

Karabatis G (2006) Using Context in Semantic Data Integration. IBIS – Interoperability in Business Information Systems, 1(3):9-21

Kelkar O, Mucha M (2004) E-Standards powered by E-Business. In: Wegweiser GmbH (ed) eBusiness-Jahrbuch der deutschen Wirtschaft 2004/2005.
Wegweiser GmbH, Berlin, pp 22-27

Kiryakov A, Ognyanov D, Manov D (2005) OWLIM – a Pragmatic Semantic
Repository for OWL. In: Proceedings of the International Workshop on
Scalable Semantic Web Knowledge Base Systems (SSWS 2005), LNCS
3807. Springer, Berlin Heidelberg New York, pp.182-192

Klein M (2001) Combining and relating ontologies: an analysis of problems
and solutions. In: Gómez-Pérez A, Gruninger M, Stuckenschmidt H, Uschold M (eds) Workshop on Ontologies and Information Sharing IJCAI01.
http://www.cs.vu.nl/~mcaklein/papers/IJCAI01-ws.pdf, 2005-06-04

Klein M, Noy N (2003) A Component-Based Framework For Ontology Evolution. In: Proceedings of the Workshop on Ontologies and Distributed Systems IJCAI03. http://www.cs.vu.nl/~mcaklein/papers/OntologyEvolution.
pdf, 2005-06-04

Klein M, Ding Y, Fensel D, Omelayenko B (2003) Ontology Management:
Storing, Aligning and Maintaining Ontologies. In: Davies J, Fensel D, van

Harmelen F (eds) Towards the Semantic Web Ontology-driven Knowledge Management. Wiley & Sons, Chichester, 47-69

Klein M (2004) Change Management for Distributed Ontologies. SIKS Dissertation Series No. 2004-11, Vrije Universiteit, Amsterdam. http://www.cs.vu.nl/~mcaklein/thesis/thesis.pdf, 2005-06-02

Knowledge Web (2005) Knowledge Web realizing the semantic web. Flyer. http://knowledgeweb.semanticweb.org/semanticportal/sewView/frames.jsp 2007-08-01

König W, Wigand RT, Beck R (2006) Germany: A "fast follower" of e-commerce technologies and practices. In: Kraemer K, Dedrick J, Melville N (eds) Global E-Commerce: Impacts of National Environment and Policy. Cambridge University Press, Cambridge, pp 141-172

Kononenko I (2001) Machine Learning for Medical Diagnosis: History, State of the Art and Perspective. Artificial Intelligence in Medicine 23(1):89-109

Kotok, Alan (2000) Extensible and More A Survey of XML Business Data Exchange Vocabularies. http://www.xml.com/pub/a/2000/02/23/ebiz/index.html, 2006-12-10

Kotok A, Webber DRR (2001) ebXML: The New Global Standard for Doing Business on the Internet. New Riders Publishing, Thousand Oaks, CA

Kubicek H (1993) The Organization Gap in Interbranch EDI Systems. EDI Europe 3(2):105-124

Lamping J, Rao R, Pirolli P (1995) A Focus+Context Technique Based on Hyperbolic Geometry for Visualizing Large Hierarchies. In: Proceedings of ACM Conference on Human Factors in Software, pp 401-408. http://sigchi.org/chi95/Electronic/documnts/papers/jl_bdy.htm, 2006-12-27

Langley P and Simon HA (1995) Applications of Machine Learning and Rule Induction. Communications of the ACM 38(11):55-64

Lawrence S (2000) Context in Web Search. IEEE Data Engineering Bulletin 23(3):25-32

Lee YH, Jeong CS, Moon C (2002) Advanced planning and scheduling with outsourcing in manufacturing supply chain. Computers and Industrial Engineering. 43(1):351-374

Lejeune MA, Yakova N (2005) On characterizing the 4 C's in supply chain management. Journal of Operations Management 23(1):81-100

Leukel J, Schmitz V, Dorloff FD (2002a) A Modeling Approach for Product Classification Systems. In: Proceedings of the 13th International Workshop on Database and Expert Systems Applications (DEXA '02), pp 868-874. http://bli.icb.uni_due.de/publications/2002_WEBH_LeukelSchmitzDorloff.pdf, 2007-01-08

Leukel J, Schmitz V, Dorloff FD (2002b) Exchange Of Catalog Data In B2B Relationships - Analysis And Improvement. In: Proceedings of the IADIS International Conference WWW/Internet 2002 (ICWI 2002), pp 403-410. http://www.bli.uni-essen.de/, 2007-08-01

Leukel J, Ondracek N, van Basten F (2005) Dictionary of Terminology for Product Classification and Description. CEN European Committee for Standardization (ed), Brussels. ftp://ftp.cenorm.be/PUB LIC/CWAs/e-

Europe/eCat/CWA15294-00-2005-May.pdf, 2006-10-11

Li H (2000) XML and Industrial Standards for Electronic Commerce. Knowledge and Information Systems 2(4):487-497

Liebig T (2006) Reasoning with OWL – System Support and Insights. Ulmer Informatik-Berichte TR-2006-04. University Ulm, http://www.informatik. uni-ulm.de/ki/Liebig/papers/TR-U-Ulm-2006-4.pdf, 2007-08-30

Lou H, Luo W, Strong D (2000) Perceived critical mass effect on groupware acceptance. European Journal of Information Systems 9:91-103

Maedche A, Motik B, Silva N, Volz R (2002) MAFRA - A MApping FRAmework for Distributed Ontologies. http://wwwneu.fzi.de/KCM S/kcms_file.php?action=link&id=39, 2005-11-18

Maedche A, Staab S (2004) Ontology Learning. In: Staab S, Studer R (eds) Handbook on ontologies. Springer, Berlin, pp 173-190

Malone TW, Grant KR, Turbak FA, Brobst SA, Cohen MD (1987) Intelligent Information-Sharing Systems. Communications of the ACM 30(5):390-402

Malucelli A, Oliveira E, (2004) Ontology-Services Agent to Help in the Structural and Semantic Heterogeneity. In: Camarinha-Matos LM (ed) Virtual Enterprises and Collaborative Networks. Kluwer Academic Publishers, pp 175-182. http://paginas.fe.up.pt/~eol/PUBLICATIONS/2004/prove04.pdf, 2006-11-09

Martin-Recuerda F, Harth A, Decker S, Zhdanova A, Ding Y, Stollberg M, Arroyo S (2004) D2.1 Report on Requirements Analysis and State of the Art (WP2 - Ontology Management) Version 1.00. http://dip.semanticweb.org/ documents/DIP-D21-v1_Public.pdf, 2005-06-02

Matthews B, Miles A, Wilson M (2004) CRISs, Thesauri and the Semantic Web. In: Nase A, Van Grootel G (eds) Proceedings of the 7th International Conference on Current Research Information Systems. Leuven University Press, Antwerp, p 113-124. http://epubs.cclrc.ac.uk/bitstream/635/Cr is2004-Mattews.pdf, 2007-05-05

McBride B (2002) The Semantic Web. Invited talk at the Euroweb 2002, http://www.hpl.hp.com/semweb/publications/Brian_euroweb02_talk.pdf, 2007-06-27

McGuinness DL (2003) Ontologies Come of Age. In: Fensel D, Hendler J, Lieberman H, Wahlster W (eds) The Semantic Web: Why, What, and How. The MIT Press, Cambridge. http://www- ksl.stanford.edu/peo ple/dlm/papers/ontologies-come-of-age-mit-press-(with-citation).htm, 2006-12-30

Meilicke C, Stuckenschmidt H, Tamilin A (2006) Improving Automatically Created Mappings using Logical Reasoning. In: Proceedings of the International Workshop on Ontology Matching collocated with the 5th International Semantic Web Conference (ISWC'06). http://dit.unitn.it/~p2p/OM 2006/6-Meilicke-TP-OM'06.pdf, 2007-06-05

Mendling J, Nüttgens M (2006) XML interchange formats for business process management. Information Systems and E-Business Management 4(3):217-220

Merriam-Webster's Online Dictionary (2007a) classification. http://www.m-w.com/cgi-bin/dictionary?book=Dictionary&va=classification, 2007-08-03

Merriam-Webster's Online Dictionary (2007b) community. http://www.m-w.com/cgi-bin/dictionary?book=Dictionary&va=community, 2007-08-02

Merriam-Webster's Online Dictionary (2007c) reason. http://www.m-w.com /dictionary/reason, 2007-08-03

Microsoft (2005) Understanding BizTalk Server 2006. White Paper. http://www.microsoft.com/technet/prodtechnol/biztalk/2006/understanding .mspx, 2007-08-14

Mika P, Akkermans H (2003) Analysis of the State-of-the-Art in Ontology-based Knowledge Management. In: SWAP EU IST-2001-34103 Project Deliverable D1.2 (WP1). http://km.aifb.uni-karlsruhe.de/projects/swap/ public/public/Publications/swap-d1.2.pdf, 2005-03-21

Miller JA (2006) Ontology Visualization. Lecture CS4050 Tool Talks, University of Georgia, USA. http://lsdis.cs.uga.edu/~ravi/academic/SoftwareEng ineering/summary.pdf, 2006-12-14

Minsky M (1975) A Framework for Representing Knowledge. In: Winston P (ed) The Psychology of Computer Vision, McGraw-Hill. http://web.med ia.mit.edu/~minsky/papers/Frames/frames.html, 2007-07-23

Mitchell TM (1997) Machine Learning. International Edition 1997. McGraw-Hill Professional

Mitchell TM (1999) Machine Learning and Data Mining. Communcations of the ACM 42(11):31-36

Mitchell TM (2006) The Discipline of Machine Learning. Technical Report CMU-ML-06-108, Machine Learning Department, School of Computer Science, Carnegie Mellon University, Pittsburgh, PA

Mitra P, Wiederhold G, Decker S (2001) A Scalable Framework for the Inter-operation of Information Sources. In: Proceedings of the 1st International Semantic Web Working Symposium (SWWS `01). Stanford University, Stanford, CA. http://infolab.stanford.edu/~prasen9/swws-bk.ps, 2006-12-28

Mizoguchi R (2003) Tutorial on ontological engineering. New Generation Computing 21(4):365-384. http://www.ei.sanken.osaka-u.ac.jp/pub/miz/P art1-pdf2.pdf, 2007-07-27

MODI (2007) About. http://www.modi-project.org, 2007-08-09

Motik B, Sattler U (2006) A Comparison of Reasoning Techniques for Query-ing Large Description Logic ABoxes. In: Proceedings of the 13th International Conference on Logic for Programming Artificial Intelligence and Reasoning (LPAR 2006), LNCS 4246. Springer, Berlin Heidelberg New York, pp 227–241

Müller-Lankenau C, Klein S (2004) Designing an EDI Solution for an Industry Segment: A Case from the Swiss Construction Industry. In: Bullen, C, Stohr E (eds) Proceedings of the Tenth Americas Conference on Information Systems (AMCIS 2004). http://www.hsw-basel.ch/iwi/publications. nsf/6f29dfc9097efd0bc12572180036eb54/0b271fec0eae4bbdc125722 e002923bc/$FILE/SIGEBZ03-1280.pdf, 2007-03-04

Murata M, Tozawa A, Kudo M (2003) XML Access Control using Static Analysis. In: Proceedings of the 10th ACM Conference on Computer and Communications Security, ACM Press, New York

Nagypál G, Lemcke J (2005) A Business Data Ontology. DIP Data, Information and Process Integration with Semantic Web Services Deliverable WP3: Service Ontologies and Service Description D3.3, http://dip.sem anticweb.org/documents/D3.3-Business-data-ontology.pdf, 2006-12-29

NATO (2007) AC/135 NATO Codification, the DNA of Modern Logistics. Brochure.   http://www.nato.int/structur/AC/135/ncs_brochure/ncs_broch ure_e/index.htm, 2007-07-04

Nichols DM (1997) Implicit Rating and Filtering. In: Proceedings of the 5th DELOS Workshop on Filtering and Collaborative Filtering. ERCIM Press, pp 31-36

Nickull D, Dubray JJ, Evans C, van der Eijk P, Chopra V, Chappell DA, Harvey B, Noordzij M, Vegt J, McGrath T, Peat B (2001) Professional ebXML Foundations. Wrox Press Inc.

Nieuwenhuis L, Bollman M, Emrich J, Alder C, Camerinelli E (2007) Improving Strategic Sourcing with SCOR at Access Business Group. Supply-Chain Council, Inc. (ed) White Paper. http://www.supply-chain.org /galleries/default-file/WPJune07.pdf, 2007-08-14

NISO (2007) National Information Standards Organization International Standards. http://www.niso.org/international/SC4/sc4gld2l.html, 2007-05-05

NLM U.S. National Library of Medicine National Institute for Health (2006) Medical Subject Headings Introduction to MeSH - 2007. http://www.nl m.nih.gov/mesh/introduction2007.html, 2007-08-09

Nonaka I, Takeuchi H (1995) The Knowledge-Creating Company: How Japanese Companies Create the Dynamics of Innovation. Oxford University Press, New York

Noy NF (2004) Semantic Integration: A Survey Of Ontology-Based Approaches. ACM Special Interest Group on Management of Data SIGMOD Record 33(4):65-70

Noy NF, Klein M (2004) Ontology Evolution: Not the Same as Schema Evolution. Knowledge and Information Systems 6(4):428-440

Nycum SH (1993) Protecting intellectual property rights in software. In: Proceedings of the conference on TRI-Ada '93 Annual International Conference on Ada. http://delivery.acm.org/10.1145/ 180000/170766/p410-nycum.pdf?key1=170766&key2=9899149811&coll=portal&dl=ACM& CFID=39489774&CFTOKEN=67304383, 2007-08-30

O'Murchu I, Breslin JG, Decker S (2004) Online Social and Business Networking Communities. DERI Technical Report 2004-08-11, Innsbruck. http://www.deri.ie/fileadmin/documents/DERI-TR-2004-08-11.pdf, 2007-07-06

O'Reilly T (2005) What is Web 2.0 – Design Patterns and Business Models for the Next Generation of Software. http://www.oreillynet.com/pub/a/oreilly/ tim/news/2005/09/30/what-is-web-20.html, 2007-07-13

OASIS (2004) UDDI Executive Overview: Enabling Service-Oriented Architecture. White Paper, http://uddi.org/pubs/uddi-exec-wp.pdf, 2007-08-14

OASIS (2006a) Universal Business Language v2.0 Standard, 12 December 2006. http://docs.oasis-open.org/ubl/os-UBL-2.0/UBL-2.0.pdf, 2007-04-05

OASIS (2006b) The Framework for eBusiness. The OASIS ebXML Joint Committee for OASIS. White Paper. http://www.oasis-open.org/committe es/download.php/17817/ebxmljcWhitePaper-wd-r02-en.pdf, 2006-12-09

Obasanjo D (2003) Understanding XML. Microsoft Corporation (ed). http://msdn2.microsoft.com/en-US/library/aa468558.aspx, 2004-04-28

OBO Open Biomedical Ontologies (2007) OBO Foundry. http://obofound ry.org/, 2007-08-01

ODETTE (2007) Odette Subsets of EDIFACT Messages. http://www.ode tte.org/html/odettesubsets.htm, 2007-08-10

ODP (2007) ODP – Open Directory Project. http://dmoz.org/, 2007-07-25

Oliver DE, Shahar Y, Shortliffe EH, Musen MA (1999) Representation of Change in Controlled Medical Terminologies. Stanford Medical Informat- ics,   MSOB   X-215.   http://smi.stanford.edu/smi-web/reports/SMI-98- 0709.pdf, 2006-12-27

Omelayenko B, Fensel D (2001) An Analysis of B2B Catalogue Integration Problems Content and Document Integration. In: Proceedings of the Inter- national Conference on Enterprise Information Systems (ICEIS-2001). http://www.cs.vu.nl/~borys/papers/OF_ICEIS01.pdf, 2006-10-30

Omelayenko B (2002) Ontology-Mediated Business Integration. In: Proceed- ings of the 13-th EKAW 2002 Conference, LNAI2473. Springer, Berlin Heidelberg New York, pp 264-269. http://borys.name/papers/ekaw02.pdf, 2005-10-30

OMG (2005) Ontology Definition Metamodel Third Revised Submission to OMG/ RFP ad/2003-03-40. http://www.omg.org/docs/ad/05-08-01.pdf, 2006-12-16

OMG (2007) Data Warehousing, CWM™ and MOF™ Resource Page. http://www.omg.org/technology/cwm/, 2007-08-09

Ontoprise (2007) OntoBroker – The Power of Inferencing. http://www.onto prise.de/content/e1171/e1231/index_eng.html, 2007-08-02

OntoWeb (2003) Mission statement. http://www.ontoweb.org/About/Mission Statement/, 2007-08-01

Open Group (2007) The UDEF. The Universal Data Element Framework. http://www.opengroup.org/udef/, 2007-08-30

OpenCyc (2006) OpenCyc just got better --- much better!. http://opencyc.org/, 2006-12-28

openRDF (2007) User Guide for Sesame 2.0 (DRAFT). http://www.open rdf.org/doc/sesame2/users/index.html, 2007-08-30

OpenTRANS (2002) Überblick. http://www.opentrans.org/, 2007-06-30

ORBI (2007) About ORBI. http://www.orbi-project.org, 2007-08-09

Otto B, Beckmann H, Kelkar O, Müller S (2002) E-Business-Standards. Verbreitung und Akzeptanz. Fraunhofer-Institut für Arbeitswirtschaft und Organisation IAO, Stuttgart

Park C, Shon J (2005) A study on the web ontology processing system. The 7th

International Conference on Advanced Communication Technology, ICACT 2005 2:1035-1038

Patil S, Newcomer E (2003) ebXML and Web Services. IEEE Internet Computing 7(3):74-82

Paulheim H, Rebstock M, Fengel J (2007) Context-Sensitive Referencing for Ontology Mapping Disambiguation. In: Bouquet P, Euzenat J, Ghidini C, McGuiness DL, de Paiva V, Serafini L, Shvaiko P, Wache H (eds) Proceedings of the 2007 workshop on Context and Ontologies Representation and Reasoning (C&O:RR-2007). Computer Science Research Report #115, Roskilde University, pp 47-56

Peña-Reyes CA, Sipper M (2000) Evolutionary Computation in Medicine: an Overview. Artificial Intelligence in Medicine 19(1):1-23

Polikoff I, Allemang D (2004) TopQuadrant Technology Briefing Semantic Technology Version 1.2 March 2004. http://www.topquadrant.com/docum ents/TQ04_Semantic_Technology_Briefing.PDF, 2006-12-28

Pols A, Etter C, Renner T (2004) eBusiness-Investitionsbarometer 2004/2005 Status quo und Perspektiven des eBusiness-Einsatzes in der deutschen Wirtscahft. In: Lorenz O (ed) eBusiness-Jahrbuch der deutschen Wirtschaft 2004/2005. http://www.bitkom.org/files/documents/eBus_Jahrbuch(1).pdf, 2005-03-04

Porter ME (1985) Competitive Advantage. Creating and Sustaining Superior Performance. The Free Press. New York London Toronto Sydney

Procter R, McKinlay A (1997) Social Affordances and Implicit Ratings for Social Filtering on the Web. In: Alton-Scheidl R, Ekhall J, van Geloven O, Kovács L, Micsik A, Lueg C, Messnarz C, Nichols D, Palme J, Tholerus T, Mason D, Procter R, Stupazzini E, Vassali M, Wheeler R (eds) Proceedings of the Fifth DELOS Workshop on Filtering and Collaborative Filtering. ERCIM Press

proficlass International e.V. (2004) Handbuch Klassifizierung Leitfaden zur Entwicklung und Pflege der Produktklassifikation proficlass International Version 2.0. http://www.proficlass.de/index.php?id=131, 2007-07-06

Provost F, Fawcett T (2001) Robust Classification for Imprecise Environments. Machine Learning 42(3):203-231

Prud'hommeaux E, Seaborne A (2007) SPARQL Query Language for RDF W3C Candidate Recommendation 14 June 2007. http://www.w3.org/TR/ 2007/CR-rdf-sparql-query-20070614/, 2007-06-27

Quantz J, Wichmann T (2003a) E-Business-Standards in Germany, Assessment, Problems, Prospects. Final Report short version commissioned by the German Federal Ministry of Economics and Labour. Berlecon Research GmbH, Berlin. http://www.berlecon.de/studien/InhaltProbe/2003 04eStandardsKF_en.pdf, 2007-08-18

Quantz J, Wichmann T (2003b) E-Business-Standards in Deutschland, Bestandsaufnahme, Probleme, Perspektiven. Report commissioned by the German Federal Ministry of Economics and Labour (BMWA). Berlecon Research GmbH, Berlin

Rahm E, Bernstein PA (2001) A survey of approaches to automatic schema matching. VLDB Journal 10:334-350

Rebstock M (2000) Elektronische Geschäftsabwicklung, Märkte und Transaktionen - eine methodische Analyse. HMD Praxis der Wirtschaftsinformatik 37(215):5-15

Rebstock M (2001) Elektronische Unterstützung und Automatisierung von Verhandlungen. Wirtschaftsinformatik 43(6):609-617

Rebstock M, Amirhamzeh Tafreschi O (2002) Secure Interactive Electronic Negotiations in Business-to-Business Marketplaces. In: Wrycza S (ed) Proceedings of the Xth European Conference on Information Systems (ECIS2002). Springer, Berlin Heidelberg New York, pp 564-572

Rebstock M, Thun P (2003) Interactive Multi-Attribute Electronic Negotiations in the Supply Chain: Design Issues and an Application Prototype. In: Sprague RH (ed) Proceedings of the 36th Annual Hawaii International Conference on Systems Sciences. IEEE Computer Society Press, New York

Rebstock M, Fengel J, Paulheim H (2007) Context-sensitive Semantic Synchronization in Electronic Negotiations. In: Proceedings of Group Decision and Negotiation (GDN) 2007, Mt. Tremblant, Canada

Rheingold H (2000) The Virtual Community Homesteading on the Electronic Frontier, 2nd. The MIT Press, Cambridge, USA

Röder P, Tafreschi O, Müller C, Eckert C (2006) History-based Access Control and Information Flow Control for Structured Documents. In: Proceedings of the First International Workshop on Security (IWSEC 2006)

Röder P, Tafreschi O, Eckert C (2007a) History-Based Access Control for XML Documents. In: Proceedings of the 2nd ACM Symposium on Information, Computer and Communications Security, ACM Press, New York

Röder P, Tafreschi O, Eckert C (2007b) On Flexible Modeling of History-Based Access Control Policies for XML Documents. In: Proceedings of the 11th International Conference on Knowledge-Based and Intelligent Information & Engineering Systems (KES 2007). Springer, Berlin Heidelberg New York

RosettaNet Consortium (2007a) Value of RosettaNet Standards. http://portal.rosettanet.org/cms/sites/RosettaNet/Standards/Value/index.html, 2007-06-20

RosettaNet Consortium (2007b) RosettaNet Dictionaries. http://portal.rosettanet.org/cms/sites/RosettaNet/Standards/RStandards/dictionary/index, 2007-06-20

RosettaNet Consortium (2007c) RosettaNet Standards. http://portal.rosettanet.org/cms/sites/RosettaNet/Standards/RStandards/index.html, 2007-06-20

RosettaNet Consortium (2007d) About RosettaNet. http://portal.rosettanet.org/cms/sites/RosettaNet/About/index.html, 2007-06-20

Russel S, Norvig P (2003) Artificial Intelligence A Modern Approach, 2nd ed. Pearson Education, Upper Saddle River, NJ

Sahami M, Dumais S, Heckermann D, Horvitz E (1998) A Bayesian Approach to Filtering Junk E-Mail. In: Proceedings of Workshop on Learning for Text Categorization. AAAI Technical Report WS-98-05. http://robotics.stanford.edu/users/sahami/papers-dir/spam.pdf, 2007-03-04

Sandhu RS, Coyne EJ, Feinstein HL, Youman CE (1996) Role-Based Access Control Models. IEEE Computer 29(2):38-47

Schafer JB, Konstan J, Riedl J (1999) Recommender Systems in E-Commerce. In: Proceedings of the 1st ACM Conference on Electronic Commerce. ACM Press, New York, pp 158-166

Schmid BF (1997) Elements of a Reference Model for Electronic Markets. In: Proceedings of Thirty-First Annual Hawaii International Conference on System Sciences. IEEE Computer Society 4:193-201

Schmitz V, Leukel J (2003) CEN/ISSS Workshop eCAT – A Step towards Multilingual Electronic Product Catalogues. In: Proceedings of the 10th ISPE International Conference on Concurrent Engineering (CE 2003), vol Enhanced Interoperable Systems, pp 321-327. http://www.bli.uni-essen.de/publications/2003_CE_SchmitzLeukel.pdf, 2006-01-01

Schulten E, Akkermans H, Guarino N, Botquin G, Lopes N, Dörr M, Sadeh N (2001) The E-Commerce Product Classification Challenge. IEEE Intelligent Systems 16(4):86-89. http://www.cs.cmu. du/~sadeh/Publicat ions/More%20Complete%20List/OntoWeb%-20Challenge.pdf, 2006-11-10

Schuster E, Allen SJ, Brock DL (2007) Global RFID The Value of the EPC-global Network for Supply Chain Management. Springer, Berlin Heidelberg New York

Searle JR (1980) Minds, Brains, and Programs. The Behavioral and Brain Sciences 3:417-457

Seen M, Rouse AC, Beaumont N (2007) Explaining and Predicting Informations Sytems Acceptance and Success: An integrative model. In: Österle H, Schelp J, Winter R (eds) Proceedings of the Fifteenth European Conference on Information Systems. University of St. Gallen, St. Gallen, pp 1356-1367

Segev A, Wan D, Beam C (1995) Designing Electronic Catalogs for Business Value: Results from the CommerceNet Pilot. CMIT Working Paper 95-WP-1005, UC Berkeley. http://citeseer.ist.psu.edu/segev95designing.html, 2007-08-20

Shannon CE (1948) A mathematical theory of communication. Bell System Technical Journal 27:379-423 and 623-656. http://cm.bell-labs.com/cm/ms/what/shannonday/shannon1948.pdf, 2007-04-30

Shapiro C, Varian HR (1999) Information Rules. Harvard Business School Press, Boston

Shardanand U, Maes P (1995) Social Information Filtering: Algorithms for Automating "Word of Mouth". In: Proceedings of ACM Conference on Human Factors in Computing Systems. ACM Press/Addison-Wesley Publishing Co., New York, 1:210-217

Shearer R (2007) Structured Ontology Format. In: Golbreich C, Kalyanpur A, Parsia B (eds) Proceedings of the OWLED 2007 Workshop on OWL: Experiences and Directions. CEUR-WS.org, Aachen. http://sunsite.inf ormatik.rwth-aachen.de/-Publications/CEUR-WS/Vol-258/, 200-7-07-31

Shvaiko P, Euzenat J (2005) A Survey of Scheme based Matching Approaches.

http://www.dit.unitn.it/~p2p/Related-Work/Matching/JoDS-IV-2005_SurveyMatching-SE.pdf, 2005-10-10

SIMAP (2007) What is the CPV?. http://simap.europa.eu/What%20is%20the%20CPV/8e7631ef-fe8e-148d-4467a6c1dd596b27_en.html, 2007-07-04

Simchi-Levi D, Kaminsky P, Simchi-Levi E (2004) Managing the Supply Chain: The Definitive Guide for the Business Professional. McGraw-Hill, Columbus

Simon, C, Rebstock, M, Fengel J (2007): Formal Control of Multilateral Negotiations. In: Proceedings of Group Decision and Negotiation (GDN) 2007, Mt. Tremblant, Canada

Sinclair P, Lewis P, Martinez K, Addis M, Prideaux D (2006) Semantic web integration of cultural heritage sources. In: Proceedings of the 15th International Conference on World Wide Web WWW '06. ACM Press, New York, pp 1047-1048

Siponen M (2006) A justification for software rights. ACM SIGCAS Computers and Society 36(3):11–20

Sirin E, Parsia B, Cuenca Grau B, Kalyanpur A, Katz Y (2006) Pellet: A Practical OWL-DL Reasoner. http://www.mindswap.org/papers/PelletJWS.pdf, 2007-08-03

SNITEM (2007) Les Industriels Adhérents Répertoire des matériels. http://www.snitem.fr/industriels-adherents/repertoires_des_materiels.php, 2007-07-30

Sowa JF (1999) Knowledge Representation: Logical, Philosophical, and Computational Foundations, Brooks Cole Publishing Co., Pacific Grove. http://www.jfsowa.com/krbook/index.htm, 2006-12-28

Sowa J (2000) Ontology, Metadata, and Semiotics. In: Ganter B, Mineau GW (eds) Conceptual Structures: Logical, Linguistic, and Computational Issues, LNAI 1867. Springer, Berlin Heidelberg New York, pp 55-81

Specht G, Kahabka T (2000) Information Filtering and Personalisation in Databases using Gaussian Curves. In: Proceedings of the IEEE 4th Int. Database Engineering and Application Symposium (IDEAS 2000). IEEE Computer Society, New York, pp 16-24

Stoimenov L, Stanimirovic A, Djordjevic-Kajan S (2006) Discovering Mappings between Ontologies in Semantic Integration Process. In: Proceedings of the 9th AGILE International Conference on Geographic Information Science. Visegrád, Hungary, pp 213-219

Stojanovic L, Maedche A, Motik B, Stojanovic N (2002) User-Driven Ontology Evolution Management. In: Proceedings of the 13th European Conference on Knowledge Engineering and Knowledge Management EKAW, 2002, LNCS 2473. Springer Berlin Heidelberg New York, pp 133-140

Ströbel M (2003) Engineering Electronic Negotiations A Guide to Electronic Negotiation Technologies for the Design and Implementation of Next-Generation Electronic Markets - Future Silkroads of eCommerce. Kluwer Academic/Plenum Publishers, New York

Stuckenschmidt H, Klein M (2003) Integrity and Change in Modular Ontologies. In: Proceedings of the 18th International Joint Conference on Artificial Intelligence. http://www.cs.vu.nl/~heiner/public/IJCAI03.pdf, 2005-06-04

Stuckenschmidt H, van Harmelen F (2005) Information Sharing on the Semantic Web. Springer, Berlin Heidelberg New York

Stuckenschmidt H, Serafini L, Wache H (2006) Reasoning about Ontology Mappings. ECAI 2006 Workshop on Context Representation and Reasoning. http://www.cs.vu.nl/~holger/Papers/stuckenschmidt_etal-06.pdf, 2007-04-06

SUMO (2006) Suggested Upper Merged Ontology (SUMO). http://www.ontologyportal.org/, 2006-12-29

Sun Microsystems (2002) Using Web Services Effectively. http://java.sun.com/blueprints/webservices/using/webservbp.html, 2007-08-09

Sure S (2003) A Methodology for Ontology-based Knowledge Management. In: Davies J, Fensel D, van Harmelen F (eds) Towards the Semantic Web Ontology-driven Knowledge Management. Wiley & Sons, Chichester, pp 33-46

Suttmeier RP, Yao X, Tan AZ (2006) Standards of Power? Technology, Institutions, and Politics in the Development of China's National Standards Strategy. NBR Special Report 10, The National Bureau of Asian Research. http://nbr.org/publications/specialreport/pdf/SR10.pdf, 2007-07-30

SWIFT (2007) Implementing Standards. http://www.swift.com/index.cfm?item_id=60001, 2007-08-01

Tanenbaum AS (1996) Computer networks. Prentice Hall International, Upper Saddle River, NJ

Tapscott D, Ticoll D, Lowy A (2000) Digital Capital: Harnessing the Power of Business Webs. Harvard Business School Press, Boston

Tennison J, Shadbolt NR (1998) APECKS: A Tool to Support Living Ontologies. http://ksi.cpsc.ucalgary.ca/KAW/KAW98/tennison/, 2007-08-01

The Apache Software Foundation (2007) Apache Tomcat. http://tomcat.apache.org/, 2007-06-13

The Jakarta Project (2007) Commons Configuration. http://jakarta.apache.org/commons/configuration/, 2007-06-20

Thurow LC (1997) Needed: A New System of Intellectual Property Rights. Harvard Business Review 75(5):95-103

Tichy WF (1985) RCS - A System for Version Control. Software - Practice and Experience 15(7):637-654

Transora (2007) Solutions. http://www.transora.com/solutions.html, 2007-06-30

Tsarkov D, Horrocks I (2006) FaCT++ Description Logic Reasoner: System Description. In: Proceedings of the International Joint Conference on Automated Reasoning (IJCAR 2006), LNAI 4130. Springer, Berlin Heidelberg New York

U.S. Census Bureau (2006) E-commerce 2005. http://www.census.gov/eos/www/2005 /2005reportfinal.pdf, 2007-05-06

U.S. Census Bureau (2007) North American Industry Classification System (NAICS). http://www.census.gov/epcd/www/naics.html, 2007-07-05

UNCTAD (2004) United Nations Conference on Trade and Development. E-Commerce and Development Report 2004, UNCTAD/SDTE/ECB/2004/1, http://www.unctad.org/en/-docs/-ecdr2004_en.pdf, 2005-03-10

UNCTAD (2006) United Nations Conference on Trade and Development. Information Economy Report 2006 The development perspective. United Nations, New York Geneva

UNECE (2006) UN/EDIFACT Introduction and Rules. http://www.unece.org/trade/untdid/texts/d100_d.htm, 2006-11-20

UNECE (2007a) UN/EDIFACT Message type : PRODAT. http://www.unece.org/trade/untdid/d03b/trmd/prodat_c.htm, 2007-08-08

UNECE (2007b) United Nations electronic Trade Documents. http://www.unece.org/etrades/unedocs/, 2007-08-16

UNSD (2007a) Central Product Classification Version 1.1, (CPC Ver. 1.1). http://unstats.un.org/unsd/cr/family2.asp?Cl=16, 2007-07-03

UNSD (2007b) Classification by Broad Economic Categories, Defined in terms of SITC, Rev.3, (BEC Rev.3). http://unstats.un.org/unsd/cr/family2.asp?Cl=10, 2007-07-03

UNSD (2007c) International Standard Industrial Classification of All Economic Activities, Third Revision, (ISIC, Rev.3). http://unstats.un.org/unsd/cr/family2.asp?Cl=2, 2007-07-03

UNSPSC (2007) Welcome. http://www.unspsc.org, 2007-06-20

Uschold M, King M, Moralee S, Zorgios Y (1998) The Enterprise Ontology. The Knowledge Engineering Review vol 13. http://www.aiai.ed.ac.uk/project/enterprise/enterprise/ontology.html, 2007-05-04

Uschold M, Gruninger M (2004) Ontologies and Semantics for Seamless Connectivity. ACM SIGMOD Record 33(4):58-64

Uszkoreit H (2005) Shallow Language Processing, Deep Language Processing and Domain Ontologies. In: Proceedings of 2005 IEEE International Conference on Natural Language Processing and Knowledge Engineering (IEEE NLP-KE 05). ieeexplore.ieee.org/xpls/abs_all.jsp?arnumber=1598697, 2007-03-18

van Harmelen F (2006) Two Obvious Intuitions: Ontology-Mapping Needs Background Knowledge and Approximation. In: Proceedings of the IEEE/WIC/ACM International Conference on Intelligent Agent Technology (IAT'06. http://ieeexplore.ieee.org/iel5/4061321/4061322/0406 1334.pdf?isnumber=4061322&prod=CNF&arnumber=4061334&arSt=11 &ared=11&arAuthor=van+Harmelen%2C+F, 2007-08-01

Visser PRS, Jones DM, Bench-Capon TJM, Shave MJR (1997) An Analysis of Ontology Mismatches; Heterogeneity versus Interoperability. In: AAAI 1997 Spring Symposium on Ontological Engineering. http://citeseer.ist.psu.edu/cache/papers/cs/699/http:zSzzSzwww.csc.liv.ac.ukzSz~pepijnz SzArticleszSzstanf-97.pdf/visser97analysis.pdf, 2006-12-19

Vlachakis J, Rex S, Otto B, Lebender M, Fleckstein T (2003) Web-Services A look into quality and security aspects. Fraunhofer IAO, Stuttgart

Voigtmann P, Zeller T (2002) Enterprise Application Integration und B2B Integration im Kontext von Electronic Business und Elektronischen Marktplätzen, Teil I: Grundlagen und Anforderungen. FORWIN report FWN-2002-013. FORWIN, Erlangen-Nürnberg

Voigtmann P, Zeller T (2003) Enterprise Application Integration und B2B Integration im Kontext von Electronic Business und Elektronischen Marktplätzen, Teil II: Integrationssysteme und Fallbeispiele. FORWIN report FWN-2003-001, FORWIN, Erlangen-Nürnberg

Vokurka RJ, Lummus RR (2000) The Role of Just-In-Time in Supply Chain Management. The International Journal of Logistics Management, 11(1):89-98

W3C (1998) Guide to the W3C XML Specification ("XMLspec") DTD, Version 2.1. http://www.w3.org/XML/1998/06/xmlspec-report-v21.htm#AEN49, 2006-11-20

W3C (2004a) OWL Web Ontology Language Reference W3C Recommendation 10 February 2004. http://www.w3.org/TR/owl-ref/, 2006-09-10

W3C (2004b) XML Schema Part 0: Primer Second Edition, W3C Recommendation 28 October 2004. http://www.w3.org/TR/xmlschema-0/, 2006-11-20

W3C (2004c) RDF/XML Syntax Specification (Revised) W3C Recommendation 10 February 2004. http://www.w3.org/TR/rdf-syntax-grammar/, 2000-12-16

W3C (2004d) RDF Vocabulary Description Language 1.0: RDF Schema W3C Recommendation 10 February 2004. http://www.w3.org/TR/rdf-schema/, 2007-08-09

W3C (2004e) OWL Web Ontology Language Overview W3C Recommendation 10 February 2004. http://www.w3.org/TR/owl-features/, 2007-08-09

W3C (2004f) RDF Test Cases W3C Recommendation 10 February 2004. http://www.w3.org/TR/rdf-testcases/#ntriples, 2007-09-02

W3C (2006a) Extensible Markup Language (XML) 1.1 (Second Edition) W3C Recommendation 16 August 2006, edited in place 29 September 2006. http://www.w3.org/TR/2006/REC-xml11-20060816/, 2007-08-01

W3C (2006b) SPARQL Query Language for RDF – W3C Working Draft 4 October 2006. http://www.w3.org/TR/rdf-sparql-query/, 2006-11-29

W3C (2007) SOAP Version 1.2 Part 1: Messaging Framework (Second Edition). http://www.w3.org/TR/soap12-part1/, 2007-06-13

Walsh A (2001) ebXML: The Technical Specifications. Prentice Hall PTR, Indianapolis. http://www.ebxml.org/specs/index.htm, 2007-07-30

WCO (2007) General Rules for the Interpretation of the Harmonized System. http://www.wcoomd.org/ie/en/topics_issues/harmonizedsystem/DocumentDB/0001E.pdf, 2007-06-30

Wigand R, Picot A, Reichwald R (1997) Information, Organisation and Management. Wiley & Sons, Chichester

WonderWeb Consortium (2003) WonderWeb – Ontology Infrastructure for the Semantic Web. http://wonderweb.semanticweb.org/, 2007-06-27

WonderWeb OWL API Consortium (2003) An API for OWL. http://owl.man.ac.uk/api/readme.html, 2007-06-27

WonderWeb Consortium (2006) Descriptive Ontology for Linguistic and Cognitive Engineering. http://www.loa-cnr.it/DOLCE.html, 2006-12-29

WordNet (2006) About WordNet. http://wordnet.princeton.edu/, 2006-12-28

WordNet (2007) WordNet – a lexical database for the English language. http://wordnet.princeton.edu/, 2007-07-25

xCBL (2006) About xCBL. http://www.xcbl.org/about.shtml, 2007-08-14

Yang H, Cui Z, O'Brien PD (1999) Extracting Ontologies from Legacy Systems for Understanding and Re-engineering. In: Proceedings of 23nd IEEE International Conference on Computer Software and Applications. ieeexplore.ieee.org/iel5/6591/17591/00812512.pdf, 2007-06-19

Zemanek H (1966) Semiotics and Programming Languages. Communications of the ACM 9(3):139-143

Zhang H, Su J (2004) Naive Bayesian classifiers for ranking. In: Proceedings of the 15th European Conference on Machine Learning (ECML2004). Springer, Berlin Heidelberg New York. doi.ieeecomputersociety.org/-10.1109/ICTAI.2005.80, 2007-06-18

Zhang S, Ford J, Makedon F (2006) A privacy-preserving collaborative filtering scheme with two-way communication. In: Proceedings of the 7th ACM conference on Electronic commerce. ACM Press, New York, pp 316-323

Zhdanova AV, de Bruijn J, Zimmermann K, Scharffe F (2004) Ontology Alignment Solution v2.0, EU IST Esperonto project deliverable (D1.4 V2.0). http://www.deri.at/fileadmin/documents/deliverables/Esperonto/De l1.4-V2.0-final.pdf, 2005-05-03

Zhdanova AV, Shvaiko P (2006) Community-Driven Ontology Matching. Technical Report DIT-06-028, Informatica e Telecomunicazioni, University of Trento

Zimmermann H (1980) OSI Reference Model — The ISO Model of Architecture for Open Systems Interconnection. IEEE Transactions on Communications (28)4:425-432

Index

Printing: Krips bv, Meppel, The Netherlands
Binding: Stürtz, Würzburg, Germany